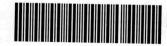

OMPACT
DISC

Jewish Musical Modernism,
Old and New

JEWISH MUSICAL

MODERNISM,
Old and New

EDITED BY **PHILIP V. BOHLMAN**

WITH A FOREWORD BY **SANDER L. GILMAN**

THE UNIVERSITY OF CHICAGO PRESS ::: CHICAGO AND LONDON

PHILIP V. BOHLMAN is the Mary Werkman Distinguished Service Professor of the Humanities and of Music at the University of Chicago and coeditor of the Chicago Studies in Ethnomusicology series, published by the University of Chicago Press.

The University of Chicago Press, Chicago 60637
The University of Chicago Press, Ltd., London
© 2008 by The University of Chicago
All rights reserved. Published 2008
Printed in China

17 16 15 14 13 12 11 10 09 08   1 2 3 4 5

ISBN-13: 978-0-226-06326-3   (cloth)
ISBN-10: 0-226-06326-7   (cloth)

Publication of this book and the accompanying CD has been generously supported by a subvention from Carol Honigberg and Joel Honigberg.

Library of Congress Cataloging-in-Publication Data

Jewish musical modernism, old and new / edited by Philip V. Bohlman with a foreword by Sander L. Gilman.
      p. cm.
    Includes bibliographical references and index.
    ISBN-13: 978-0-226-06326-3 (cloth : alk. paper)
    ISBN-10: 0-226-06326-7 (cloth : alk. paper) 1. Jews—Music—History and criticism. 2. Modernism (Music) 3. Jewish musicians. 4. Music—20th century—History and criticism. I. Bohlman, Philip Vilas.
ML3776.J42 2008
780.89'924—dc22

2007045221

CONTENTS

Are Jews Musical?

Historical Notes on the Question of Jewish Musical Modernism

::: SANDER L. GILMAN

As early as Shakespeare the stereotypical Jew is denied any special relationship to Western (read: civilized and civilizing) music. The Jew in *The Merchant of Venice* is devoid of any moral and therefore aesthetic sensibility. As Shylock says:

Lock up my doors; and when you hear the drum
And the vile squealing of the wry-neck'd fife,
Clamber not you up to the casements then,
Nor thrust your head into the public street
To gaze on Christian fools with varnish'd faces,
But stop my house's ears, I mean my casements:
Let not the sound of shallow foppery enter
My sober house.

(*Merchant of Venice*, act 2, scene 5)

But just so that we do not miss the message, Lorenzo conveys to Shylock's daughter that her father is insensible to music:

The man that hath no music in himself,
Nor is not moved with concord of sweet sounds,
Is fit for treasons, stratagems and spoils;
The motions of his spirit are dull as night
And his affections dark as Erebus:
Let no such man be trusted. Mark the music.

(*Merchant of Venice*, act 5, scene 1)

"Mark the music" is the key to one powerful image of the stereotypical Jew that is part of English as well as European culture. To be civilized the Jews had to learn to love the music of their wider world, to identify with and participate in a high culture beyond the Shakespearean fantasy of Jewish incomprehensibility and the myth of the noise of the synagogue and the *Judenschule* (Jews' school). They had to accept music as part of the decorous world of high culture that improved the human being.

In the eighteenth century Moses Mendelssohn and the German Jewish Enlightenment argued that Jewish transformation into citizens of a nation-state would enable Jews to be both Germans and Jews. Unlike the liberals of his time, such as Wilhelm von Humboldt, who demanded the extension of civic emancipation to the Jews without any qualification, on the basis that all human beings shared these rights, the Haskalah, or Jewish Enlightenment, model demanded observable change. For Germany one of the changes demanded of the Jews was that they so alter their "Jewish" mentality that they begin to experience the ethical dimensions attributed to "high culture" (*Bildung*), dimensions from which they were felt to have excluded themselves because of their religious beliefs rather than their innate incapacity (see, in general, Sorkin 2000; Meyer 2001; Hess 2002; Herzig 2002; Dauber 2004). Music, especially the music of modern high culture, what is today called "classical" as opposed to popular music, becomes one of the places that such transformation is seen to take place. If "music" indeed "hath charms to soothe the savage breast, / To soften rocks, or bend a knotted oak," as William Congreve (1670–1729) observed in *The Mourning Bride* (act 1, scene 1), the "Jew," however, was capable neither of comprehending nor of producing such an effect.

Certainly for the nineteenth century the formulation that most strongly resonated was in Richard Wagner's 1850 essay "Judaism [i.e., Jewry] in Music." This essay, republished in edited form by Wagner in 1869 and widely reprinted at the close of the century, summarized nineteenth-century anti-Semitic images of the Jewish lack of any innate musicality:

Our modern arts had likewise become a portion of this culture, and among them more particularly that art which is just the very easiest to learn—the art of music, and indeed that Music which, severed from her sister arts, had been lifted by the force and stress of [the] grandest geniuses to a stage in her universal faculty of Expression where either, in new conjunction with the other arts, she might speak aloud the most sublime, or, in persistent separation from them, she could also speak at will the deepest bathos of the trivial. Naturally, what the cultured Jew had to speak, in his aforesaid situation, could be nothing but the trivial and indifferent, because his whole artistic bent was in sooth a mere luxurious, needless thing (88). . . . The Jew has never had an Art of his own, hence never a Life of art-enabling import ("ein Leben von kunstfähigem Gehalte"): an import, a universally applicable, a human import, not even to-day does it offer to the searcher, but merely a peculiar method of expression. . . . Now the only musical expression offered to the Jew tone-setter by his native Folk, is the ceremonial music of their Jehova-rites: the Synagogue is the solitary fountain whence the Jew can draw art-motives at once popular and intelligible to himself.[1]

It was into this world that Jews of the early nineteenth century, such as Giacomo Meyerbeer (born Jakob Liebmann Beer, 1791–1864), against whom Wagner fulminated in his essay, entered to show that they too could and did contribute to European high culture. Jews, however defined, could show that they had the sensibility and sensitivity to be full-fledged members of a world of ethics and aesthetics. Yet the more that they actually did so, the more anti-Semitic stereotypes held that they were incapable of contributing anything of value. In the end they were inhibited by their Jewishness from comprehending the true nature of "classical" music.

In 1850 in London Robert Knox, accused grave robber and medical hack, sat down and wrote the first systematic anthropology of the Jews in English. His book *The Races of Men* picked up this thread when he observed that "the real Jew has no ear for music" (Knox 1850: 131). Knox was not merely paralleling Wagner. Both were perpetuating a view well-known from the early modern period, as Shakespeare's Shylock illustrates. Benjamin Disraeli, novelist and politician manqué, had countered that view in his novel *Coningsby* (1844) in which Sidonie, the embodiment of all that is positive among the Jews, forcefully declares that "musical Europe is ours!," for every time a Christian listens to a [Gioacchino] Rossini[2] [1792–1868] or a Meyerbeer or is "thrilled into raptures at the notes of an aria by a [Giuditta] Pasta [1798–1865] or a [Giulia] Grisi [1811–1869], little do they suspect that they are offering their homage to 'the sweet singers of Israel!'" The Jews are endowed "with the almost exclusive privilege of MUSIC" (Disraeli 1983: 271; see also Schwarz 1979). What is vital in reading Disraeli as against Wagner and Knox is that Disraeli stresses the Jew's preeminence in the music of European high culture, of the opera and the concert stage. Neither synagogue liturgy nor Jewish themes, but the most cutting-edge high culture of the music of the day defines Jewish preeminence (for the contrast in the twentieth century, see Schiller 2003).

In general the notion that the Jew could not command the realm of high musical culture is undercut in the popular mind by the presence of "Jewish" performers (rather than composers) during the course of the late nineteenth century. Francis Galton's view of "hereditary genius" in 1869, documenting his interest in the "mental peculiarities of different races," includes only one Jewish "genius," and that is the poet Heinrich Heine.[3] No musicians at all make the grade. But twenty years later, in 1889, Joseph Jacobs, the Australian-born anthropologist who wrote extensively on Jews and race in Victorian London, commented that in "Grove's *Dictionary of Music* [there is] a far larger proportion of executants than composers. . . . [There is] clear evidence of general musical ability among Jews" (cf. Jacobs 1889: 13). In his statistical survey of Jewish professions he commented, "That a Jew obtained one of the fifty scholarships at the new Royal College of Music, whereas one in five hundred would represent a proper proportion, seems to confirm the popular impression of the Jewish love and aptitude for music, and this may be further confirmed by the fact that of the six musical knights in England no less than three are of Jewish blood" (Jacobs 1891: 45). He later lists the musical "geniuses" of "Jewish blood," enumerating the three knighted composers, Julius Benedict (1804–1885), Michael Costa (1810–1884), and the famed composer of "Onward Christian Soldiers" (1871) and Savoy operettas Arthur Sullivan (1844–1900),[4] but placing most of his emphasis on performers such as the violinists Joseph Joachim and Hermann Cohen (Jacobs 1891: lix–lx).

The rationale behind such a claim is not merely that there are more Jewish performers than composers (Disraeli can easily pair them), but rather that the nature of music seems to be divided between the "creators" and the "interpreters." The latter fulfill the anti-Semites' expectation of "mere Jewish mimicry," while philo-Semites ascribed "genius" to such interpreters. Georg Simmel, in his oft-quoted essay on the "Stranger" (1908), put this in terms of the general economy:

> Trade [here we can read: performance] can always absorb more people than primary production [here we can read: composition]; it is, therefore, the sphere indicated for the stranger, who intrudes as a supernumerary, so to speak, into a group in which the economic positions are actually occupied—the classical example is the history of European Jews. The stranger is by nature no "owner of soil"—soil not only in the physical, but also in the figurative sense of a life-substance which is fixed, if not in a point in space, at least in an ideal point of the social environment. [This would be the notion of the inherent creativity of the "rooted" composer that Wagner represents.] Although in more intimate relations, he may develop all kinds of charm and significance, as long as he is considered a stranger in the eyes of the other, he is not an "owner of soil." (Simmel 1950: 404)

The Jew had to show that he was not merely in trade, but also a creative genius.

This debate raged among Jews on the Continent. Heinrich Berl picked up on the question of the originality of the Jews in music in a series of essays in Martin Buber's *Der Jude* ("The Jew") and then in a published collection of these essays in 1926 (Berl 1921, Berl 1923, Berl 1926). Berl argued, against Max Brod's concept of Jewish music as well as his strong espousal of Gustav Mahler's work, that Jews reflect an "Asian" relationship to music because of their inherent psychology (Brod 1916). Music for them is form, not content. It is best exemplified by the rise of "New Music" that dominates modernity, from Georges Bizet (1838–1875) (a "half Jew" in whom the Jewish half dominates, according to Berl [Berl 1926: 69]) to Gustav Mahler and Arnold Schoenberg. Jews are a "form creating people," not a "cultural people" (ibid.: 86). They had already shown this in their own musical tradition of the liturgy, which had infiltrated their attempts to write modern music as early as Meyerbeer. This could not be transformed into Western classical music (ibid.: 87). Thus they created modern music (Mahler and Schoenberg) without melodic quality, because the Jews lack the melodic capacity that provides the "sense of space" in music. As a people without "space," this affects their musical creativity. Berl's views echo the general principles of Wagner's son-in-law Houston Stewart Chamberlain's understanding of Germanic music in his 1899 anti-Semitic polemic against the Jews (Chamberlain 1934: 1166–71).

Jewish virtuosi show similar qualities to composers. They may have genius in invention but are not creative as performers, for they cannot make music truly sensual (Berl 1926: 84). The audience is enraptured by their playing because they are actors who transmute music into the visual world of appearances. Music, Berl stresses, is not visual: "it does not paint, it sings" (ibid.: 189). The Jewish performer, however, can only perform, not inhabit, the work of art. Berl's example is the Prague-born pianist Ignaz Moscheles (1794–1870), the teacher of Felix Mendelssohn and great opponent of Franz Liszt.

A number of Jewish contemporaries struck out against Berl's rigid position. Arno Nadel argued that there is no "Jewish" music beyond the liturgical (Nadel 1923). He denied the existence of any secular Jewish music except in the most recent attempts to evoke "Jewishness" in Western musical forms. Alfred Einstein's image of "Jews in Music" moved from the complex interaction between Jewish and non-Jewish musicians in Europe during the early modern period to the figures of the Jew on the musical stage, as in Eugen d'Albert's *Golem* (Einstein 1927). He argued that there is little specifically "Jewish" among either the composers or, he added, the characters. Berl's views were answered in part by the Prague musicologist Paul Nettl (1889–1972), who dismissed the underpinnings of Berl's so-called phenomenological analysis and replaced the view of a "Jewish" music with the notion that Jews adapt the music of the worlds they inhabit quite well to their own liturgical and cultural needs (Nettl 1923). Whether Jews occupy high culture and "have" music is central to this debate. Do they mimic, do they borrow, and have they an inherent musical ability that is different from the Western underpinnings of musical creativity?

One can note here that a number of anti-Semites of the late nineteenth century answered the hypothetical question, "Do we not have many notable figures among the Jews?" (Fritsch 1892a: 27). In challenging the assumption that Jews have greater facility for music, Theodor Fritsch, perhaps the most widely read of these polemicists, replied that when any Jewish performer shows a modicum of talent, the Jewish press and Jewish agents immediately make them world famous. In a later account of "Jewish Statistics" Fritsch's list of the "Jews in the Musical World" concluded with Hermann Wolff, the concert manager (Fritsch 1892b: 30). Simultaneously, Fritsch bemoaned the fact that this emphasis on Jewish virtuosity signifies the disappearance of the German performer from the stage.

In the debate about Jewish cultural competency it was usually the violinist, more than anyone else, who represented Jewish musical accomplishment at the close of the nineteenth century. When we think of the nineteenth century and the rise of the violin virtuoso, prior to Wagner, it was Nicolò Paganini (1782–1840) who dominated the public's imagination as the essential violinist. He played so extraordinarily that he was said to have been aligned with the devil, as, of course, was also said of the Jews (de Saussine 1953: 113). This emphasis changed by the end of the nineteenth century. A "Jewish" cast to the image of the violinist began in the generation of Johannes Brahms's friend Joseph Joachim (1831–1907), the son of a Jewish merchant family, who was not only the premier violinist of his age, but a composer and conductor. By the 1930s the role of the Jew as a major contributor to or destroyer of high culture focused to no little extent on his (and they are all men) ability to play the violin. The violinist as the exemplary figure of Jewish participation in high art is a reflex of the age of the multicultural.

At the end of the nineteenth century societies to combat anti-Semitism arose. Central to their mission was to "prove" that Jews were as good if not better citizens than non-Jews, because the anti-Semites had made the argument that Jews were an inherent evil in Western society. Books were published to show that Jews did not dominate the "criminal classes," that they took part in civic obligations such as the military, and that they were a positive force in society. Especially after the accession to power of the Nazis in 1933, a spate of books and pamphlets appeared to chronicle the contributions of "Jews" (often very loosely defined) to Western high culture (the best-known of these publications is Zweig 1934)—as if such proof answered the Nazis' claims of the overrepresentation of the Jews in high culture and their baneful effect on it. High culture, more than any other realm, became the place for this debate, for it was widely accepted that exposure to high culture improved the moral quality of individuals and of society as a whole. Theater, music, art, and literature were inherently ennobling unless—and here the anti-Semites' voice rang out—practiced by the Jews, who used claims of individual and civic improvement to poison the society in which they lived through undermining true (read: German) culture.[5]

The Russian cellist Gdal Saleski (1888–1967) published a comprehensive catalog of Jewish musicians in 1927 as a direct answer to the Wagnerian claim of Jewish musical parasitism (Saleski 1927). It is basically a catalog of composers, conductors, and instrumentalists. Saleski stressed that he was not interested in a religious or political definition of the Jew but "purely a racial one" (ibid.: vii). He argued through his biographical catalog that "Jewish musicians have undoubtedly contributed their mite to the world's music" (ibid.: viii). They have done so, however, as human beings, not as Jews: "In the realm of music there are no artificial racial and religious divisions. In this realm there reigns only talent and genius," which Jews show in great abundance. Saleski's views were quickly translated into popular form. In the mid-1930s the Anti-Defamation League of B'nai Brith published a series of pamphlets under the title of the "Fireside Discussion Group." (The echo of Franklin Roosevelt's "fireside chats" is unmistakable.) One, published in 1936 but typical of a wide range of such texts from the 1890s to the 1950s, is titled *Jews in Music.* "Jews have taken an even greater place," the pamphlet claimed, "as interpreters of music and instrumentalists than they have as composers. It has been estimated that out of every twelve musical artists, vocalists, violinists and conductors, eight are descendants of the people of Israel" (Fireside Discussion Group XVI n.d. [1936]: 3). Two full pages of the pamphlet's seven are devoted to violinists. "Violin virtuosity has become almost synonymous with Jewish musical genius. Saleski, in *Famous Musicians of a Wandering Race,* lists 73 violinists who have achieved recognition: prominent among them are Leopold Auer, Mischa Elman, Jascha Heifetz, Fritz Kreisler, Yehudi Menuhin, Erika Morine, Max Rosen, Toscha Seidel, and Efrem Zimbalist." The pamphlet's author continued in this vein for two pages with the biographies of Elman, Zimbalist, and Kreisler ("the greatest violinist who ever lived")[6] and ended with the then nineteen-year-old Menuhin. In Saleski's own work, the section on violinists is by far the longest. Jews made an important contribution to Western culture as violinists, even if their own "relationship" to being Jewish was truly tenuous. But the link between musical high culture and Jewish identity, so strongly denied until the close of the nineteenth century, had by the 1930s become an intrinsic part of the self-definition of Central European Jewry.

The myth about being Jewish as an incomprehensible mental construct that leads to creative antagonism was answered in the early twentieth century by myths about music of necessity leading to other forms of creativity. Both myths sought to answer the question of why Jewish "genius" arises. One viewed the scientific creativity of the Jews as stemming from their imposed position as marginal to established science (*Wissenschaft*); the other saw their musicality as a key factor central to their lives as educated citizens (*Bildungsbürgertum*) and as Jews.

Theodor Herzl wrote in January 1898 that in 1895

> during the last two months of my residence in Paris I wrote the book *The Jewish State*. . . . I do not recollect ever having written anything in such an elevated frame of mind as that book. . . . I worked at it every day until I was completely exhausted; my

only relaxation in the evening consisted of listening to Wagner's music, especially to *Tannhäuser*, an opera I went to every time it was performed. Only on the evenings when there was no performance at the Opera did I feel doubts about the correctness of my ideas. (cited in Robertson 1999: 150)

The Phantom of the Opéra is in point of fact the centrality of musical culture for the definition of Jewish creativity. Herzl imagined a Jewish state, first in Argentina, and then in Palestine, with a side trip to Uganda, where European culture would dominate—a world imagined to look like Switzerland or the Austro-Hungarian Empire, without the nationalist conflicts and bound together by Jewish identity and Western high culture. Indeed he saw the projected "Jewish State" (*der Judenstaat*) in his programmatic pamphlet of that title from 1896 through the metaphor of music:

> presuppos[ing] the application of scientific methods. We cannot journey out of Egypt today in the primitive fashion of ancient times. We shall previously obtain an accurate account of our number and strength. The undertaking of that great and ancient gestar of the Jews in primitive days bears much the same relation to ours that some wonderful melody bears to a modern opera. We are playing the same melody with many more violins, flutes, harps, violoncellos, and bass viols; with electric light, decorations, choirs, beautiful costumes, and with the first singers of their day. (Herzl 1946)

The world of Zionism is in an odd way the orchestra at the Paris Opéra bringing together all of the instruments that now represent the heterogeneity of world Jewry. The Jewish state was in one way the ultimate acknowledgment of the centrality of music in the mental lives of modern Jews. The irony, of course, is that the British Zionist Israel Zangwill (1864–1926), in his extraordinarily popular play *The Melting Pot* (published 1909), used the very same image of the orchestra, now composed of all of the nationalities of the world, including the Jews of Eastern Europe, to represent the ideal American state. Music in Zangwill's drama represents the ability of Jews to integrate into the world of the New World. All nationalities in the end are incorporated in the "New World Symphony" composed by his Jewish protagonist.

As modern music history followed its course toward modernism in the twentieth century, there could be little doubt that Jews had been assigned multiple roles that would shape the future of music, by both their detractors and supporters, by both Jews and non-Jews. If there was no single answer to the question I pose in my title, echoing with that question the era that unfolds in the pages of this book, nonetheless the question had never been more critical and public in the ways music's presence in a high culture was increasingly destabilized by the historical events inseparable from modernity's twentieth-century course: the dissolution of the long nineteenth century in World War I; the rise of fascism between the world wars; the Holocaust; and processes of return and revival accompanying European reunification at the end of the century. The essays in this book are themselves neither univocal nor unequivocal in the ways they respond to this common question of music and Jewish history. The essayists draw our attention to Jewish roles in modern music that are barely recognized; they also identify tendencies to overestimate the Jewish role in musical modernism. Above all, they illustrate the need to close the space between the question of Jewish identity in the musics of modernity and the Jewish question itself. On the eve of musical modernism, when the music history of one century gave way to another, Jews were making music in all the domains of a modern world.

Here the battle lines were set: The twentieth-century musical experience, as articulated by Jewish (however defined) composers and performers, was profoundly shaped by their quiet awareness of the real question: Can Jews make music in a Western context? And what happens when they do?

::: **NOTES** :::

1. See Wagner 1894: 88 and 90. On the background and reception of Wagner's "Das Judentum in der Musik" see Fischer 2000.

2. Again it is interesting to note the attribution of a Jewish identity to a figure such as Rossini. Philip Gossett, the dean of Rossini scholars, wrote to me privately that

"I cannot for the life of me imagine where Disraeli got that idea. It's a unicum, to my knowledge. Indeed the frequently quoted remark of Rossini's about Meyerbeer, Halévy, and the Opéra was that Rossini had given up composing for that august institution until 'the Jews finish with their Sabbath.' That's more likely to be the way he thought about it! Rossini, by the way, DID have a world of respect for Meyerbeer and showed it in many different ways."

3. Cf. Galton 1869: 23 (on race); 4 (on Jews and Italians); 234 (on Heine). Galton's views were critiqued in his own days because of his inability to consider class as a factor; see Constable 1905. On the persistence of Galton's views see Osborn 1952–53: 39–40. See also Cowan 1969, Walter 1983, and Kosacoff 1986.

4. Sullivan's inclusion seems as odd as Rossini's, but the intent was to show the quality of "Jewish music," not to present any real lineage. See Sullivan's genealogy at http://math.boisestate.edu/gas/other_sullivan/genealogy/sul_genealogy.html (accessed June 20, 2007).

5. See Spotts 2002. In this regard see the anti-Semitic compilation of "Jews in Music" in Stengel and Gerigk 1999.

6. Amy Biancolli's biography of Fritz Kreisler (Biancolli 1998) contains an extensive discussion of Kreisler's Jewish background, which he never acknowledged and which his wife adamantly denied (see chapter 8, "Kreisler the Catholic, Kreisler the Jew"). Biancolli cites a 1992 interview by David Sackson of Franz Rupp, Fritz Kreisler's piano accompanist in the 1930s. Rupp states that he once asked Kreisler's brother, the cellist Hugo Kreisler, about their Jewish background, to which Hugo responded simply, "I'm a Jew, but my brother, I don't know." According to Biancolli, Kreisler's father, Salomon Severin Kreisler (also called Samuel Severin Kreisler), a physician and amateur violinist from Kraków, was almost certainly Jewish. Fritz Kreisler's mother, Anna, was a Roman Catholic, and probably an "Aryan." According to Louis Lochner's 1950 biography, *Fritz Kreisler*, Kreisler was reared as a Roman Catholic. However, according to unpublished parts of the manuscript uncovered by Biancolli in the Library of Congress, he was baptized only at the age of twelve. The bottom line seems to be that Kreisler was at least half Jewish, and his reticence on the subject was primarily an attempt to placate his highly anti-Semitic wife, Harriet. ("Fritz hasn't a drop of Jewish blood in his veins!" she is said to have vehemently responded to an inquiry from Leopold Godowsky. Godowsky retorted: "He must be very anemic.")

::: WORKS CITED :::

"Are You Related to Sir Arthur Sullivan?" http://math.boisestate.edu/gas/other_sullivan/genealogy/sul_genealogy.html, accessed July 26, 2007.

Berl, Heinrich. 1921. "Das Judentum in der abendländischen Musik." *Der Jude* 6: 495–505.

———. 1923. "Zum Problem einer jüdischen Musik." *Der Jude* 7: 309–20.

———. 1926. *Das Judentum in der Musik*. Stuttgart: Deutsche Verlags-Anstalt.

Biancolli, Amy. 1998. *Fritz Kreisler: Love's Sorrow, Love's Joy*. Portland, Ore.: Amadeus Press.

Brod, Max. 1916. "Jüdische Volksmelodien." *Der Jude* 1: 344–45.

Chamberlain, Houston Stewart. 1934. *Die Grundlagen des neunzehnten Jahrhunderts*. Munich: F. Bruckmann.

Constable, Frank Challice. 1905. *Poverty and Hereditary Genius: A Criticism of Mr. Francis Galton's Theory of Hereditary Genius*. London: A. C. Fifield.

Cowan, Ruth Leah Schwartz. 1969. "Sir Francis Galton and the Study of Heredity in the Nineteenth Century." Ph.D. dissertation, Johns Hopkins University.

Dauber, Jeremy Asher. 2004. *Antonio's Devils: Writers of the Jewish Enlightenment and the Birth of Modern Hebrew and Yiddish Literature*. Stanford, Calif.: Stanford University Press.

Disraeli, Benjamin. 1983. *Coningsby, or The New Generation*. Harmondsworth: Penguin.

Einstein, Alfred. 1927. "Der Jude in der Musik." *Der Morgen* 2: 590–602.

Fireside Discussion Group XVI. N. d. [1936]. *Jews in Music*. Chicago: Anti-Defamation League of the B'nai Brith.

Fischer, Jens Malte. 2000. *Richard Wagners "Das Juden-tum in der Musik": Eine kritische Dokumentation als Beitrag zur Geschichte des Antisemitismus.* Frankfurt am Main: Insel Verlag.

Fritsch, Theodor. 1892a. *Fragen und Antworten über das Juden-Thema.* Leipzig: Verlag von Theodor Fritsch.

———. 1892b. *Statistik des Judenthums.* Leipzig: Verlag von Theodor Fritsch.

Galton, Francis. 1869. *Hereditary Genius: An Inquiry into Its Laws and Consequences.* London: Macmillan.

Herzig, Arno. 2002. *Judentum und Aufklärung: Jüdisches Selbstverständnis in der bürgerlichen Öffentlichkeit.* Göttingen: Vandenhoeck & Ruprecht.

Herzl, Theodor. 1946. *The Jewish State.* Trans. Sylvie D'Avigdor. New York: American Zionist Emergency Council. http://www.geocities.com/Vienna/6640/zion/judenstaadt.html, accessed July 26, 2007.

Hess, Jonathan M. 2002. *Germans, Jews and the Claims of Modernity.* New Haven, Conn.: Yale University Press.

Jacobs, Joseph. 1889. *The Jewish Race: A Study in National Character.* London: N. p.

———. 1891. *Studies in Jewish Statistics: Social, Vital and Anthropometric.* London: D. Nutt.

Knox, Robert. 1850. *The Races of Men: A Fragment.* London: H. Renshaw.

Kosacoff, Michael I. 1986. "A Critical Examination of Some Assumptions of Psychometric Theory (Galton, Eugenics)." Ph.D. dissertation, New York University.

Lochner, Louis Paul. 1950. *Fritz Kreisler.* New York: Macmillan.

Meyer, Michael A. 2001. *Judaism within Modernity: Essays on Jewish History and Religion.* Detroit, Mich.: Wayne State University Press.

Nadel, Arno. 1923. "Jüdische Musik." *Der Jude* 7: 227–36.

Nettl, Paul. 1923. *Alte jüdische Spielleute und Musiker.* Prague: J. Flesch.

Osborn, Frederick. 1952–53. "Galton's 'Hereditary Genius.'" *Eugenics Review* 44: 39–40.

Robertson, Ritchie, ed. 1999. *The German-Jewish Dialogue: An Anthology of Literary Texts, 1749–1993.* Oxford: Oxford University Press.

Saleski, Gdal. 1927. *Famous Musicians of a Wandering Race: Biographical Sketches of Outstanding Figures of Jewish Origin in the Musical World.* Trans. by Maurice M. Altermann and Celia Krieger. New York: Bloch.

de Saussine, Renee. 1953. *Paganini.* New York: Hutchenson.

Schiller, David M. 2003. *Bloch, Schoenberg, Bernstein: Assimilating Jewish Music.* Oxford: Oxford University Press.

Schwarz, Daniel R. 1979. *Disraeli's Fiction.* London: Macmillan.

Simmel, Georg. 1950. "The Stranger." In Kurt Wolff, ed. and trans., *The Sociology of Georg Simmel*, 402–8. New York: Free Press.

Sorkin, David. 2000. *The Berlin Haskalah and German Religious Thought: Orphans of Knowledge.* London: Vallentine Mitchell.

Spotts, Frederic. 2002. *Hitler and the Power of Aesthetics.* London: Hutchinson.

Stengel, Theo, and Herbert Gerigk. 1999. *Ausgemerzt! Das Lexikon der Juden in der Musik und seine mörderischen Folgen.* Cologne: Dittrich.

Wagner, Richard. 1894. "Judaism in Music." In *Richard Wagner's Prose Works*, trans., William Ashton Ellis. 7 vols. 3:79–100. London: Kegan Paul Trench Trubner. Orig. publ. 1850.

Walter, Wolfgang. 1983. *Der Geist der Eugenik: Francis Galtons Wissenschaftsreligion in kultursoziologischer Perspektive.* Bielefeld: Universität Bielefeld.

Zweig, Arnold. 1937. *Insulted and Exiled: The Truth about the German Jews.* London: John Miles.

ACKNOWLEDGMENTS

The transitions that rendered Jewish history modern in the nineteenth century and that engendered Jewish modernism in the twentieth century were more often than not the results of unexpected, even extraordinary, juxtapositions of aesthetic and intellectual resources. The present book also owes much to the confluence of perspectives from scholars and musicians who were accustomed to taking account of the impact of Jewish music on modern cultural history in quite different ways. Accordingly, the book is not so much the product of traditional disciplines of musical scholarship—historical musicology, ethnomusicology, or music theory—as of unexpected and, we dare to hope, extraordinary disciplinary juxtapositions that result when Jewish music is fully embraced as a subject of modern Jewish studies.

From the outset the lectures and concerts that began to shape the core of *Jewish Musical Modernism, Old and New* were responses to an idea and a gift, both generous in their own ways, from Joel Honigberg and Carol Honigberg. It was the Honigbergs' hope that a new series of lectures in Jewish Studies at the University of Chicago might open productive areas of discussion about modern Jewish history and the arts, particularly in what has come to be known as fin-de-siècle Central Europe. It was perhaps inevitable that music should have found its way into a central position in the planning of the Honigberg Lectures because, on one hand, the Honigbergs are a family of distinguished musicians, and because, on the other, Jewish music enjoys distinctive support at Chicago from both the Department of Music and the Committee on Jewish Studies. We were in a position not just to talk about Jewish music but to make it sound in very distinctive ways. The Honigbergs recognized this possibility, and this book—its words and its sounds—is a tribute to their vision and generosity.

The University of Chicago gave free rein to the planning of the Honigberg Lectures and concerts and to their transformation into a book and CD. Philip Gossett, Dean of the Humanities at the University of Chicago at the time of the Honigberg Lectures in the autumn of 1999, characteristically urged us to take on more rather than less, and it was with his encouragement that the lectures themselves came to parallel a graduate seminar in Jewish music, which in turn integrated the Honigberg lecturers into the classroom. Not surprisingly, the participants in that seminar, especially Rich Jankowsky, Bertie Kibreah, Yossi Maurey, Joshua Pilzer, and Loraine Schneider, enhanced the Honigberg Lectures through their enthusiastic engagement with the diverse paths it followed and their challenging inquiry, which has served as a counterpoint to many of the ideas in this book, particularly those in my own contributions. Chicago colleagues also contributed in substantial ways to the discussions accompanying the lectures, and I should particularly like to thank Sander Gilman, David Levin, Martin Stokes, and, this time as a musicologist, Philip Gossett.

This book underwent the transition from lectures to essays to chapters at the same time that the New Budapest Orpheum Society underwent a transition from a troupe of interested musicians for whom Jewish cabaret was still perhaps more exotic than anything else to an ensemble committed to the diverse musical repertories of Jewish modernism. The concept behind the book has benefited enormously from the more experimental stage of the New Budapest Orpheum Society—appearances at University of Chicago conferences or synagogue performances—to the current semiprofessional stage at which our successes threaten to catch up with us as we take to the boards at the United States Memorial Holocaust Museum, the Neue Galerie, Symphony Space, and the YIVO Institute for Jewish Research. This book owes much, beyond the accompanying CD itself, to the members of the New Budapest Orpheum Society: Deborah Bard, Julia Bentley, the late Peter Blagoev, Stewart Figa, Iordanka Kissiova, Stewart Miller, Hank Tausend, and, last but not least, Ilya Levinson.

Concerts, rehearsals, arrangements, and lyrics do not just happen, so we also wish to thank Matthew Zuckerbraun, Robert Kendrick, chair of the Chicago Music Department, and Mary Jean Kraybill, associate dean for Development in the Humanities, for investing their trust in the New Budapest Orpheum Society. Nicholas J. Yasillo skillfully recorded and engineered the Hanns Eisler and Bertolt Brecht *Hollywooder Liederbuch* songs on the accompanying CD. We were particularly fortunate that James Ginsburg was willing to take us on as a project for Cedille Records, helping us sound better not only because he knows the ropes of sound engineering, but also because he really cares about what it is the New Budapesters have to say. The anonymous readers of the book responded with thoughtfulness and that balance of criticism and engagement that inspired us to take their challenges very seriously indeed. We thank those readers for sharing their time and thoughtfulness with us. With each detailed exchange about proofs and production with Erik Carlson I learned more not only about this book but also about the care and thoughtfulness necessary for publishing the best books today. As an opera scholar in her own right, Kathleen K. Hansell also cares about what musical troupes that take to the stage have to say, but she also takes pains to ensure that words about and within music speak with equal eloquence. We were surely lucky that she was willing to take this project of words and music under her wing at the University of Chicago Press.

As I have worked with the contributors to this book, discussing with them their lectures and the carefully crafted prose of their chapters, I have realized that I was unusually fortunate to muster such a distinguished team of colleagues. The chapters and the diverse approaches, in many ways, do not constitute a typical book on Jewish music; rather, they push the study of Jewish music in new directions by raising questions that elude those in search of the typical. The results

of their critical thinking are nonetheless no less convincing; indeed, they are particularly convincing about the potential for Jewish music scholarship to achieve much more by drawing upon the unexpected and extraordinary perspectives of those outside an otherwise inchoate field. Thanks to Mitchell G. Ash, Pamela M. Potter, Edwin Seroussi, Kay Kaufman Shelemay, and Michael P. Steinberg for setting in motion the critical transitions that this book marks.

Jewish music research has never failed to provide me with an opening toward the issues of modernity and modernism and beyond to the most compelling intellectual challenges of our own day. More often than not, it has been my privilege to turn outward to embrace new intellectual domains, rather than inward to be ensnared by the narrow debates of disciplinary provincialism. No one gains the opportunities of turning outward without sustained encouragement from others, that is, from those who travel along. In my case, that encouragement has been sustained even more by the love and trust of my family. To Andrea, Ben, and Christine, I cannot say thanks often enough.

Chicago, Illinois

The Transcendent Moment of Jewish Modernism

::: PHILIP V. BOHLMAN

Until now, there has never been a "Jewish" opera. . . . If in Berlin, for the first time outside Palestine, an attempt is made to establish a Jewish opera, what is "Jewish" now lies in the performers and in the audience, which together create a sort of unspeakable atmosphere that in an especially curious way envelops a Jewish community. . . . Suddenly, we have before us a Jewish national theater. . . . Many in the midst of all this might not really want it to be this way. But it really is.

"Oper im Kulturbund," *Jüdische Rundschau*,
17 November 1933

A moment when music became Jewish. A transcendent moment when to become Jewish meant being freed by music from the crisis of history. This is the moment of Jewish modernism, revealed by the transcendence unleashed by music in European Jewish society from the closing decades of the nineteenth century until the Holocaust. It is the moment into which the essays in this book draw us.

The considerable contribution of Jews to the historical underpinnings of modernity and to the aesthetic conditions of modernism has, at least since the mid-twentieth century, focused one of the crucial arguments in modern historiography. Modernity, as an emancipatory transformation of Western culture, was by no means specific to European Jewish society in any way, but it is Jewish society that often provides one of the most clear-cut bodies of empirical evidence to illustrate modernity (see Katz 1987; Meyer 1988; Cheyette and Marcus 1998; Vital 1999). Modernism—broadly speaking, the cultural, artistic, and scientific products of modernity and the expressive form these take—is no less inseparable from discussions of Jewish intellectuals and artists. Indeed, a discussion of any group of modernists from which Jews were absent is quite unimaginable. Marx, Freud, Kafka, Schoenberg, Wittgenstein—their contributions are inseparable from the very metaphysics of modernism (see Botstein 1991; Bell 1999; Karady 1999; Volkov 2001).

Modernity and modernism, however, are but the points of departure for the new and different story this book narrates. Whereas Jewish modernism emerged from and, at least in its initial stages, overlapped with modernity and modernism, its historical trajectory was distinctive in several decisive ways. Jewish modernism did not move toward and participate in the universal; rather, it gathered its impetus by a centripetal movement toward the local. Born of emancipation and spurred on by assimilation, Jewish modernism did not seek to free itself from its origins. Jewish modernism did not so much collapse time as it recalibrated history, seeking to establish a place in history rather than to liberate itself from history. Indeed, the historical telos of Jewish modernism differed in one very fundamental way from modernism at large: It neither moved toward nor did it give way to postmodernism of any kind, much less to something we might call Jewish postmodernism. To the extent that Jewish modernism was propelled by an historical telos at all, it does not lend itself to being defined by an endpoint. Jewish modernism was not simply the culminating moment in what Friedrich Battenberg (1990) has called the "European era of the Jews"; it opened toward a transcendence of that age altogether.

The language of modernism aspires toward the conditions of music. Modernism engenders a reconfiguration of time, and music both embodies and encodes many of the processes that reconfigure time. Because of its temporal ambiguity—music absorbs and articulates time, but it unwillingly represents time through narrative meaning—it lends itself to wide-ranging modernist vocabularies and experiments. The modernist appropriation of time, nonetheless, draws attention to music by privileging it. Other forms of artistic expression adopt the conditions of music, for example, rhythm in poetry and painting. Modernism marks music in special ways, thus empowering it as never before (see Albright 2000).

In Jewish modernism the empowerment of music was even more striking and sweeping because of its potential to effect transcendence. The point here is deceptively simple. One of the signals that determined the beginning of the historical moment to which I refer as Jewish modernism occurred when the diverse expressive practices of sacred and secular Jewish society were called "Jewish music." In fact, both components of the designation, "Jewish" and "music," and, above all, their combination reflected a metaphysical sea change. For one thing, the two terms drew attention to their essential contradiction, "Jewish" as a reflection of the religious character of cultural and ethnic identity, "music" as secular cultural practices. Perhaps because of this contradiction the revolution in nomenclature happened quickly: it began around 1880 and was fully in place by the turn of the century (see Bohlman 2005 for a documentary study of the discourse history that unfolded after "Jewish folk music" was named).

The act of naming did not so much create a different music as intensify the level of discourse about music as a phenomenon of defining and ascribing Jewish identity, particularly in a modern context where that identity was increasingly complex and ambiguous. The debates about what Jewish music was or might be were sometimes acrimonious and at other times mustered for high political stakes, for example, in early Zionism, whose history was in most respects coeval with that of Jewish modernism. It was not only discourse, moreover, that emerged from the debates. Folklorists went about the task of collecting volumes of Jewish folk song; popular songsmiths went about publishing Jewish popular music; cantors, choir directors, and organists went about revolutionizing the performance practices of the synagogue. The physical and ontological boundaries that determined just where Jewish music took place could no longer contain it as Jewish music's presence in modern Jewish society exploded (Bohlman 2004).

The suddenness with which Jewish music appeared on the landscape of modern Jewish society was also emblematic of crisis, indeed, of internal and external crises with varying magnitudes. The moment of Jewish modernism was anything but a period for the celebration of selfness. In its early

decades, the 1880s and 1890s, anti-Semitism actually intensified as a counterpart to the feverish gathering of Jewish music. Pogroms spread through Eastern Europe (Karady 1999: 174–79), and fin-de-siècle Vienna's *Sezession* provided an aesthetic mechanism for placing distance between liberal Jews and rising anti-Semitism in the public sphere (Schorske 1980: 116–80). The promise of emancipation was thwarted repeatedly as Jewish modernist composers failed to make inroads into official musical circles. As the discourse of Jewish modernism intensified, so too did the sense of crisis. The counterhistory of crisis forming a counterpoint with Jewish modernism was not wanting for a teleological impetus of its own, the ineluctable pull toward a crisis of catastrophic proportions, the Holocaust (see the essays in Postone and Santner 2003).

The epigraph that begins this introduction appeared at a moment of crisis, and yet its tone of crisis is barely audible. Instead, the anonymous author of this review describing the opening opera performance in Berlin's Jüdischer Kulturbund (see Akademie der Künste 1992), a racial and cultural ghetto imposed on the Jews of Germany in 1933, responds to what appears to him (or her) as revelation: Jewish opera had come into being, in a place and in a musical form where one might least expect it. The moment itself—embodied by the performers and the audience far more than the place and musical form—somehow overwhelmed the increasingly present crisis, the translation of German anti-Semitism into the physical imprisonment of the Kulturbund. The voice we hear had not lost its capacity to marvel at the transcendence of the moment. The end of Jewish modernism was undeniably imminent, yet its historical telos had been forestalled through the perception of Jewishness—of modern Jewishness—in a musical space Jewish music had not previously occupied.

Alt/Neu: The Ancient Modernism of Jewish Music

The prayer following the Passover meal had been recited, the end of *hagadah* had been reached, and the *seder* had come to its conclusion. Everyone passed into the living room, where a phonograph with Joseph's narrative on a cylinder stood on the table. . . . David sat down beside the machine, turned the horn toward the listeners, and announced, "Our friend, Mr. Joe Levy, will now speak." For a moment, the machine shuddered, then a strong, masculine voice spoke clearly from it. "Welcome to everyone here tonight! I shall now report to you about the modern migration of the Jews."

Herzl 1935 [1902]: 314

A change in voice marks the passage from the *alt* to the *neu*, from the old to the new, at the opening of the second chapter of the fourth book in Theodor Herzl's novel, *Altneuland* (Old/New Land), one of several works of fiction, drama, and skits for the cabaret published by the founder of modern Zionism.[1] This passage, hardly isolated as a juxtaposition of the "old" and the "new" in the novel's title, envoices the narratives marking the passage between myth and history. Song and prayer performatively mark myth, that is, the story of Passover. History enters the evening through

the recording horn, which closes the spaces of the Diaspora through a mechanical ingathering of modern voices. Joe Levy's report on the "modern migration of the Jews" (*neue Judenwanderung*) unfolds over the course of the entire fourth book of the novel, "Passover," a disembodied voice able to claim a long-playing quality of recorded technology not yet realizable in 1902.

Throughout *Altneuland*, written and published at the fin de siècle that is so often invoked to locate modernism in time and space (see, e.g., Seroussi in this volume), music and narrative define the space between the past and the future, reconfiguring the chronotope of old and new.[2] When Herzl's characters finally reach the goal of their journey to modern Israel, they metaphorically enter the space of the rebuilt temple, where Friedrich Löwenberg experiences the chorus and orchestra of the temple, which, however, in the first instance reminded him of Heinrich Heine's *Hebräische Melodien*. The juxtapositions of old and new would seem not to make sense, because they so repeatedly serve as emblems for what at first glance seem to be opposites. The narratives of myth and history, the symbols of past and present, the ancient melodies and the "new songs" presaged in the Bible—all these provide the moment of Jewish modernism in the preoccupation of Herzl and his generation with the ancient modernity of the future to which they so hopefully turned.

Theodor Herzl's search for the modern in the narrative space between old and new was by no means limited to the Zionist movement, if indeed Zionism provided one means of politicizing Jewish modernism by propelling it into the public sphere. The mythic-historical pair, old-new, had an extensive currency in the Diaspora, for example, in the designation of one of the most historically significant synagogues (often referred to as Europe's "oldest" synagogue), the *Altneusynagoge* (Old-New Synagogue) of Prague. Crucial to the coupling of past and present was the conviction that Jewish history was at any given moment transitory, passing from past to future, and constructing the future from the past. The modernity of the old-new chronotope was always explicit, for example, in the titles and subjects of Herzl's various writings, in the fine arts and politics. The "new ghetto" of his most famous play was in the Vienna of 1893 (Herzl 1935 [1897]: 1–124). The subtitle of his most important political tract, *Der Judenstaat* (The Jewish State), is "the attempt at a modern solution to the Jewish Question" (Herzl 1896). The call for Jewish modernism spread across Europe, connecting East and West, and historicizing the Diaspora in works such as Nathan Birnbaum's *Die jüdische Moderne* (Jewish Modernism), which historicized the past and reimagined it as the future (Birnbaum 1989; reprint of articles published 1893–1905 and reprinted in collection [Czernowitz: Birnbaum & Kohut, 1910]). Music inevitably found its way into these modernist narratives (see, e.g., Botstein and Hanak 2004). A double process of naming accompanied the integration of music into Jewish modernism as prayer and recitation, folk and popular music, cantorial and classical music, secular and sacred music all became Jewish the moment they became modern.

Sacred song and liturgy, folk and popular music, became Jewish and modern at the same historical moment, so much so that Jewishness and modernism were mutually dependent by the early decades of the twentieth century (see the essays in Mendelsohn 1993). The concepts of Jewishness and modernism I employ here and the authors employ elsewhere in the book are marked categories of identity. Jewish music does not simply refer to all music made by Jews, as some scholars have dismissively claimed; rather, it identifies a music that reflects the conditions and identities that accrue to Jewish communities in their encounter with modernity. That encounter, furthermore, was mediated, through the fictional imagination of Theodor Herzl writing about the past in the present, through the wax-cylinder recording machines used by A. Z. Idelsohn to record the past in the present,[3] or through the historical modes and modalities mustered by modern cantors and modernist composers, such as Arnold Schoenberg.

In the search for the modern, the ancient provided the critical connective. Music, because of its temporality and narrativity, provided an almost ideal connective. According to traditional theories of orality, music survived because of its time-boundedness, the unbroken performance of ritual and liturgical cycles that stretched from ancient Jerusalem to modern Jerusalem. Although modern Jerusalem had not yet been reached, the modernist transformation of music offered a compelling opportunity, all the more so because of a conviction that orality and literacy were inextricably linked in Jewish tradition. It was modernity, as the phonographs of Herzl and Idelsohn were to symbolize, that would mediate that link. It was in Jewish modernism that the new musical language for that link would find its most complex and arresting expression.

Jewish Modernism at the Border of Transcendence

The transcendence with which this book concerns itself takes place at the border between myth and history. In the broadest sense, the essays that follow examine what happens during a moment and in the space of transition. In the course of the moment, indeed, in the process of bringing that moment into being, history and geography, time and place are transcended. The transition between myth and history does not move in any single direction, say, from myth to history, as if the latter superseded the former. Throughout the course of Jewish history, particularly in the Diaspora, myth has often symbolized a powerful alternative to history. *Eretz yisrael*, the "land of Israel," occupies a position on both sides of diasporic history, with exodus and return framing history in mythological counterpoint. The moment of Jewish modernism that we consider here arose nonetheless from a particularly complex calculus of transition between myth and history.

Jewish modernism consciously and subconsciously drew upon the past and even depended upon the possibility of recuperating the past as the present and future. Myth is crucial for history because it provides palpable and powerful symbols for revival, the ancient modernity toward which the aesthetics of modernism drew Jewish music. Jewish modernism also depended on the sense of loss and destruction that accompanied Jewish history. We witness this most vividly in the historical symbol that defined the Diaspora at both its ancient beginning and its modern ending, the destruction of the two temples in Jerusalem, particularly the Second Temple in 70 CE. The loss of musical instruments and musical professionals with the Temple unleashed the striving for their recovery, which in turn reinstated the telos of modern Jewish music history. Ironically, loss and nostalgia afforded meaning to modernism, though not because of the ways they salvaged the past, but because of the paths along which they provided salvation in the future.

Modernism itself embodied a set of distinctive historical processes converging in the late nineteenth century: emancipation and acculturation in Central Europe; pogrom and migration in Eastern Europe; colonialism and orientalism in Sephardic and Eastern communities; nationalism and Zionism within European Jewry. Each of these modernist phenomena, moreover, was predicated on myth as well as history. The full achievement of emancipation and the realization of the Zionist state required a capacity to believe in myth. The vocabulary of easternness that increasingly distinguished Jewishness in the arts also resulted from the encoding of myth in modern forms (Gilman 1993; Stein 2004). If the border articulated by myth and history that we examine in this book became particularly pronounced between 1880 and 1950, it also proved particularly fertile for new possibilities of transcendence, and these together constituted the moment of Jewish modernism.

Abundant dichotomies form at the border between myth and history, and many of these seem to display doubleness and dialectic. Myth and history often assume the character of dialectic. The modernist border also separated the Jewish community, which maintained its own polity and cultural life, from a political and economic public sphere to which European Jews were increasingly making significant contributions. In the realm of music, too, dichotomies came into sharper focus and in turn became significant factors in the representation of the borders between myth and history. On one side of those borders were the practices of Jewish music that were entirely limited by religious, ritual, and community functions, whereas on the other side was a growing movement toward autonomous musical practices, which benefited exceptionally from the contributions of Jews.

The borders between myth and history at once engendered a growing reconfiguration of self and other. Within the Jewish community the sense of self became more problematic as local forms of Jewishness, for example in liturgical music, were enriched by encounter with practices that were more global in scope. Collectors of Jewish music, such as Abraham Zvi Idelsohn (1882–1938), undertook massive projects to gather all the musics of the Jewish people into a systematic whole, and in so doing they remapped the borders between Jewish communities and, by extension, among Jewish communities and the diverse cultural influences on them. Jewish music during this period began to mean anything from the written practices of the Ashkenazic synagogue to the oral traditions of Sephardic sacred musicians who had full command of Arab or Turkish classical systems. The meanings of these musical borders multiplied, and they therefore provided a template for remapping the Diaspora and turning the dichotomies of self versus other and myth versus history inside out. Jewish music, as a result, increasingly became a music in which the identity of selfness was largely a product of difference. Unquestionably, such reconfigurations of borders within and without the Diaspora struck many as counterintuitive, but it was precisely for that reason that the musical diversity of a recharted Diaspora so powerfully contributed to the representation of Jewish modernism (see Bohlman 2002).

The destabilization of the relation between self and other intensified the sense of self-consciousness that characterized Jewish modernism. Just to what extent did emancipation undermine the Jewishness of European society? How Jewish does liturgy remain once Hebrew texts are replaced with modern vernaculars? To what extent can aesthetic autonomy retain traces of meaningful Jewish identity? The debates and public discussions about the impact of fin-de-siècle culture and modernism on Jewish society proliferated in the closing decades of the nineteenth century. Not only was great concern directed toward a much wider range of cultural topics, among them music, but the very public nature of the debates and discussions was amplified as never before. On one level, these debates responded to the growing consciousness of self through pragmatic solutions. The systematization of modern Hebrew, which began in the 1880s on the very threshold of

Jewish modernism, was one of the first and most sustained responses to what was increasingly viewed as a crisis of self-consciousness. Political solutions occupied another level of response, and among these the founding of political and cultural Zionism in the 1890s is the most obviously modern. Creating a modern Hebrew language, as a project of Zionism, was highly political, but so too were the invention and canonization of a music with modern Hebrew texts, even when these were used in folk songs from a past in which modern Hebrew did not exist, much less lend itself to orally transmitted folk song (see, e.g., the transitions from Hebrew folk song to art song in the *shireh chalutzim*, or "pioneer songs," gathered as an anthology in Nathan 1994).

In the temporal and geographical space of transition Jewish music comes into existence but is not weighed down by the usual threadbare dichotomies (e.g., whether Jewish music can be both sacred and secular). The usual dichotomies, instead, undergo a process of negation, falling victim at the border region between myth and history. Theodor Adorno has referred to this process as one of negative dialectics (Adorno 1973), which Jürgen Habermas has extended even more pointedly as a condition, if not precondition, of modernism (Habermas 1985).[4] The power of the space of transition to diffuse the preexisting historical dichotomies becomes sweeping and crucial if modernism is to supplant the crushing hegemony of a global history that is presumed to culminate in Europe. European history, with its anti-Semitism and rejection of otherness, is negated in this space. Crossing it as a border region,

thus, might afford the possibility of entering into the reconfigured public spaces beyond, where Jewish identity is no longer a liability and restriction, the expression of otherness that contrasts with Europeanness.

The turn toward self-consciousness in Jewish music was no less public and passionate, and it was distinctly modern in its focus on the border between myth and history. In an era of growing nationalism, it was Jewish folk music that first demanded attention as a topic for public discussion and debate. Motivated by a sense of impending loss, philologists, folklorists, and musicologists set out in search of repertories they could place in anthologies of Jewish folk song (see Bohlman 2005). The significance of establishing a canon of Jewish folk song captured the attention of almost every Jewish intellectual working in both secular and theological traditions (e.g., Max Brod, Martin Buber, and Fritz Mordechai Kaufmann). It is significant that the public debate and discussion about Jewish folk song produced very little unity. It was not unity (e.g., the identification of a core repertory or even of a single language, such as Yiddish) that drove the discussions. When Jewish songs were wanting, particularly for use by newly emerging social organizations, they could be composed. The more compelling and disturbing question was whether composition was no more than invention, whether the structural components of Jewishness were sufficient to claim that modern Jewish folk song still retained the identity of an earlier Jewish folk song. The concern that it did not was great indeed, and it is hardly surprising that the discourse of self-consciousness it generated was equally great, all the more so be-cause it adapted the language of transcendence (Bohlman 2002).

The discourse of self-consciousness quickly yielded a panoply of representational practices in the arts (see Cohn 1998: 186–219). These prac-tices spread across the visual and decorative arts, where they again spawned questions about the extent to which claims of Jewishness could be ap-plied in the representational domains previously excluded from Jewish visual aesthetics.[5] By the late nineteenth century architecture, too, had de-veloped distinctive vocabularies for representing Jewishness, most notable among them the use of arabesque on the internal and external surfaces of synagogues built in the form of mosques. As extraordinary as it may seem that synagogues should resemble mosques in order to be recog-nizably Jewish, Moorish-style synagogues spread throughout the Diaspora, effectively closing the gap between traditional Jewish symbols of the East and the modernist fantasy of orientalism, and then locating the space of Jewish worship it-self in the secular space of the metropole, literally on the city streets that gave the synagogues their names, such as Oranienburgerstraße Synagoge in Berlin or Dohány utca Synagogue in Budapest.[6]

The emergence of a Jewish belles lettres with Yiddish as a literary language was another case of modernism in the arts that took a decisively Jewish turn. Crucial to the writers of the Yid-dish literary movement in the second half of the nineteenth century was the capacity to transform Yiddish itself from an oral, vernacular language in numerous regional dialects into a written, elite language, suitable for a literature that crossed regional languages. Jewish journalists, too, dis-played a heightened degree of self-consciousness, and it is not surprising that the number of news-papers and journals explicitly drawing attention to the Jewish themes that filled their pages would expand exponentially in the early decades of the twentieth century. Some of these journals, such as *Ost und West* and Martin Buber's *Der Jude*, at-tracted contributions from Jewish intellectuals from throughout the world (cf. Brenner 1998; Lappin 2000). Others, especially Jewish newspa-pers, were local, but no less effective in emphasiz-ing the Jewish transformation of everyday culture (Stein 2004).[7]

Folklore and folk culture imagined to be Jew-ish and, by extension, authentic, provided crucial elements to the discourse of self-consciousness. On one hand, establishing the nature of Jewish folklore was a prerequisite for nationalist claims; therefore, folk songs, to take an obvious case in point, were incorporated into repertories of Zion-ist song. On the other hand, folklore enhanced the vocabulary of modernism, affording it a universal quality that wrenched artistic expression from the limitations of specific historical contexts. Folklore, by its very nature, should have provided a means of representing the authentic; when the authentic was not immediately available, folk-lore provided tools for its invention (see Brenner 1996: 129–52). Modernism in general emerged during a moment of increased exploration of folk culture, and Jewish modernism in specific relied on the explosion of interest in Jewish folk culture, ranging from Martin Buber's translation and publication of Hasidic folktales (1949) to the institutionalized endeavors of the St. Petersburg Society for Jewish Folk Music (cf. Ginsburg and Marek 1901). For the modernists, the documentation of Jewish folklore was not an end in itself, but rather the first stage in renegotiating the distinctions between folk and elite practices. As these practices converged because of a common aesthetic of Jewishness, they provided the impetus for new forms of modernist expression that transcended the two practices' former contradictions.

By around 1920 Jewish modernism itself had begun to demonstrate a palpable autonomy. It had, for example, acquired its own history, the result of another negation of the border between myth and history. The discourse of self-consciousness had come to describe Jewishness and "the Jew" as modern phenomena, capable of creativity in the arts or possessing an independent will responsive to a highly personal aesthetic.[8] The discourse history of Jewish modernism began to unfold as a series of distinct stages, with invention and discovery characterizing the late nineteenth century, consolidation and canonization distinguishing the early decades of the twentieth century, and a "renaissance of Jewish culture" emerging during the Weimar period (see especially M. Brenner 1996). In order to undergo a renaissance, Jewish culture necessarily acquired a history that drew upon the sundry ways in which categories of Jewish culture may have been reified. Ongoing musical revival is but one of the most striking of the mythico-sacred categories that found aesthetic and secular realization as Jewish modernism took shape. Such categories, in turn, grew from

the other process of autonomy, which shaped interpretive approaches to Jewish culture (see Gilman and Shain 1993).

Scientific principles borrowed from the physical sciences, such as acoustics, as well as from the humanistic sciences were mustered to identify the underlying structure and integrity of Jewish culture.[9] The study of Jewish music made possible by the systemization of musical repertories and scientific experimentation with them underwent what amounted to a scientific revolution during World War I and the decade that followed. In the ten volumes of his *Thesaurus of Hebrew-Oriental Melodies* (1914–32), Idelsohn used the acoustic methods of comparative linguistic analysis to design elaborate typologies of modal structure for Jewish music in Mediterranean and Eastern communities, thereby charting the presence of *maqām* (mode in Arab classical music, pl. *maqāmāt*) in Jewish sacred and secular practice. The Russian music theorist Joseph Yasser proposed an analytical system for what he called "Jewish harmony" (1938), thus extending the concept of Jewishness in music to a theoretical domain where it had not previously existed.[10]

The essays in this book provide very different answers to the question, How did different forms and practices of music making—obviously or obliquely Jewish—come to constitute the moment of Jewish modernism? Without essentializing music itself, the essays reveal the ways in which music draws attention to the border region between myth and history. Some of these ways are specific, if not unique, to music, whereas others require that music join together with other cultural practices. The authors do not ignore the possibility, however, that music's temporality plays a particularly important role in the reconfiguration of history that must take place if modernism is to emerge. Music reflects and provides a language for the various dichotomies that accrue to the moment of Jewish modernism. Music also makes possible the detachment from that moment, the phenomenon to which I refer in this introduction as transcendence.

Jewish Modernism: Three Acts Framed by Beginnings and Endings

Jewish modernism unfolded on the stage of European history from the 1880s until the 1940s in three successive acts. "Stage," in this sense, has both literal and figurative meanings that together suggest the complex and contradictory tensions of confrontation and border crossing between the community and the public sphere, between Jewish and non-Jewish worlds. The stage was, crucially, a place of performance, indeed, musical performance. The stage was literally the *bima* (Hebrew, "pulpit" *and* "stage"),[11] on which the cantor appeared in the late eighteenth century to personalize and professionalize the cantillation and liturgy of the synagogue (see Seroussi in this volume; Bohlman 1994). Many of the musical practices, moreover, that came to occupy center stage during the moment of Jewish modernism were themselves traditions of the stage: Jewish cabaret and popular song, Yiddish musical theater, and opera and film in the high modernism of the new Viennese School.[12]

Figuratively, the stage of history provided a setting for encounter, on one hand, and for experimental aesthetic forms and unexpected patterns of musical cross-fertilization, on the other. The stage transformed the nature of spectatorship in modern European society. Giving structure to the framework for each of the acts were larger events of European and world history and events within Jewish society itself. It is especially appropriate to interpret these events as responses and to look to modernism as a vessel that shaped and contained—and ultimately failed to contain—events and the responses to them.

Act 1 (ca. 1880–1914): Discovery and Invention

> The songs themselves contain the mode and style in which they are performed. In some cases, these are highly Jewish in character. Because the songs live as sung phenomena among the people, and because it is the poet or composer who shapes the melodies, they give the impression of being genuine only when sung in the correct mode and style.
>
> Dalman 1891: VIII

Suddenly, almost overnight, Jewish music was everywhere in Europe in the 1880s. Cantors and other synagogue musicians realized that they shared a common art, so much so that they established international cantorial societies. As Gustaf Dalman reported in the first account of Jewish folk music, in the epigraph above, Jewish melody was unique, and Jewish song emerged from the conjunction of a tradition that had always been a part of folk culture and yet took shape through the artifice of the modern poet and composer (ibid.). The cantors of the Austro-Hungarian Empire, for example, established their own journal in 1881, the *Österreichisch-ungarische Cantoren-Zeitung*, which, according to its masthead, was dedicated to "all the interests of Jewish cantors" (cf. Schmidt 1998; Seroussi in this volume). Popular music swept across Europe, borne by the troupes of theater musicians who left the small cities of Eastern Europe to seek fame and fortune in Western Europe. In the mid-nineteenth century the troupes had made only occasional forays into the public sphere, where the fame of such theater singers as the "Broder Singer" and the "Brothers Herrnfeld" (Dalman 1891) was at best ephemeral. By the 1880s and 1890s, however, they were settling down, at least to the extent this was possible, by performing with regularity in the hotels and theaters of the major cities (Dalinger 1998: 16–36; cf. the CD accompanying this volume). Choruses had become fairly regular features of synagogues, especially those of the metropole, where they provided the sacred dimensions for a cosmopolitan *city music*. The secular Jewish chorus, too, had begun to enjoy the aesthetic privileges of full membership in the singing-society movement. Above all, it is the fact that all these musical phenomena fell under the rubric of Jewish music that was so remarkable in the 1880s and 1890s. Jewish music, in all its diversity, had achieved European dimensions and had become a phenomenon of modernity (see Bohlman 2002).

The moment during which Jewish music fully achieved its historical presence was one in which many Jewish communities were suffering from a heightened sense of threat. The troupes of theater and popular musicians migrating across Europe from the east followed paths similar to those of migrants fleeing the proliferation of pogroms in 1881 and the ensuing 1882 "May laws" in Russia, which hardened the already heavy-handed restrictions on Russian Jews. Anti-Semitism was not only on the rise during this period, but it was more wantonly public and openly directed toward stemming the gains Jews had won by accepting the possibilities of assimilation.

Paradoxes abound, but paradoxes also help us understand the contradictory roles exposed through the rapidly growing visibility of Jewish music in the European public sphere. When Jewish music made its sudden appearance, it was accompanied by an immediate nostalgia. Jewish music appeared as a shadow—or better, an echo—of the past, phenomenologically instilling a feeling of loss. The discovery of Jewish music in the late eighteenth century came at a time many believed it was disappearing. Its loss posed a threat of a different order when compared to anti-Semitism, but it threatened nonetheless. To stem the threat, attempts to salvage the endangered music arose almost overnight. By the turn of the century Jewish folklorists, amateur and professional, were setting out in search of disappearing Jewish folk songs. Jewish musical scholars, many working within sacred traditions, threw themselves into massive editorial projects that would yield new histories and make anthologies available on an expanding cultural market. The Russian collections of Shaul Ginsburg and Pesach Marek (1901) succeeded remarkably in salvaging Yiddish song from Russia, while Moritz Levy's cultural history of Balkan communities drew Sephardic Jews into the modernist sphere of public discourse (1996).

The activist agenda of recuperating the past, however, could not deflect the further paradox that Jewish music had entered the European public sphere as it was moving historically toward an event that would radically alter the course of its history: World War I. The cataclysm of war would be no less a crisis for Jewish modernism. Ironically, the entr'acte of the war itself would be one of the most intensive moments for discovering Jewish music in its most modernist ontologies.

Act 2 (1918–1933): The Experimental Stage

World War I profoundly altered the relation of Jewish society to European culture. The war brought about the end of the long nineteenth century, both undermining and buttressing the several forms of nationalism that had dominated the century. For Jews in Europe the war had fundamentally dismantled the cultural barriers between communities in Western and Central Europe and those in Eastern Europe. The dual framework of East versus West, so vital in both positive and negative senses to the migration of Jews from the shtetls of Poland and Russia to the metropoles of Wilhelmine Germany and Habsburg Austria and Hungary, had been dismantled, making it possible to breach the bulwark between the two parts of Jewish Europe at any point.

Just as the discovery of Jewish music had played a decisive role in setting the first act in motion, it would not diminish during the next stage. Translated into a modernist vocabulary, it would come to play quite a different role, namely by expanding the possibilities for musical experimentation. In a very basic sense, experimentation began with attempts to mix and juxtapose the differences that had previously left fissures between the Jewish communities of Europe. It was during the second act of Jewish modernism, for example, that Jewish folklorists employed new recording technologies to embark upon radically new forms of fieldwork. In folklore Max Grunwald used the framework of his Society for Jewish Folklore to develop new standards for detailed field studies of the customs and music in regions of intensive Jewish settlement (e.g., Grunwald 1924–25). The Berlin comparative musicologist Robert Lachmann used several different types of recording technology to conduct fieldwork in the putatively isolated Jewish communities on the island of Djerba, then transcribed the recordings and exposed them to an analytical scrutiny that eventually challenged Jewish ethnographers to rethink the historical contact between Jewish communities and the non-Jewish cultural mainstream of which they were a part (Lachmann 1940). Moreover, Lachmann gathered his recordings as an "Archive of Oriental Music," first at the University of Berlin and then in the late 1930s in Jerusalem, where they were to form the basis for the Jewish music collections of the Phonoteca, or National Sound Archives, at the Hebrew University.

Experimentation also assumed a different shape as a necessary impetus in the high modernism that characterized the new music of the interwar period. High modernism, indeed, relied on the sort of scientific impulse that led to the systematization of musical vocabularies and the implementation of a scientific discourse, drawn especially from mathematics and acoustics, allowing composers to move beyond the restrictions of harmonic practice (see Ash in this volume). It is necessary to use some caution when referring to the modernism of Arnold Schoenberg and his circle as Jewish—though Jews contributed in critical ways, non-Jews constituted a substantial part of the circle—but it is also a fact that in several cases, not least among them Schoenberg himself, the modernist experiments of the 1920s and 1930s created a trajectory toward the most obviously Jewish works of the 1940s (see Potter in this volume). A different type of experimentation is evident in the ways composers deliberately plumbed folk-music sources in order to gather melodic and harmonic materials that would make their works deliberately Jewish. Several music publishers, such as Jibneh-Juwal, a subsidiary of Universal Edition in Vienna, began to devote special series to these works of Jewish music, thus providing a context for works that were deliberately contemporary but to which Jewish identity could still be ascribed. The period between the two world wars was indeed one of political and economic instability, but the experimentation that opened the canon of Jewish music to entirely new repertories and genres, far from leaving it mired in that instability, succeeded in transcending it and investing it with new modernist potential.

Act 3 (1933–1945): Denouement and Destruction

The final act was constituted of scenes of finality. It was, indeed, with the initial scenes of the Holocaust that the final act began. These did not eradicate the moment of Jewish modernism but, paradoxically, intensified it. Beginning in Germany in 1933, immediately after the National Socialist ascent to political control of the country, an official policy of isolating Jewish cultural activities from those of the non-Jewish sector of society was implemented. The German archetype for a cultural ghetto, the Jüdischer Kulturbund [Jewish Cultural Union], spread in various forms to other fascist states during the 1930s, effectively imposing boundaries that would force Jewish identity upon virtually everything that occurred within them. The script for the cultural ghettos was implicit, if not explicit, in their formation: the boundaries would grow ever more restrictive until the life of the cultural ghetto was choked off entirely. It is not even a question of whether the Jüdischer Kulturbund was or was not a prototype for the concentration camp. More to the point, the Kulturbund facilitated, directly and indirectly, what the concentration camps would attempt to achieve as a "final solution" to the Jewish presence in Central Europe.

The Jewish response to the cultural ghettos contradicted the script the Germans had forged for them, and it is this response that exhibits, if tragically, the transcendence that emerged from the moment of Jewish modernism. Jewish creativity in the arts thrived during the first years of the final act, and in some remarkable instances it continued to thrive into the years of greatest crisis and eventual destruction (see, e.g., Belke 1983). Elsewhere in this introduction I examine in greater detail some of these remarkable instances, but here I wish to emphasize the fact that the chronicles and survivor testimonies that comment upon the growth of Jewish musical activity in the camps uniformly stress the transformation from European, even universal, musical practices to those that explicitly reflect a Jewish identity. It is incumbent upon us at the beginning of the twenty-first century not to explain away such responses as naive or inexplicably blind to what lay ahead. The moment of Jewish modernism engendered a transcendent narrative of its own, one of the most stunning cases of which is the subject of Michael Steinberg's essay in the present volume. These responses were the products of the moment of Jewish modernism itself and the transcendent release from history, the very history that was in the process of terminating the moment.

Epilogue

Had transcendence at the moment of Jewish modernism possessed the power to overwhelm European history, to reroute or derail its teleology, there would be no epilogue to consider. The epilogue contains the traces that were left once the moment reached its end. Traces though they be, however, they reflect the capacity to survive that is also inseparable from transcendence. Many of them survived with the Jewish musicians

and émigrés who managed to transplant Jewish modernism to mandatory Palestine and then after 1948 to Israel. The epilogue continued to take shape from the works that came into existence in the ghettos and concentration camps but only after many decades reached the stage through performance. The epilogue also forms along the border between myth and history, but in this case the border does not expedite transition; it is a border that contains rather than releases transcendence. Understanding the response of Jewish musicians and music at that border, nonetheless, is crucial if the modernist transformation of music in Jewish life between 1880 and 1950 is to begin making sense.

Narratives of Jewish Modernism: Confluence, Convergence, Coalescence

The moment of Jewish modernism coalesced when a surfeit of historical fragments—events and individual actions, genealogies and discourses, technological innovations and global encounters—converged. Whereas some of these events bore relationships to each other, most did not. In some ways their confluence was random, even unexpected; in other ways, it was their persistent unpredictability that engendered the transcendence of Jewish modernism. As distinctively individual as the many fragments that coalesced to form Jewish modernism were, it was more often than not an act of radical juxtaposition, even revolutionary transformation, that brought them together. From 1880 until 1900, in the space of a generation, Jewish modernism had undergone a transformation from being indistinct and inchoate to fully articulated expressions of self-consciousness in European Jewish society.

The coterminous conjunction of randomness and revolution was nothing if not paradoxical, and accordingly it is not possible to explain Jewish modernism as a single cultural, aesthetic, and scientific movement. Rather than a unifying grand narrative, we experience Jewish modernism as a collection of stories and a collectivity of narrators, whose own responses to the increasingly public nature of Jewish self-identity varied vastly. The essays in the present book do not try to identify and weave together all the historical narratives from which Jewish modernism took shape. The authors focus not so much on individual narratives, in fact, as on the points of their convergence and the impact of their coalescence.

The point of convergence, however, is also a point of departure for each of the essays. Moments of beginning and ending are crucial to the ways in which the essays attempt to provide a new type of depth to illumine a period in Jewish history celebrated for both triumph and ultimate tragedy. As a group the essays in this book focus collectively on a moment in modern Jewish history that has traditionally been interpreted as foreshadowing its own end through the destruction of the Holocaust. The focus, however, falls on the transformation of identity, particularly the intensification of Jewish self-consciousness and the belief that modernism could assume identifiably Jewish dimensions. It is in these dimensions, then, that the essayists locate another possibility

for coalescence, namely of the diverse forms of Jewish musical expression that would empower a new conscious conviction in self and liberate an unprecedented transcendence of the historically imposed conditions of being Europe's other.

At first glance the historical contexts of Mitchell Ash's exploration of "multiple modernisms" would seem to defer to a set of historical narratives quite unlike those of the other essayists. Ash draws his empirical evidence from the history of science and the politically charged debates that accompanied the radical transformations and paradigm shifts occurring around the turn of the century. The details of the debates and the scientists passionately committed to them rarely make an appearance in the historiography of modernism in the arts, humanities, and social sciences, but this is precisely one of Ash's points of departure for suggesting that we stand to enrich our understanding of modernism by formulating an inclusive historiography, one that recognizes the convergence of multiple modernities. Modernism in the sciences and modernism in the arts, then, do not exist in opposing historical universes, but rather demonstrate many similarities, which may in turn reflect the common subjectivities of a cast of historical agents whose thinking and experimentation—in the sciences and the arts—brought modernism into historical perspective.

Modernism in the sciences does not simply follow from extended processes of experimentation that yield new results that in turn make new experiments possible because systems of representation—in the sciences and the arts—become self-referential. Modernism, first and foremost, represented a revolution, not only in experimentation but in how new scientific methods and data transformed the ways in which humans perceived nature, matter, and the world around them. In their debate about the mathematical models used in physics, for example, Ernst Mach and Ludwig Boltzmann were not so much arguing that matter existed in different forms as advancing claims about the possibilities for different ways of viewing matter, that is, of perceiving it through mathematical or technological means so that the objects of scientific inquiry could be represented in their own, self-referential terms.

Ash further stakes out the common territory of multiple modernisms by drawing our attention to technology's role in making revolutionary moments possible. The impact of recording technology at the end of the twentieth century was profound, and modernism in music would be unthinkable without it. Recording technology provided early ethnomusicologists and comparative musicologists—many of them acousticians and psychologists—with ways of encountering all the musics of the world, at least in principle, thus destabilizing and ultimately undermining a metaphysics of music dependent entirely on European constructions. Recording technology, we now realize, made it possible to approach music as a science and to sort out the patterns that served as the frameworks for systems. Jewish music, too, became scientific because of technological advances, notably the systematic fieldwork conducted by Abraham Zvi Idelsohn in Jerusalem during the half dozen years prior to World War I,

which then became the basis for his highly systematic *Thesaurus* (Idelsohn 1914–32).[13]

Systems of a different order emerge in the compositions of Arnold Schoenberg, whose seminal presence in high modernism and Jewish modernism should not mask the scientific logic with which he laid the groundwork for his 1911 *Harmonielehre* (Theory of Harmony), making that work, too, one of the modernist tracts connecting music and science (Schoenberg 1978). Schoenberg's deliberate crafting of his system proved to be a conduit for one of the primary modernist transformations of representational language, namely the creation of self-referential symbol systems. Significantly, Ash's examination of multiple modernisms in the sciences and the arts does not strip modernism of its ideological implications, but rather accentuates the modernist reformulation of art's political functions in society. Symbol systems, however self-referential, are not innocent, nor are they inept, as Ash trenchantly demonstrates (cf. Herf 1984; Hentschel 1996). Once modernisms become plural, they also have the power to unleash views of the world that can be dangerously at odds with each other.

Historical thresholds and borders bump up against each other throughout Edwin Seroussi's reflections on Sephardic liturgical music in a sacred tradition of music that traditionally formed the cornerstone for an Ashkenazic historiography of European modernity. Seroussi deftly enters the late-nineteenth-century world of the Viennese Sephardic community at a moment that at once heralds its most visible musical achievements and witnesses the signs of decline. On one hand,

Seroussi forcefully makes a case for the presence of Sephardic music at the historical moment of full-blown modernism in fin-de-siècle Vienna. Spurred on by the efforts of the community and its musical leaders, the publication of *Schir Hakawod* in 1889 symbolized a process of canonization under way since the mid-nineteenth century. Its impact was all the greater because of the expansion of the choral forces in the Sephardic synagogue, the selective use of an organ, and the fulfillment of the conditions of decorum that guided the liturgical and musical reforms of Salomon Sulzer, the *ḥazzan* and composer who had brought the "Viennese rite" into being. On the other hand, the publication of *Schir Hakawod* could stifle the oral liturgical traditions that were central to Sephardi musical identity. The moment of modernism had arrived, and to embrace it meant perilously abandoning the community to the "end of the century."

Seroussi asks us to consider just how the crossing of a threshold at the end of the century really does alter identity. Does the encounter with modernism, in the guise of liturgical reform, really eliminate the community's identity? Are modernism and tradition at critical historical junctures such as that in fin-de-siècle Vienna mutually exclusive? How does the end of tradition—oral tradition, Sephardic liturgical history, an Austrian-Jewish engagement with southeastern Europe and the Mediterranean—form a border with the beginning of modernism? Does the recognition of a Sephardic presence around the peripheries of the canonic Viennese rite actually introduce another presence of plurals, this time

in the historical singularity imposed on modernism by the concept of the fin de siècle? Seroussi does not content himself with rhetorical answers to such questions. Instead, he illustrates the ways in which the newly canonized liturgical tradition, especially through the activities of the community's distinguished cantor, Jacob Bauer, opened the borders to the entire Jewish culture at the epicenter of the Austro-Hungarian Empire and, perhaps even more significantly, to the public sphere of Viennese musical life.

Ends of centuries, Seroussi claims in his ethnographic and self-reflexive epilogue, are not isolated events. They return, and in so doing they call the very notion of ending into question. The traditions of the Sephardic community in Vienna did not, in fact, disappear, neither with the intersection of reform and high modernism in Vienna after World War I nor with the virtual elimination during the Holocaust of the modern Central European liturgical tradition adapted by the Sephardic community. Its traces remain in the liturgy of a congregation of Bulgarian Sephardic Jews in their small synagogue in Jaffa, and the border between Sephardic and Ashkenazic identities that characterized fin-de-siècle Viennese Jewish modernism has complex political dimensions for the ways in which religion divided Israeli society at the end of the twentieth century. Sephardic modernism has refused to detach itself from the borders between the present and past.

The irony of identity takes a very different turn in Pamela Potter's essay, which seems to depart along a journey through the familiar—the intense intellectual investment by Germans, Jews and non-Jews, in the foundation of modern musical science, or musicology, in the early twentieth century—but then insists on a recharting of the seemingly well-known musicological terrain that defamiliarizes it in very disturbing ways. On the terrain of the familiar, it was Jewish music that represented the specter of strangeness, not only for mainstream German and Austrian musicologists, whose interests were predicated on maintaining the philological purity of their science, but also for Jewish scholars, who, for various reasons, chose not to study the music that ascribed self-identity as a part of their scholarly domain. Jewish music occupied a position on the periphery, together with popular music and "modern music" itself—in other words, all musics that bore the modernist stamp. Paradoxically, Jewish music joined the ranks of modernism-as-otherness, which Austro-German musicology fostered as a means of affording what it imagined to be scientific legitimacy.

If Jewish music was initially excluded by musicology, a discipline that was very much the product of modern European intellectual history, it did not disappear from the contested landscape of modern Europe. Quite the contrary, as the crisis of Jewish modernism intensified in the 1930s and then culminated in the 1940s, Jewish music became the target of the racialized, scientized musicology of the Nazis. Whereas the racialization of Jewish music required a certain pseudoscientific compromise of musicology, it nonetheless redirected the discipline to the service of more horrendous goals, not least among them the creation of an aesthetic justification for the elimination of

Jews from European, especially German, history. Potter's essay disturbs us even further by illustrating the continuity that characterized the transition of Austro-German musicology through the Holocaust even to the present. As unmistakably racialized as the language of many German musicologists had been, notably Hans Joachim Moser but also scores of scholars who commanded respect in prestigious positions, critical reassessment was very slow in coming. Arguably, Jewish music has been excluded from the German and Austrian sciences of musicology until the present (see the essays in John and Zimmermann 2004, which are notable because of the extent to which they redress the exclusion).

The questions about identity—Jewish identity in modern Europe—are indeed very complex, even haunting when measured against the history of the twentieth century. Potter eloquently problematizes the conjunction "and" in her title by moving the various attributes in the title around, again defamiliarizing what at first glance seemed entirely familiar. The shifting assaults on Jewish music, she suggests, formed a counterpoint to the attempts to elevate German music (cf., e.g., Blessinger 1938; Waldmann 1938). The Germanness of science might well have seemed too seductive in its familiarity to Jewish musicologists in the early decades of the century, who were in search of public, not just religious or ethnic, identity. The calculus of Potter's title is underscored at the end of her essay, when she questions recent attempts to redress the exclusion of Jewish music and revive it from its absence. Does this recent penance, Potter wonders as she leaves the questions in the final part of her essay open, erase the sins of the modern discipline? "Was anything of this really bringing German scholars closer to knowing something about Jewish music?" The crisis of modern Austro-German musicology, so trenchantly emblematized by the exclusion of Jewish music, has left more than traces on the intellectual terrain of musicology's history as it enters a new century.

Was the modernist teleology toward Europe experienced by Jewish communities universal? Was it unavoidable? Was the crisis of Jewish modernism, therefore, European, Jewish, or both? These are among the disturbing questions that Kay Kaufman Shelemay's essay raises, and for which she employs the narrative metaphors of *midrash* to elucidate, and to some degree to answer. Shelemay invites us to listen to the echoes of a Jewish community that had virtually no contact with Europe prior to the nineteenth century, the Beta Israel of Ethiopia,[14] whom Shelemay positions against modernity by locating them at the farthest diasporic reaches beyond Europe's borders. The periphery of the Diaspora, however, was not to be spared the crisis of the center, and Beta Israel history could not resist the centripetalizing pull of the modernism that European Jews were embracing as a means of enhancing what they perceived as Jewish self-identity.

The "echoes," or overlapping historical narratives, that constitute Shelemay's midrashic explication of the Beta Israel *longue durée*, however, defiantly belie easy interpretation. She examines two primary sets of historical evidence, the first set critical to the Beta Israel's own sense of self-ness, the other constructed by European Jews to implement what they perceived as an absent Jewishness in the Ethiopian way of Beta Israel life. The traditional role of craftsperson and artificer may well have guided the response of the Beta Israel toward outside encouragement to regard tradition as malleable and ultimately to mold it to express what we might understand as "pan-Jewish" culture. In liturgical music, for example, this would mean replacing texts sung in the traditional Ge'ez language of the Beta Israel with Hebrew texts. For the Jewish agencies that urged such changes on traditional music, there was a clear modernist agenda. For the Beta Israel, as Shelemay has shown in her rich ethnographies of Beta Israel sacred music (e.g., 1986), the oral tradition they had maintained since the arrival of Jews in Ethiopia in biblical times would necessarily come to an end, disrupting and even severing their own historical connections to Jewishness. The transformation of the Beta Israel into Ethiopian Jews, which took place at several distinct stages during the course of the twentieth century, underscored the dominance of European and modernist narratives.

Shelemay's essay also succeeds in re-posing questions about the geographical and temporal spheres in which Jewish modernism took place, for she turns the question of modernism outside in. The Beta Israel were not simply victims of modernism; rather, their own responses—through *aliya* to Israel or entering into a European diaspora—blurred the ways in which the modernist narrative begins and ends. Now, at the beginning of the twenty-first century, new musical practices represent the Ethiopian Jews of Israel that reflect the struggle for identity in the multiethnic society of that modern nation, and new generations of Ethiopian Jews contribute to global practices of Jewish popular music. No longer authentic representations of Beta Israel tradition, these musical practices nonetheless resound for the modern community as echoes from its past, echoes still traditional insofar as they emanate from self-consciously constructed history. Traditional Beta Israel society has not disappeared, but it has assumed different shapes, requiring us to listen to and perceive it as a Jewish counterhistory that has become modern in its own way.

No essay confronts the paradox of transcendence in modern Jewish history more directly than that of Michael Steinberg. The transcendence that Steinberg examines is historically situated at the end of Jewish modernism, and it therefore requires us to recognize that meaning coalesces most powerfully within the most brutal and inhuman circumstances. Therein lies its paradox. The transcendence that artistic expression makes possible, in this case the signature work of Charlotte Salomon (1917–1943), a complex of paintings, texts, and melody-as-memory created in the final years of her life, when she was in exile in southern France before being deported to and murdered in Auschwitz. Steinberg's work contributes a critical fulcrum to the volume's essays by drawing us into the concluding years of Jewish modernism. Its end was imminent, and Salomon's *Life? Or Theater?* reveals too that it was immanent (cf. Felstiner 1997). Jewish modernism, nonetheless, had reached a threshold, indeed, was straddling a threshold, on which the present had not yet given way to the paradoxical paths ahead: history or memory.

Steinberg's essay is an interpellation of the finality of historical closure. The essay itself is imprinted with a strong sense of telos, for it draws us to the geographical and historical center, Germany during the 1930s, after the Nazi ascent to power. At the center we can choose from numerous contradictory historical frameworks, all of which had provided responses to Salomon's counterpoising of life and theater. Steinberg charges us to think about the moment of closure not in the absolutist terms of either history or memory, representation or presentation of life. At the center and at the end transcendence was also possible when it most directly confronted, as Steinberg observes about the Salomon's images of windows—with their own midrashic echoes in paintings by Caspar David Friedrich and Mark Rothko—to portray the convergence of death and transcendence, the language of modernism, specifically the tension provided by the simultaneity of the engagement with transcendence and at the same time the refusal to fall under its spell, in other words the refusal to agree to the representation of the transcendent.

By weaving numerous historical threads into his essay—from art and music history, from psychoanalysis, from the reception of the Holocaust, from studies of memory and meaning—Steinberg reveals both the wholeness of the fabric of Jewish modernism in the 1930s and the deterioration of its seams. The Jüdischer Kulturbund provided the setting for artistic experimentation, but only as a staging of the paradox of authenticity that the moment of Jewish modernism heightened rather than resolved. The production of authenticity in German-Jewish modernity could only be an engagement with the world that strives neither for an essential Germanness nor for an essential Jewishness but to be culturally and existentially authentic in a multiple and flexible manner adequate to the multiplicity and transitoriness of the modern world.

In the final chapter of the book I examine the problem of ending from the perspectives set in motion by beginning. The burden of beginnings and endings is heavy in the Jewish scriptural tradition, first and indeed also foremost in the foundational texts of Jewish myth and history, the Torah, the five books of Moses. The ends of Jewish history—accelerated by pogrom and holocaust, displaced through diaspora and migration, delayed and deflected through the dissonance of reconciliation and prejudice—are ever elusive, metaphorically located on the horizon of Canaan in the promised land of Israel, which Moses sees but does not reach at the end of his life and the end of the Torah. Similarly, the closing chapter of the book begins by returning hermeneutically to the biblical texts that return repeatedly through their historical teleology to the beginning, *bereshit*.

The final chapter, however, does not forestall the ending of Jewish modernism, for it calls attention to the ways in which the boundaries of Jewish music—fully modern after being named so often and so problematically in the twentieth century—fail to contain the tide of history. Whereas the beginnings of Jewish modernism emerge because of musical and historical responses to the end of the nineteenth century, thus bringing Jewish modernism into harmony with other moments of European modernity, in the arts, politics, and science, the path toward their endings is distinctive because of the ways it circumvents the endings of modernism that define cultural history in the first half of the twentieth century. Scholars locate the end of modernism variously, literally making modernism local, for example, when Walter Frisch equates the closure of German modernism with the close of the long nineteenth century at the end of World War I, or when Carol J. Oja examines the heightened conditions for American musical modernism in the 1920s (cf. Frisch 2005; Oja 2000).

Again, paradox intervened and inflected the teleology that directed the local history of Jewish modernism. At the moment of most profound closure, the Holocaust, a new creativity was unleashed. Propelled by the historical telos of the end of history, the musicians and intellectuals shaping that creativity transcended the historical conditions of modernism—naturalism, nationalism, historicism, the irony of self-referentiality. In the Jüdischer Kulturbund of Germany, in the ghettos and shtetls of Eastern Europe, in the kibbutzim of the Yishuv in mandatory Palestine, and ultimately even in the musical life of the concentration camp, a new music vigorously and apocalyptically sounded the ending as a new beginning. The end of Jewish modernism shared much with its beginning. Jewish self-consciousness was real, but transitory; it was enriched because of the confluence of distinctly Jewish narratives, and yet it revealed that those narratives were inherently constructions, in other words representations. The transcendence that so powerfully ushered in Jewish modernism blurred its end. It was, instead, history that provided the final acts of closure.

Resistance to Coda:
Modernism without Postmodernism

Aesthetic transcendence and disenchantment form their unity through silence.

                                                    Adorno 1970: 123

It is one of the most unsettling ironies of historical thinking that endings are most clearly defined by what follows them. We reckon with ending retrospectively, after the fact, which is to say, after we perceive an absence of what once existed. This irony becomes all the more unsettling when we set about trying to imagine and write histories of modernity, for we put ourselves in the position of distancing ourselves from those whose telos necessarily begins to include us. How does one write the history of an era that in some measure remains one's own? Where does the past end and the present begin (Picard 2004)?

Reckoning with the end of Jewish modernism only intensifies the irony, for the historical practice of defining ends by recognizing beginnings offers few options. Whereas the historiographies of modernism and postmodernism have become mutually dependent, we search hard to find what might amount to a "Jewish postmodernism," which followed from the moment of Jewish mod-

ernism. Postmodernism should pick up where modernism left off. The need to find historical closure in modernism is negated by assuming that postmodernism simply picks up the strands of a modernism that had naturally entered a period of denouement and decline. Both modernism and postmodernism are movements that equally stress fragmentation, and unexpected juxtapositions are therefore neatly sutured together.[15] In modern Jewish history, however, there is no neat suturing, no transition, no clear sense of closure and ending. Jewish modernism did not give way to postmodernism.

The absence of closure results from a number of different factors. It must be stated unequivocally that the absence of closure for Jewish modernism is overwhelmed by the brutal enforcement of closure that lay at the core of what the Nazis achieved with the Holocaust. The end of history that the Holocaust has come to symbolize profoundly complicates the need to reckon with a closure on a more psychological and aesthetic level. We also find it vexing to deal with the end of Jewish modernism because, as I have argued at various points in this introduction, there was no grand narrative that unified the diverse narratives that converged as Jewish modernism. One of the most striking motifs unifying the essays in this book, moreover, is that modernism is constitutive of many different parts and that we witness, as Mitchell Ash states, multiple modernisms. Its psychological framework, as Michael Steinberg argues, might also arise from the multiplicity of personality conditions that modern psychoanalysis unveils. We ask ourselves, nonetheless, whether such conditions of multiplicity might equally explain postmodernism. How could they remain the privileged domain of modernism, especially when we introduce psychological dimensions as well?

The historical argument the essays in this book formulate, however, is not that the diverse elements and multiplicity of Jewish modernism formed in spite of disjuncture, but rather that they coalesced around unpredictable points of convergence. Risking an essentialist explanation, I should like to suggest that it was convergence that made it possible for modernism to be inflected as Jewish. It was at points of convergence that a Jewish self-consciousness took shape, thereby having the effect of suturing, even negating, disjuncture. Unexpected juxtapositions—of sacred and secular elements, of disparate ethnic identities, of contradictory musical ontologies—proved not to be dysfunctional, but rather highly fertile for the formation of modern subjectivities.

The essays in this book, in raising the question of Jewish modernism, also pose another question, namely whether modernism can be Jewish (or, for that matter, have any form of ethnic, religious, or national identity). In its strictest interpretations, modernism should possess a universal character. Indeed, the modernist writer, artist, or psychoanalyst is engaged in determining a language that belies the local and enhances the universal. Jewish modernism, should such a thing exist, would then seem to be parochial, individual, even existing outside of history, exceptional. Why, given the signal presence of Jews in the full range of modernist activities, would there be any reason to succumb to the seemingly more limited agendas of Jewish modernism? Admitting that, to some degree, there were Jewish modernists who were parochial and whose vision was severely limited, I return at the end of the introduction, before the essays constituting the body of the book begin, to two of the most troubling conditions of Jewish modernism: paradox and its antithesis, transcendence.

Paradox permeated every layer and every moment of Jewish modernism. The experimental languages of Jewish modernist literature were made possible only by stripping tradition of some of the most elemental symbols of Judaism. Jewish folk music was modernized by setting it with a harmonic vocabulary that had no precedent in tradition. Jewish tradition, in effect, was abandoned to create a space for Jewish self-consciousness. In that space of paradox, which Adorno would describe as disenchanted, transcendence took shape. Transcendence through modernism negates the possibility of moving on to the next historical moment, in other words, of passing from modernism to postmodernism. The transcendence that emerged in the space opened by paradox would mean that Jewish music had to be untethered from the historical conditions that had engendered Jewish modernism. Jewish music could only be retethered when different historical and aesthetic conditions were in place, among them the nationalism of modern Israel and the multiculturalism that followed the reconfiguration of Jewish communities after the Holocaust. Transcendence, however, does not inherently lend itself to connections with new beginnings.

Rather, it calls attention to the historical space and aesthetic conditions from which it was untethered, reminding those who will listen that the silence they experience is possible only when the process of historical closure has not come to an end.

::: **NOTES** :::

The review cited in the epigraph is of the first opera staged by the Jüdischer Kulturbund (Jewish Cultural Union) of Berlin, published as "Oper im Kulturbund" in the Kulturbund's newspaper, *Jüdische Rundschau* (17 November 1933). The opera arousing the feeling of a first Jewish opera was Mozart's *Marriage of Figaro*. See Dahm 1988: 133–34.

1. In the most literal sense, alt/neu translates as "old/new," and I use this translation in the course of the present introduction. The juxtaposition of alt/neu, however, carries more weight, for it consciously marks paradox, thereby heightening the symbolism of alt as "ancient" and neu as "modern." It is that heightened symbolism with which we most often concern ourselves in this book.

2. Mikhail Bakhtin's concept of chronotope draws upon the power of narrative to juxtapose time and space, that is, the past as time and the past as place. Chronotope takes the shape of several binarisms in the essays of Bakhtin 1981, particularly the central book-length essay in that collection, "Forms of Time and Chronotope in the Novel" (ibid.: 84–258). Herzl's narrative realization of an "old/new land" has a particularly rich and complex chronotopic texture, employing a single concept wherein the modern relies on the past as well as on the locality of a specific geography.

3. Idelsohn's recordings from 1911 to 1913 are now available on digitized CDs in Lechleitner 2005.

4. Habermas refers to the formulation of this negation by Adorno as the "Verschlingung von Mythos und Aufklärung" (Habermas 1985: 130). The German *Verschlingung* itself embodies a sense of dichotomy, meaning both "entwinement" and "swallowing up,"

thus evoking a contradictory set of images to apply to the border between myth and, in Habermas's case, enlightenment.

5. Traditionally, representation of human figures in Jewish sacred art was unacceptable. Human figures, for example, do not appear in the decorative designs in a synagogue, which at once exaggerate abstract pattern and negate suggestions of human form.

6. The Moorish synagogue served as a symbol of the East (Hebrew: *mizrakh*), hence the historical geography of *eretz yisrael* as the site of return. The arabesque and minarets of such synagogues were stripped of their specific Muslim meanings and given a more general iconic significance. The transformation of representational form to nonrepresentational meaning is an essential component of modernism. The Oranienburgerstraße Synagoge was and still is known also as the Neue Synagoge, the "New Synagogue."

7. In his memoirs the Hungarian newspaper publisher Lajos Szabolcsi described the growing influence that followed his newspaper's enhancement of Jewish themes as "a miracle" (see Szabolcsi 1999: 86).

8. Historically, it was common to speak of the Jewish musician or artist as primarily reproductive rather than creative (see Sander L. Gilman's foreword to the present volume). This distinction was no less common in Jewish writings on Jewish musicians and artists than in anti-Semitic tracts, such as Richard Wagner's *Das Judentum in der Musik* (1850/1869), which made a great deal of such distinctions. Not insignificantly, Wagner also assigned the explicit traits of modernism (*Moderne*) to Jews in general (see Frisch 2005: 12).

9. There was a growing interest in the formation of scientific societies for the study of Jewish music. The best-known case of these was the so-called World Centre for Jewish Music in Palestine, which enjoyed short-lived successes in the mid- and late 1930s. For a documentary history of the World Centre, see Bohlman 1992.

10. Traditional discussions of Jewish music, from cantillation to liturgical music to folk song, rested on the presumption that it was monophonic. In the heated debates about the appropriateness of choral music in the synagogue during the nineteenth century, moreover, there were those who argued that harmony was anathema to the very possibility of Jewishness in music. In light of such traditional discussions, the extent to which Yasser's proposal for a system of Jewish harmony moves toward the possibility of an autonomous Jewish music is even more remarkable.

11. It would be an oversimplification to suggest that the two meanings of *bima* distinguish between sacred and secular functions. Whether as the area before the Torah ark at the front of the synagogue sanctuary or as the stage of a theater, as in Habima (literally, "The Stage," the national theater of Israel), the *bima* is a raised platform from which specialists and professionals perform. The performers on the *bima* invest new meaning in the texts they perform, effecting a type of aesthetic autonomy. On the *bima* the cantor enhances cantillation and liturgy by emphasizing their musical qualities; the actor, too, brings out the theatrical aspects of text, originally biblical texts, as in the traditional *purimshpil* of the medieval Jewish theater. The contradictory functions of the stage are further complicated in Yiddish, where the terms *bima* and *bina* (from the German *Bühne*) are used interchangeably.

12. Many of the diverse social and aesthetic functions that the stage makes possible are evident in the performances on the CD that accompanies this volume. For a discourse history of the stages during which Jewish folk music first emerged as a concept and then stimulated collection and performance, see Bohlman 2005.

13. Idelsohn spent most of World War I in Vienna, where he ran linguistic experiments on the wax-disc recordings he had collected in Jerusalem and Palestine. The tabular comparisons and comparative transcriptions of those experiments were published by the Imperial Academy of Sciences, which financed and supported the original fieldwork (see Idelsohn 1917).

14. For a detailed discussion of the meaning of the designation "Beta Israel" and of the distinctive practices that constitute traditional Beta Israel culture and history, see Shelemay's essay in this volume and Shelemay 1986.

15. Here I am concerned not so much with whether modernism and postmodernism are movements or eras or even collective responses to history, but rather that they exhibit ontological kinship and are thus genealogically connected. I quite agree with Michael Bell, who observes that "the change from Modernism to postmodernism is not a difference in metaphysic so much as a different stage in the digestion of the same metaphysic" (1999: 9).

::: WORKS CITED :::

Adorno, Theodor W. 1970. *Ästhetische Theorie*. Ed. by Gretel Adorno and Rolf Tiedemann. Frankfurt am Main: Suhrkamp.

———. 1973. *Negative Dialektik: Jargon der Eigentlichkeit*. Frankfurt am Main: Suhrkamp. (Gesammelte Schriften, 6)

Albright, Daniel. 2000. *Untwisting the Serpent: Modernism in Music, Literature, and Other Arts*. Chicago: University of Chicago Press.

Akademie der Künste, ed. 1992. *Geschlossene Vorstellung: Der jüdische Kulturbund in Deutschland, 1933–1941*. Berlin: Edition Hentrich.

Bakhtin, Mikhail M. 1981. *The Dialogic Imagination: Four Essays*. Ed. by Michael Holquist. Trans. by Caryl Emerson and Michael Holquist. Austin: University of Texas Press. (University of Texas Press Slavic Series, 1)

Battenberg, Friedrich. 1990. *Das europäische Zeitalter der Juden: Zur Entwicklung einer Minderheit in der nichtjüdischen Umwelt Europas*. Darmstadt: Wissenschaftliche Buchgesellschaft.

Belke, Ingrid, ed. 1983. *In den Katakomben: Jüdische Verlage in Deutschland, 1933–1938.* Special edition of *Marbacher Magazin* 25.

Bell, Michael. 1999. "The Metaphysics of Modernism." In Michael Levenson, ed., *The Cambridge Companion to Modernism,* 9–32. Cambridge: Cambridge University Press.

Benz, Wolfgang. 1988. *Die Juden in Deutschland, 1933–1945: Leben unter nationalsozialistischer Herrschaft.* Munich: C. H. Beck.

Birnbaum, Nathan. 1989. *Die jüdische Moderne: Frühe zionistische Schriften.* Augsburg: Ölbaum-Verlag.

Blessinger, Karl. 1938. *Mendelssohn, Meyerbeer, Mahler: Drei Kapitel Judentum in der Musik als Schlüssel zur Musikgeschichte des 19. Jahrhunderts.* Berlin: Hahnefeld.

Bohlman, Philip V. 1992. *The World Centre for Jewish Music in Palestine, 1936–1940: Jewish Musical Life on the Eve of World War II.* Oxford: Oxford University Press.

———. 1994. "Auf der Bima—Auf der Bühne: Zur Emanzipation der jüdischen Popularmusik der Jahrhundertwende im Wien." In Elisabeth T. Hilscher and Theophil Antonicek, eds., *Vergleichend-systematische Musikwissenschaft: Beiträge zu Methode und Problematik der systematischen, ethnologischen und historischen Musikwissenschaft: Franz Födermayr zum 60. Geburtstag,* 417–49. Tutzing: Hans Schneider.

———. 2002. "Inventing Jewish Music." In Eliyahu Schleifer and Edwin Seroussi, eds., *Studies in Honor of Israel Adler,* 33–68. Jerusalem: Magnes Press of the Hebrew University. (Yuval Monograph Series, 7)

———. 2004. "Die Entdeckung des jüdischen Volkslieds als Signum musikalisch-jüdischer Identität." In John and Zimmermann, *Jüdische Musik?,* 77–99. Cologne: Böhlau.

———. 2005. *Jüdische Volksmusik: Eine mitteleuropäische Geistesgeschichte.* Vienna: Böhlau. (Schriften zur Volksmusik, 21)

Botstein, Leon. 1991. *Judentum und Modernität: Essays zur Rolle der Juden in der deutschen und österreichischen Kultur, 1848 bis 1938.* Vienna: Böhlau.

———, and Werner Hanak, eds. 2004. *Vienna: Jews and the City of Music, 1870–1938.* Annandale-on-Hudson, N.Y.: Bard College; Vienna: Wolke Verlag.

Brenner, David A. 1998. *The Invention of Jewish Ethnicity in Ost und West.* Detroit, Mich.: Wayne State University Press.

Brenner, Michael. 1996. *The Renaissance of Jewish Culture in Weimar Germany.* New Haven, Conn.: Yale University Press.

Buber, Martin. 1949. *Die Erzählungen der Chassidim.* Zurich: Manesse.

———. 1985. *Pfade in Utopia: Über Gemeinschaft und deren Verwirklichung.* 3rd revised ed. Heidelberg: Lambert Schneider.

Cheyette, Bryan, and Laura Marcus, eds. 1998. *Modernity, Culture and "the Jew."* Stanford, Calif.: Stanford University Press.

Cohn, Richard I. 1998. *Jewish Icons: Art and Society in Modern Europe.* Berkeley and Los Angeles: University of California Press.

Dahm, Volker. 1988. "Kulturelles und geistiges Leben." In Benz, *Die Juden in Deutschland,* 125–267.

Dalinger, Brigitte. 1998. *Verloschene Sterne: Geschichte des jüdischen Theaters in Wien.* Vienna: Picus.

Dalman, Gustaf H. 1891. *Jüdischdeutsche Volkslieder aus Galizien und Russland.* 2nd ed. Berlin: Evangelische Vereins-Buchhandlung. (Schriften des Institutum Judaicum, 12) Orig. publ. 1884.

Felstiner, Mary Lowenthal. 1997. *To Paint Her Life: Charlotte Salomon in the Nazi Era.* Berkeley and Los Angeles: University of California Press.

Frisch, Walter. 2005. *German Modernism: Music and the Arts.* Berkeley: University of California Press.

Gilman, Sander L. 1993. *Inscribing the Other.* Lincoln: University of Nebraska Press. (Texts and Contexts, 1)

———, and Milton Shain, eds. 1993. *Jews at the Frontiers: Accommodation, Identity, Conflict.* Urbana: University of Illinois Press.

Ginsburg, S. M., and Marek, P. S. 1901. *Evreiskie narodnye pesni v Rossii* [Jewish Folk Music in Russia]. St. Petersburg: Voskhod.

Grunwald, Max. 1924–25. *Mattersdorf.* Special edition of *Jahrbuch für jüdische Volkskunde.* Berlin and Vienna: Benjamin Harz.

Habermas, Jürgen. 1985. *Der philosophische Diskurs der Moderne: Zwölf Vorlesungen.* Frankfurt am Main: Suhrkamp.

Hentschel, Klaus, ed. 1996. *Physics and National Socialism: An Anthology of Primary Sources.* Boston: Birkhäuser. (Science Networks, Historical Studies, 18)

Herf, Jeffrey. 1984. *Reactionary Modernism: Technology, Culture, and Politics in Weimar and the Third Reich.* Cambridge: Cambridge University Press.

Herzl, Theodor. 1896. *Der Judenstaat: Versuch einer modernen Lösung der Judenfrage.* Leipzig and Vienna: M. Breitenstein.

———. 1935. *Das neue Ghetto, Altneuland, Aus dem Nachlaß.* Vol. 5: *Theodor Herzl, Gesammelte zionistische Werke.* Berlin: Jüdischer Verlag.

Idelsohn, A. Z. 1914–32. *Hebräisch-orientalischer Melodienschatz.* 10 vols. Berlin, etc.: Benjamin Harz, etc.

———. 1917. *Phonographierte Gesänge und Aussprachsproben des Hebräischen der jemenitischen, persischen und syrischen Juden.* Vienna: Alfred Hölder. (Mitteilung der Phonogramm-Archivs-Kommission der kaiserlichen Akademie der Wissenschaften in Wien, 15)

John, Eckhard, and Heidy Zimmermann, eds. 2004. *Jüdische Musik? Fremdbilder—Eigenbilder.* Cologne: Böhlau.

Karady, Victor. 1999. *Gewalterfahrung und Utopie: Juden in der europäischen Moderne.* Frankfurt am Main: Fischer Taschenbuch Verlag.

Katz, Jacob, ed. 1987. *Toward Modernity: The European Jewish Model.* New Brunswick, N.J.: Transaction Books.

Lachmann, Robert. 1940. *Jewish Cantillation and Song in the Isle of Djerba.* Jerusalem: Archives of Oriental Music of the Hebrew University. Publication of the full original German text: *Gesänge der Juden auf der Insel Djerba.* Ed. by Edith Gerson-Kiwi. Jerusalem: Magnes Press of the Hebrew University, 1976. (Yuval Monograph Series, 7)

Lappin, Eleonore. 2000. *Der Jude: Die Geschichte einer Zeitschrift.* Tübingen: Mohr Siebeck.

Lechleitner, Gerda, ed. 2005. *The Collection of Abraham Zvi Idelsohn (1911–1913).* 3 CDs and CD-ROM, plus booklet. Vienna: Verlag der Österreichischen Akademie der Wissenschaften. (Tondokumente aus dem Phonogrammarchiv der Österreichischen Akademie der Wissenschaften, Gesamtausgabe der Historischen Bestände 1899–1950, Series 9)

Levy, Moritz. 1996. *Die Sephardim in Bosnien: Ein Beitrag zur Geschischte der Juden auf der Balkanhalbinsel.* Klagenfurt: Wieser. (Bosnisch-österreichische Beziehungen, 1) Orig. publ. 1911.

Mendelsohn, Ezra, ed. 1993. *Modern Jews and Their Musical Agendas.* Special edition of *Studies in Contemporary Jewry* 9. New York: Oxford University Press.

Meyer, Michael A. 1988. *Response to Modernity: A History of the Reform Movement in Judaism.* New York: Oxford University Press.

Nathan, Hans, ed. 1994. *Israeli Folk Music: Songs of the Early Pioneers.* Madison, Wisc.: A-R Editions. (Recent Researches in the Oral Traditions of Music, 4)

Oja, Carol J. 2000. *Making Music Modern: New York in the 1920s.* New York: Oxford University Press.

Picard, Jacques. 2004. "Profane Zeit, sakrale Zeit, virtuelle Zeit? Über jüdische Kultur in der Moderne." In John and Zimmermann, *Jüdische Musik?*, 339–59. Cologne: Böhlau.

Postone, Moishe, and Eric Santner, eds. 2003. *Catastrophe and Meaning: The Holocaust and the Twentieth Century.* Chicago: University of Chicago Press.

Schmidt, Esther. 1998. "Die Idee von Professionalismus in der musikalischen Welt des Judentums: Wien im neunzehnten Jahrhundert und die Gründung der Oesterreichisch-ungarischen Cantoren-Zeitung." Master's thesis, University of Vienna.

Schoenberg, Arnold. 1978. *Theory of Harmony.* Trans. by Roy E. Carter. Berkeley and Los Angeles: University of California Press. Orig. publ. 1911.

Schorske, Carl E. 1980. *Fin-de-siècle Vienna: Politics and Culture.* New York: Random House.

Shelemay, Kay Kaufman. 1986. *Music, Ritual, and Falasha History*. East Lansing: African Studies Center, Michigan State University.

Stein, Sarah Abrevaya. 2004. *Making Jews Modern: The Yiddish and Ladino Press in the Russian and Ottoman Empires*. Bloomington: Indiana University Press. (Modern Jewish Experience)

Szabolcsi, Lajos. 1999. *Zwei Generationen*. In Peter Haber, ed. and trans., *Jüdisches Städtebild: Budapest*, 85–86. Frankfurt am Main: Jüdischer Verlag.

Vital, David. 1999. *A People Apart: The Jews in Europe, 1789–1939*. Oxford: Oxford University Press.

Volkov, Shulamit. 2001. *Das jüdische Projekt der Moderne*. Munich: C. H. Beck.

Waldmann, Guido, ed. 1938. *Zur Tonalität des deutschen Volksliedes*. Wolfenbüttel: Kallmeyer.

Yasser, Joseph. 1938. "Foundations of Jewish Harmony." *Musica Hebraica* 1–2: 8–12.

1

Multiple Modernisms?

Episodes from the Sciences as Cultures, 1900–1945

::: MITCHELL G. ASH

Introduction: The Plurality of Modernity and Modernism

At the beginning of the twenty-first century, after the storm of controversy over the question of "postmodernity" appears to have calmed somewhat, it seems appropriate to reconsider both the concepts of modernity and its alleged crisis, as well as the historical realities to which these concepts supposedly refer. Any effort to approach this task seriously, however, raises the question of whether the collective singular is actually the appropriate form of address, in view of the variety of political, economic, societal, and cultural developments that have been called "modern." Perhaps it would be better to speak instead of modernities and modernisms in the plural. The notion of multiple modernities has recently been advanced in the context of postcolonial theory, for example in

discussions of so-called Islamic, East Asian, and Indian modernities (see, e.g., *Multiple Modernities* 2000). Such claims often appear to accept postmodernism's assertion of Western modernity as a totalizing project, in order to claim that postcolonial cultures have created entirely new modernities, or hybrids of Western and non-Western cultural constructs, forms of life, and so on. In this chapter I question a central position of postmodernism and advance instead the thesis that so-called Western modernity itself—or, more precisely, cultural modernism in the West—has always been plural.

The collective singular noun "modernism" (*die Moderne* in German) is the established property of the humanities and refers to developments in literature, music, the visual arts, and architecture. Without wishing to question this use, I nonetheless believe it appropriate to point out that it is equally established usage to speak also of modern physics, mathematics, chemistry, or biology. The term "modern" can hardly mean the same thing in all of these contexts. Indeed, as I will show, the term "modern" had multiple meanings even within the sciences. It therefore seems prudent to employ a descriptive rather than a normative approach to the concept of modernity, specifying what was considered modern, or modernistic, in particular contexts and then searching for common ground, rather than presenting one particular definition of modernism as such (for further discussion see Ash 1999; for a more unitary view of science and modernity, see Forman 2007).

My intention here is twofold. I wish to argue, first, that there are certain affinities between the breakthrough to modern ways of thinking in the natural sciences and mathematics and the radical changes in the arts that occurred at the same time. I should also like to argue, second, that modernism, and hence cultural modernity, in all these fields was nonetheless fundamentally plural. The larger agenda that I want to advance is to continue work begun by many others on the establishment of a historically grounded and therefore pluralistic concept of modernity as the most effective antidote to the rhetorical excesses of postmodernism, but one that is neither limited in advance to particular social systems, political regimes, or canonical cultural forms, nor prejudiced in advance by ideals of what we wish modernity could or should be (see, e.g., Giddens 1990; Münch 1993).

In order to provide a rudimentary conceptual basis for this discussion, I introduce here without extensive elaboration a threefold distinction originally made by the historian of science Herbert Mehrtens between modernity, countermodernity, and technocratic modernity (Mehrtens 1990a; Mehrtens 1990b). Modernity as an intellectual style in science, as in many of the arts, involves a break with direct, supposedly pictorial representation of nature and a turn toward giving free play to abstraction and theoretical imagination. In order to characterize the affinities involved in at least a preliminary way, I propose to speak here of the breakthrough to "modern" thinking as *the emancipation of self-referential symbol systems* from the tyranny of supposedly realistic representationalism. In opposition to such emancipatory moves, advocates of countermodernity insisted on what they called *Anschaulichkeit*, by which they meant ways of thinking that preserved what they took to be the holistic connectedness of mind, or rather *Seele*, with nature. In contrast to both these styles of thinking, technocratic modernity presupposes a concept of knowledge based less on self-referential abstraction than on what can be done with, or to, nature as well as other human beings. It should be evident that I am speaking here of ideal types.

In the following remarks I hope to present examples to make these broad-brush characterizations more specific. In the first part of the chapter, I bring out affinities between modernity in the sciences and modernism in the arts at the turn of the century. In the second part, I briefly discuss controversies between modern and countermodern movements in the 1920s and the widespread talk of "crisis" of which these controversies were supposed to be symptoms. In the third and final part, I discuss very briefly the attacks on modernism in the sciences, the triumphs of technocratic modernity under Nazism, and the scientific transformations created by expelled Jewish scientists and scholars who reflected actively on the consequences of their persecution. This narrative structure corresponds in many respects to the three-act drama proposed in the introduction to this volume: act 1, discovery and invention of modernism; act 2, the age of cultural experimentation and open controversy; act 3, denouement, expulsion, and transformation.

Modernism in the Sciences and the Arts around 1900

The common context for the breakthroughs to modern styles of thought in both the sciences and the arts at the turn of the century are the technological transformations of the lived world resulting from the second industrial revolution. I name only two of these transformations here to set the scene for what follows: the abolition of the distinction between day and night by gas and then electric lighting; and the opening of the cities to the countryside and suburbs by means of horse-drawn, then electric street cars and later the automobile (see, e.g., Schivelbusch 1995; Rabinbach 1992). Both developments mark the emergence of the city as an artificial universe of sound and light, seemingly emancipated from any direct dependence on nature and its rhythms—a nature that was itself being transformed by the encroachment of the city. Already here, in these transfor-

mations of the lived world, we see how difficult it is to separate the emancipation of self-referential symbol systems from technocratic modernity.

A third transformation that is particularly relevant here is the one wrought by the entry of mechanized recording devices and communication systems into both the sciences and economic life. This development manifested itself in a wide range of objects, from the microscope and photography as instruments for expanding the range of the observable to data recording and processing apparatus, mechanical calculators, and the like (Kittler 1995). These machines transformed both the representation and the perception of nature while simultaneously revolutionizing the banking and insurance industries. The social counterpart to these changes was the emergence of new groupings, called the *neuer Mittelstand* in German and white-collar workers in English, the primary function of which was to manipulate such technologies.

A fourth development that reflected the others was the extraordinary acceleration in the speed of knowledge acquisition and concomitant specialization in the sciences and technology, a development noted with some anxiety by contemporaries and often directly linked with the social, technical, and cultural transformations just named. For example, in a lecture entitled "On the Development of Theoretical Physics in Our Times," given in Munich at the close of the old century, Ludwig Boltzmann contrasted the situation with that of an earlier era:

> In earlier centuries science progressed steadily, if slowly, due to the work of the finest minds, in the

way that an old city constantly grows due to new construction by busy and enterprising citizens. By contrast, the current century of steam and the telegraph with its nervous, overly hasty activity has made its mark on the progress of science as well. Especially the development of the natural sciences in our time appears more and more similar to the most modern American city, growing in a few decades from a village to a metropolis with a population of millions. (Boltzmann 1905: 198)

The trope of "nervousness" and the comparison of Europe's old cities and their supposedly steady, organic growth with America's rapidly burgeoning communities were both common devices of the time (Radkau 1998). The fear of fragmentation, paired with fantasies of progress including dreams of air travel and space flight, were characteristic of the ambivalence of modern consciousness.

How did all this affect the intellectual content of the sciences? Let me provide a few specific examples. In each case, I try to bring out basic features that link the cases in question to one or another of the definitions of modernity as a style of thought sketched at the beginning of these remarks.

In the so-called foundational crisis (*Grundlagenkrise*) in geometry, the aspect that links modern mathematics and modern art is the emancipation of symbol systems from any directly representational function. In mathematics the dispute began with the debate over the mathematical and philosophical implications of non-Euclidean geometry. From this emerged a battle between the supporters of symbolic and "intuitionistic" conceptions of number at the turn of the century. The controversy concerned the relation between mathematical symbol systems and the experience of counting. Around 1900 the Göttingen mathematician David Hilbert proposed what he called "axiomatics," which treated both mathematics and logic as complex symbol systems, neither of which need have any pictorial relation to the outside world. Like the physicist Max Planck, Hilbert believed that only such symbol systems could liberate science from any traces of what Planck called "anthropomorphism" and reveal the invariant laws of nature; accordingly, the unity, objectivity, and general validity of these sciences would be firmly grounded. Both the metaphor of liberation and the claim that symbol systems had their own integrity independent of any link with empirical facts were the bases of the claim to modernity in this instance (Mehrtens 1990a: passim, but esp. 117 ff.). There is a certain irony here, for the turn of the century saw a revival of idealism in philosophy, which is usually portrayed as a countermodernist position. However, the advocates of the "new" geometry emphasized the significance of abstract intellectual constructs for their logical consistency and coherence, which gave them in their view an admirable sublimity and superiority over all merely empirical descriptions of nature. In these senses they understood themselves not as cultural conservatives, but rather as productively renewing the German idealist tradition (Sigurdsson 1991).

The leading proponent of the intuitionistic answer to Hilbert's program, the Dutch mathematician L. E. J. Brouwer, based his work on an analysis of mathematical continua. For Brouwer, series like that of so-called natural numbers are not discrete groupings, as they are in set theory, but rather undivided wholes. Because such continua cannot be regarded as composita of parts, according to Brouwer, no judgment can be made about the existence or nonexistence of a number with a particular characteristic (e.g., an even number) without counting through the entire series; this is, however, impossible by definition, because such series are infinite. Thus, in this analysis, mathematics, if it is to retain any connection in principle with the experience of counting, must reject the traditional rules of logic, in this case the law of the excluded middle term.

Briefly summarized, for modernist mathematicians such as Hilbert the general validity of mathematical propositions lay in their abstraction from the merely empirical, in their logical consistence as symbol systems and not in their exact depiction of the intuitively lived world. Not for nothing did they often use the term "transcendence," as did many advocates of modernism in the arts, such as Wassily Kandinsky. The relation of this controversy to modern physics, in particular to relativity theory and later to quantum mechanics, which also emphasized the consistency of mathematical symbol systems often going beyond experimental data, is obvious in retrospect. For intuitionists such as Brouwer, on the other hand, the intuitive experience of counting was the source of

the validity of all mathematical propositions. The relation of such claims to contemporaneous pessimistic views of culture, whose advocates often complained about what they called the "distance from life" (*Lebensferne*) of modern mathematics and natural science, seems equally obvious. However, though the emancipation of self-referential symbol systems appeared to mark the "modern" position, the situation was in fact not quite so simple. The philosopher Gottlob Frege, for example, complained in his reply to Hilbert's program that he no longer knew whether or not his pocket watch—or even the earth—could be regarded as a point for mathematical purposes, as had been the case in the physics of Newton and Galileo (Mehrtens 1990a: 121). This would seem to make Frege, one of the founders of modern logic, an "antimodernist."

The complications become still greater when we examine turn-of-the-century controversies in physics. I focus here not on relativity (see Galison 2003), but rather on the debate between Ernst Mach and Ludwig Boltzmann on the status of mathematical and particularly statistical models in physics, which constituted an important part of the background to the reception of relativity theory and quantum mechanics. In a major historical work on the foundations of mechanics, Mach—a physiologist, psychophysicist, and experimental physicist, who was professor of "Philosophy, with emphasis on the history and theory of the inductive sciences" in Vienna from 1895 to 1901—presented the development of mechanics as a story of evolutionary progress from the "practical mechanics" of the great pyramids in Egypt to Newton, Leibniz, and beyond, in which the history of physics and that of human technology intertwined. Specifically, he argued that mechanics developed into a science only when repeated use of handcrafted tools extended the capacity of the senses and eventually drove the intellect to a higher level:

> The doctrines of mechanics have developed out of the collected experiences of handcraft by an intellectual process of refinement. . . . The simple machines—the five mechanical powers—are without question a product of handcraft. . . . The making of rollers (for example) must have gained a great technical importance and have led to the discovery of the lathe. In possession of this, mankind easily discovered the wheel, the wheel and axle, and the pulley. (Mach 1960: 612–13)

In an essay entitled "The Economical Nature of Physical Inquiry," Mach argued further that mathematical formulations, too, are no more than convenient tools to summarize sense impressions or laboratory observations (Mach 1943: 186–213). He did not deny the importance of hypotheses or thought-experiments like those of Galileo and Newton as aids to discovery, but he opposed going any further beyond direct observation and measurement than necessary, a standpoint characterized at the time as "phenomenological." Thus, he argued, for example, that because we experience the external world as a continuum, we should imagine underlying physical reality as consisting of continuities, not particles. Mach op-

posed physical atomism in part because there was as yet no direct observational evidence of the existence of any such hard, massy, bounded bodies as ultimate components of matter. Finally, Mach argued, using Darwinist imagery, that following simple rules of theoretical self-restraint yields advantages in the struggle for existence, by which he meant competition in science itself.

It is important to note here that for Mach sense impressions were plainly not limited to what the naked eye can see and the unaided ear can hear. An example of what he did mean is the photographs of projectiles he made with Peter Salcher and published in 1887 (Hoffmann 1997; Hoffmann 2001; see fig. 1.1). The avowed aim of this study, according to Mach, was to "make the process perceivable"—in this case to capture photographically the pressure waves caused by the movement of an object through air at high speed (Mach 1910: 357; see fig. 1.2). The similarity of these photos to those in Eadweard Muybridge's widely known movement studies seems obvious, and it was not accidental. Mach later defined the aim of the recording apparatus in general as the "thickening of immediate perception" (*Verdichtung der Anschauung*) (Hoffmann 1997: 45; see also Stiegler 1998). To put it in a nutshell, for Mach the term "sense impressions" included extensions of ordinary sensation by means of technology. The apparent difference between how things appeared to the unaided senses and these technologically produced images was, in Mach's view, merely quantitative, despite the extraordinary difficulties he encountered when he attempted to create such images. Thus, if Mach was a modernist—and he surely was—then he is plainly to be classed as an adherent of technological modernity.

A primary opponent of Mach on these issues was Ludwig Boltzmann, professor of theoretical physics in Vienna. In contrast to the polymath Mach, Boltzmann stood for the institutionalization of theoretical physics as an independent field and thus embodied the specialization he himself diagnosed in the statement cited above. Boltzmann consistently advocated the independent status of mathematical models in physics, asserting that their importance went far beyond the mere summation of measurement data. In an encyclopedia article on mathematical and physical models, apparatus, and instruments, he called such models "instruments" and acknowledged that the "need to save labor" was an important

reason for their use (Boltzmann 1905: 1). But he scornfully compared Mach's Darwinist "economy of thought" with the businessman's need to save time and money. The real purpose of mathematical models, in his view, was "the need to make results of calculation observable [*anschaulich*]"; elsewhere in the same text he used the term "sensorization" (*Versinnlichung*) (ibid.: 2).

By terms such as *anschaulich* and *Versinnlichung* Boltzmann clearly meant something quite different from Mach's sense impressions or Brouwer's intuitionism. Boltzmann meant to give priority to theory, not observation, and to argue that the former guided the latter, not the other way around. Ever since the time of great Paris mathematicians, he wrote, "one has conceived matter as a sum of mathematical points," not as a continuum. Atomism thus became a practical necessity

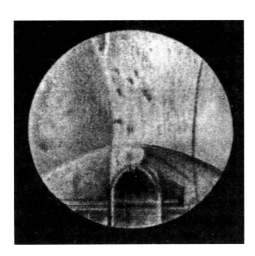

Figure 1.1 Ernst Mach and Peter Salcher's photograph of hyperbolic pressure wave from the tip of a projectile passing through air (1887). Source: Hoffmann 1997, p. 44, fig. 3.

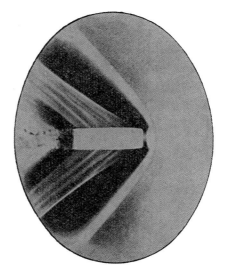

Figure 1.2 Mach and Salcher's photograph of hyperbolic pressure wave, retouched. Source: Mach 1910, p. 370, fig. 52.

for doing physics at all, quite independent of the observability of atoms:

> One does not believe, however, that one has really created a clear concept of what a continuum is merely by employing the word, continuum, and writing out a differential equation! On closer examination the differential equation is only the expression for the fact that one must begin with a finite number. (Boltzmann 1905: 144; author's translation)

The labor involved was not the convenient summary of sense impressions, but the development of "mental images" (*Gedankenbilder*); indeed, Boltzmann argued that broad collections of facts (*umfassende Tatsachengebiete*) could never be described directly, but could only be depicted by such *Gedankenbilder*—that is, by mathematical equations (ibid.: 142). Though he spoke of images, representation, and *Versinnlichung*, Boltzmann plainly did not mean any analogy to photographic imagery. Rather, theories are symbol systems that stand on their own and are testable only as wholes; they are images of nature only in a very abstract sense. Boltzmann nonetheless calls them "instruments" and emphasizes that they are not entirely self-referential, but rather subject to experimental testing.

Boltzmann's emphasis on the independence of mathematical theory and on abstract theoretical rather than photographic pictures of nature has come to be regarded as central to the modern standpoint in physics. It is important to note, however, that the synthesis of theoretical physics with high technology in the form of the atomic bomb was hardly dreamed of by anyone involved at the time. Thus, the turn-of-the-century positions I have outlined do not form an opposition in principle between "modern" and "countermodern," but rather are two versions of the "modern" in physics. The two styles of thinking lived alongside one another at first and could even become competitors, but it was also possible to blend them.

Modernity in Music

What relevance, if any, has any of this to modernity in music? Though I am not a musicologist, perhaps I may be allowed to note some suggestive references in the writings of Arnold Schoenberg that may provide starting points for discussion. In "Composition in Twelve Tones," for example, Schoenberg speaks of the "emancipation of dissonance" and explicitly rejects the designation "atonal" as a description of his system, speaking instead of a "system of components relating only to one another" (Schoenberg 1984: 217–18). Specifically, he described the twelve-tone method in terms of mirrored notes similar to the abstraction of mirrored numbers, as shown in the diagram (fig. 1.3). Such remarks appear to place this particularly formalistic version of modern music squarely in the camp of modernity as the emancipation of self-referential symbol systems. Caution is needed here, since one might well say that music itself is a self-referential symbol system. Nonetheless, the contrast of Schoenberg's willfully austere twelve-tone approach with the

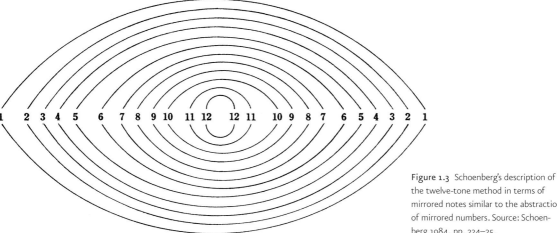

1 2 3 4 5 6 7 8 9 10 11 12 12 11 10 9 8 7 6 5 4 3 2 1

Figure 1.3 Schoenberg's description of the twelve-tone method in terms of mirrored notes similar to the abstraction of mirrored numbers. Source: Schoenberg 1984, pp. 224–25.

highly evocative, definitely referential texts Richard Strauss and Gustav Mahler—and Schoenberg himself—attached to their tone poems is obvious.

Care is needed also for another reason: Schoenberg refers to non-Euclidean geometry only occasionally and vaguely, whereas his references to Mach's phenomenological and evolutionary conception of physics were more frequent and precise, though he does not mention Mach by name. He constantly wrote of the development of musical ideas from lower to higher stages and regarded his own twelve-tone system as a result of gradual evolutionary development. Still more interesting in this regard are Schoenberg's frequent references in the *Theory of Harmony* to the psychological effects of tones and chords (e.g., Schoenberg 1978: 19 ff.).

Though Schoenberg was not a trained scientist, such discussions show a familiarity with the work of the physiologist and physicist Hermann Helmholtz and the philosopher and psychologist Carl Stumpf on the psychology of hearing (Helm-

holtz 1862; Stumpf 1883). Mach, too, worked on these subjects. There is no evidence that Schoenberg met Mach, but he certainly knew two people who had done so, Guido Adler and David Joseph Bach; Bach was one of the formative influences in Schoenberg's youth by his own account and a doctoral student of Mach and Friedrich Jodl in Vienna (Kwiram 1999). There is an intriguing similarity between this diagram of Mach's, showing differences between pure and tempered tuning that would remain on a circular keyboard (fig. 1.4), and the following diagrams by Schoenberg. The first diagram, a design for Berlin streetcar tickets (fig. 1.5), shows Schoenberg as a craftsman. The second (fig. 1.6) depicts Schoenberg's *Zwölftondrehscheibe*, a "tool," as he called it, for generating twelve-tone series. I do *not* claim that Schoenberg "borrowed" his design from Mach. Rather, the issue is the way in which they embodied figuratively their shared belief in the evolution of "higher" creative forms from handcrafted work. Situated within the argument I advance in

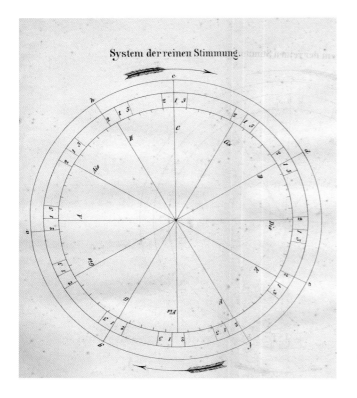

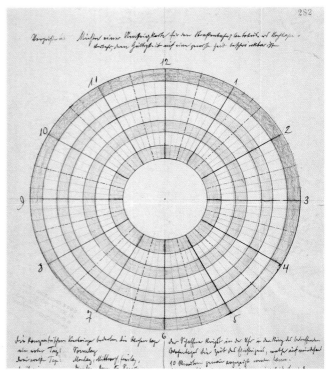

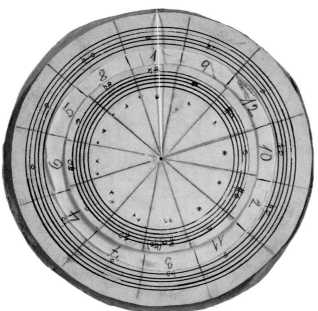

Figure 1.4 (*top left*) Diagram by Ernst Mach showing differences between pure and tempered tuning on a circular keyboard. In this model, the octave C returns to itself, and most intervals preserve their alignment. Source: Mach 1985, "System der reinen Stimmung," appendix.

Figure 1.5 (*top right*) Arnold Schoenberg's design for Berlin streetcar tickets. (Courtesy of the Arnold Schönberg Cener, Vienna. Used by permission of Belmont Music Publishers.)

Figure 1.6 (*bottom*) Arnold Schoenberg's *Zwölftondrehscheibe*. (Courtesy of the Arnold Schönberg Center, Vienna. Used by permission of Belmont Music Publishers)

this chapter, both diagrams exemplify syntheses of formalist and technological modernity.

"Jewish" Modernism?

I have discussed turn-of-the-century trends in the sciences and music at such length because they created the intellectual and cultural resources for subsequent controversies and transformations. Before proceeding to these, I would like to comment on so-called Jewish contributions to modernity. Here it is vitally important to distinguish between two possible meanings of this expression, which are often confused with one another. To put the point as clearly as possible: contributions by ethnic Jews to modernity in the sciences or the arts need not, and usually did not, have anything to do with Jewish religion or culture. It is true enough that many of the authors named above were ethnically Jews, but it seems to me to be mistaken to jump to any simple conclusions from that fact about affinities between content of their creations and Jewish thought, which was and remains a rather complex entity in itself. Though it is surely correct that traditional Jewish culture held *religious* learning in high regard, this hardly explains why large numbers of Jews in a single time and place—German-speaking Europe in the late nineteenth and early twentieth centuries—suddenly made the *secular* learned professions their own.

More plausible to me is the view that the evident preference of many—though by no means all—artists and scientists of Jewish ethnicity for abstraction, formalism, and universalistic or cos-mopolitan viewpoints in this period can best be explained as part of a complex acculturation strategy (Beller 1989, part 2; Beller 1996; Hacohen 2001). The physicist Leopold Infeld, for example, remarked in his autobiography that when his parents prevented him from enrolling in the local Gymnasium, "I realized that what my parents had done was to close to me the easiest exit from the ghetto" (cited in Fischer 1998: 103). For ethnic Jews who chose this path, acculturation meant choosing cultural values taken to be abstract or universal over specifically Jewish constructions of culture. Polemical denials, for example by Ernst Gombrich (1997), that there was any such thing as a separate Jewish culture or any identifiably Jewish influence on the culture of fin-de-siècle Vienna are themselves excellent examples of this acculturation strategy. It is well-known that these Jews came from highly educated families, which tended in any case to buy into the perceived values of the host culture wholesale.

Elsewhere, continuing a productive line of research begun by Shulamit Volkov (2001), I have argued that the relatively high percentage of Jewish scientists in psychology and the social sciences is a specific expression of what Amos Funkenstein once termed "the modernization of German (-speaking) Jewry" (Funkenstein 1994). Funkenstein meant by this the increasing secularization of Jewish as well as modern life, and the concomitant reorientation of the majority of German-speaking Jews from a diaspora identity to identification with a state and culture "which they took to be their own" (ibid.: 8). In the case of Jewish psychologists and social scientists, modernization meant two things: the rewriting of traditional discursive elements of the German philosophical tradition; and participation, along with many non-Jews, in the rationalization and technologization of the social sphere by applying scientific techniques to personnel selection, the study of labor processes, or social and economic policy analysis. Common to both moves is the tendency to avoid issues that might be taken to be specifically Jewish and to participate instead in discourses and practices taken to be objective and therefore modern (Ash 2004).

There appears to be no obvious difference between natural scientists, humanists, and creative artists in this regard. The introduction to this volume makes an eloquent case that there were ways of constructing cultural modernity within Jewish religious and ethnic life, and some scholars and scientists surely felt and expressed an affinity with Judaism and Jewish culture (see below). Nonetheless, scientists such as Sigmund Freud were much more often utterly secular, even antireligious. Of course that did not prevent their work from being defamed as "Jewish" by their opponents with increasing frequency and intensity in the interwar period, to which I now briefly turn.

After World War I

The interwar period saw a continuation and intensification of the trends and controversies already in motion before World War I, with two important differences, both clearly attributable to the radically changed political situation. First, explicitly political terminology entered the discussion, and second, the controversies came to be regarded ever more widely as signs of a general cultural crisis.

The centrality of Weimar Germany to this topic is obvious. Since the 1960s a dualistic interpretive schema has dominated discussions of Weimar culture (Gay 1969; Laqueur 1974: esp. chaps. 3 and 6; for a similar interpretation of developments in physical science, see Forman 1971). According to such views the ideological and cultural disputes of the time are depicted as struggles between modernism and antimodernism, with a corresponding tendency to link avant-garde aesthetics or scientific innovations with the progressive side of the political spectrum. More recently, however, such dualisms have been questioned from a variety of perspectives.

Particularly significant in this context is the fact that, as recent research has shown, it is not possible simply to link avant-garde culture as firmly with progressive politics as earlier writers once tried to do (see Peukert 1993; Bialas 1996). Just as there were left-wing adherents of Nietzsche around 1900 and later, there were also socialist interpretations of Darwinism and eugenics (Weingart, Kroll, and Bayertz 1988; Weindling 1989; Weikart 1999). In the discourse of technology as well there were "reactionary modernists," as Jeffrey Herf (1984) called them. Oswald Spengler, for example, was no enemy of technology, but he argued for a healthy German technics, which, in connection with the peasantry, soldiers, and artists, would constitute the formative forces (*Gestaltungskräften*) of cultural renewal (Spengler 1977, 1: 130–31 and 135 ff.; 2: 660 ff.; cf. Herf 1984: esp. 52 ff., 63). Holistic thinking has long been considered a clear sign of countermodernity that could easily be linked with conservative or reactionary circles. There were, however, many efforts, for example in biology and psychology, to make concepts such as intuitive meaning (*Sinn*), *Ganzheit*, *Gestalt*, and other elements of holistic thought compatible with modern natural science and also with democratic, even socialist politics (Harrington 1996; Ash 1995: esp. chap. 17; cf. Ringer 1969: 375 ff.).

The popularity, moreover, of various technocratically oriented modernisms, from the so-called New Objectivity in the visual arts to the idea of "rationalizing" industrial production—both hotly debated during the relatively stable middle years of the Weimar Republic from 1923 to 1929—speaks against any presentation of such strivings for wholeness and meaning as merely a reflexive response to the precarious social situation of German *Bildungsbürger*. In this period state support for research recovered much of the ground lost during World War I, despite continuing talk of a "crisis of science"; by 1928 the financial support for basic research in Germany had reached pre–World War I levels (Forman 1974). The fundamental insights of Max Weber or Sigmund Freud into the depths of modern life—whether it was the perceived loss of intrinsic meaning in a thoroughly rationalized society or the unhappy effects of so-called civilized sexual morality—surely cannot be dismissed as nothing more than the products of upper- or petit-bourgeois *ressentiments* (Peukert 1993: 186).

For my consideration of science as culture in the present chapter, the most important criticism of any simple dualism between "modernism" and "countermodernity" is the fact that the cultural contents that are termed "modern" differ so greatly from one discipline and branch of the arts to another that any attempt to differentiate the modern from the countermodern in any generally valid way is doomed to failure. For example, the conceptual contents and argumentative structures of the modern approaches in mathematics, physics, and psychology differed. In physics and mathematics, as explained above, the modernists, like the modernists in the arts, moved to liberate their thinking from the conventions of representationalism in favor of the abstract, the symbolic, and the self-referential. In psychology, however, the members of the so-called Berlin School of Gestalt psychology, who certainly understood themselves as modernizers in their field, emphasized the immanent structure of immediate experience itself and claimed that intrinsic meaning could be apprehended directly in the phenomena themselves (Wertheimer 1925; cf. Harrington 1996; Ash 1995). That sounds like a return to romanticism, but Gestalt theory was based on laboratory research and strict natural-scientific explanation and was regarded internationally as an innovative approach. Even though they borrowed concepts such as "frame of reference" from relativity theory, the Gestalt theorists' version of modernity in science was clearly not based on the emancipation of self-referential symbol systems. Rather, this approach exemplified one of the two acculturation strategies described in the "'Jewish' Modernism?" section above—the rewriting of traditional discursive elements of the German philosophical tradition.

Radically different from both of these variants of modernism in the sciences during the Weimar era was the discourse of technocratic modernity, which, like "modern" mathematics and relativity theory, also began to emerge before 1914. Examples include eugenics or "race hygiene," the debate over Taylorism, Fordism, and the "rationalization" of industrial labor, as well as the aviation craze, the passion for rocketry, and popular fantasies of flying to the moon (Weindling 1989; Rabinbach 1992; Nolan 1994; Fischer 1991; Neufeld 1990). Common to all of these technocratic initiatives were the related hopes of dominating nature and achieving social control by technical means. Counterparts to all this in the arts were Italian Futurism and especially the so-called New Objectivity (*Neue Sachlichkeit*) of the mid-1920s (Willet 1978). The Social Democrats who supported the rationalization of factory labor surely had little affinity for abstract art or quantum mechanics.

Concomitant with these varied modernisms was the widespread talk of cultural crisis that began at the turn of the century and became endemic during the Weimar era. Whether the talk was about a crisis of modernity or about modernity itself as a crisis depended on the speaker's point of view (see vom Bruch 1989; Ash 2000). There are many social, economic, and political reasons for the spread of crisis talk in this period, but equally important was the inability to find a common language that could unite the hopeless plurality of developments in economy, society, politics, and culture. Precisely the fragmentation of what—at least to nostalgic eyes—had once been an organically structured society into social milieus and interest groups, as well as the splintering of the sciences into specialized disciplines and specialties, emerged as the most often diagnosed symptoms of crisis. It could be argued that crisis talk itself became a kind of metaphorical glue, producing unity where none existed, and that slogan words such as *Ganzheit*, *Gestalt*, "meaning" (*Sinn*), and "synthesis" were frequently employed by authors with different political orientations.

Even the political coding of crisis talk was by no means fixed. Talk of cultural crisis was by no means limited to Weimar Germany, nor was it limited to a single discipline or political viewpoint. It was a common diagnosis of the time; cultural conservatives such as Spengler as well as Marxists used the term, albeit with very different intentions and interpretations. The same is true of the idea of a "third way," offered in many versions as a way out of the crisis. The categories of fragmentation and totality as well as attempts to provide a "synthesis" or to "overcome" old antagonisms were central to the thought of Marxist theoreticians such as Georg Lukacs and Ernst Bloch (Jay 1984). After 1933 the Nazis attempted to resolve the political, social, and cultural crises of the Weimar era simultaneously, and by force.

After 1933

For many years, accounts of the sciences under Nazism, like that of Weimar culture, rested on a series of simple dualisms that, taken together, formed the framework of a master narrative. Because the components of that narrative are still very much with us, it may be useful to state two of them as succinctly as possible at the outset. First, it was often a story of pseudoscience, against which the forces of good—that is, good science—were eventually victorious. Implicit in this narrative component was the hope that the morally good, the politically progressive, and the scientifically innovative might coincide. Second, it was a tale of regression to barbarism, a story of the misuse of modern science and technology.

Here, if not sooner, the discussion makes contact with much wider debates on the general significance of the Nazi era in German history and in the history of modernity itself. For general historians, too, the standard story remains that of the perversion of essentially value-neutral achievements of modern society and culture by the Nazis. Hans Mommsen, for example, argues that even in the military, where no one doubts the modernity of the technology and strategic thinking that was available to the Nazis, the National Socialist leadership lived parasitically off of earlier innovations. Yet this is surely not the case for the breakthrough in rocketry achieved at Peenemünde (see below), and Mommsen himself must admit that in the case of forced sterilization for eugenic purposes, in the so-called euthanasia program, and in the Holocaust the regime achieved a "specific" and horrifically effective form of modernization (Mommsen 1991: 423). In his final publication, Detlev Peukert went still further, arguing that these crimes, though they were not inevitable, originated in the "spirit of science" itself; in his

view they were "not fatal outbreaks of barbarism . . . but one of the possibilities of modern civilization in crisis" (Peukert 1989: 104).

For the past twenty years, all variants of the master narrative just outlined have been subjected to detailed scrutiny and criticism (Harwood 1997; Szöllöszi-Janze 2001). These simple dualisms, nonetheless, are still very much with us. In the concluding pages of this chapter I turn to three related areas: the impacts of the dismissal of scientists identified as Jews and socialists; transformations of so-called normal science in Germany; and scientific changes following emigration, particularly those resulting from reflections by émigrés on their own circumstances.

Forced Migration: An Expulsion of Modernism?

The significance of the break in 1933 is hard to exaggerate. The so-called Law for the Reconstitution of the Professional Civil Service of 7 April 1933, which authorized the release or premature retirement from government service of persons who were not of "Aryan" descent or who were associated with groups considered politically undesirable in the new German state, was only the beginning of a massive, forced exodus, mainly of Jewish scholars and scientists from Nazi Germany. The Nuremberg Laws of 1935, the invasion of Austria in March 1938, the pogroms in Germany in November of that year, and finally the Nazi conquests in the rest of Europe led to a mass emigration of scientists and scholars unprecedented in the modern history of academic life.

Recent research, however, has led to a surprisingly differentiated picture. For example, the distribution pattern of dismissals among German-speaking universities is quite uneven. From a list of 614 university teachers dismissed in the first year of the civil service law, for example, three universities—Berlin, Frankfurt, and Breslau—accounted for fully 40 percent of the total, while the universities of Rostock and Tübingen had as few as two each, and Erlangen only one (Liste 1934; see also Gerstengarbe 1994). The numbers are thus indicators of the uneven concentration of Jewish academics in Germany—and of the presence or absence of structural anti-Semitism in German higher education. More comprehensive studies have confirmed this result (Grüttner and Kimas 2007).

Similar differences have emerged from studies of dismissals and emigration in individual disciplines. In physics and psychology, for example, the larger and generally more innovative institutes were the hardest hit. Thus, in these fields Nazism's racist policies left noticeable, and in some places considerable, quantitative gaps in Germany's scientific institutions. The qualitative losses, though, were often still more significant. Not for nothing does Alan Beyerchen (1983) speak, in a deliberately ironic reference to Martin Heidegger's inaugural address as rector in Freiburg, of the "self-decapitation" (*Selbstenthauptung*) of German culture, as opposed to the "self-assertion" (*Selbstbehauptung*) advocated by Heidegger.

And yet, that is not the whole story. As recent research on science under Nazism has shown, emigration rates were not the same for all disciplines. Recent studies of the dismissal and emigration of medical scientists from Berlin, for example, present a highly differentiated picture, from complete destruction in the case of Magnus Hirschfeld's Institute for Sexual Research to nearly complete continuity in university and extra-academic institutes concerned with public health and population policy (Fischer et al. 1994). It now appears exaggerated to speak in any simple or general sense of an "exodus of reason" or even of modernity as such from Nazi Germany after 1933. Such a view has the effect of distracting us from examining more closely just what kinds of modernity not only survived but flourished under Nazism.

Science under Nazism: Triumph of Technocracy?

When we turn more critically toward an assessment of science under the Nazis, we soon recognize that recent research results have forced us to question earlier views. It has long been known that in many areas of culture, Nazis proved themselves to be supportive of certain modern trends, despite their hostility to others. Modern political campaign organization, the use of radio and film, the skillful organization of sound and light at party rallies filmed by Leni Riefenstahl—all these and other examples show clearly enough that the Nazis' avowed hostility to "degenerate" art did not extend to the modern media. In the sciences and technology, too, the relationships are far more complex than the simple dichotomy of modern and countermodern would suggest.

Successors were found often enough for those dismissed academics who emigrated, and the science that replaced their work cannot be dismissed simply as Nazified ideology disguised as science, though there surely was plenty of that. In the well-known case of "German physics," physicists opposed to relativity theory and quantum mechanics were able for a time to mobilize support in the Nazi party and the SS and thus acquire important positions within the German science policy administration; but they were effectively opposed from within the discipline, and their influence waned during World War II (Hentschel 1996). Ute Deichmann's study of biologists under Hitler (Deichmann 1996) shows that funding for basic research in genetics did not diminish but in fact increased during the Nazi period. Herbert Mehrtens and Helmuth Trischler (in Renneberg and Walker 1994) note a shift to "technoscience"—meaning technology-oriented basic research—before and during World War II in fields as disparate as mathematics and aerodynamics, a shift that paralleled trends in the West (see also Epple and Rennert 2000; Epple 2002). Finally, Michael Neufeld's study of the German rocketry project (Neufeld 1995) clearly shows that despite the mass emigration of Jewish scientists and technicians, neither personnel, resources, nor the will to invest in them was lacking when it came to programs deemed central to Nazism's eugenic or expansionist aims—and to creating and unleashing a modern war machine to achieve them.

As Robert Proctor (1999) shows in his study of Nazi-era cancer research, this was not merely an instrumental relationship in which the Nazis used supposedly neutral science for evil ends. In this case, epidemiological proof that habitual smoking causes lung cancer and large-scale propaganda campaigns against smoking were aimed at "purifying" the so-called Aryan people's body (*Volkskörper*). Slogans such as the infamous claim that National Socialism was nothing more than "applied biology" presupposed a natural-scientific-technological worldview, even though at the same time many leading Nazis appeared to be at odds with relativity and quantum mechanics. As Herbert Mehrtens writes: "Let us conclude, in a very general way: One basis of the Nazi belief system is a scientomorphic worldview, which implies a technical treatment of nature"—and, I would add, of other human beings as well (Mehrtens 1990b: 115).

Mehrtens finds numerous examples of both countermodernity and technocratic modernity under Nazism: "A strange aversion to abstraction can be found among the ideologists of 'Germanic' science, quite similar to the relationship of National Socialism to modern art. At the same time the chemical industry, fighter planes, and radio sets were 'German' enough" (ibid.: 113). Joseph Goebbels was referring to the Volkswagen when he said at the opening of the 1939 German auto show: "National Socialism never rejected or struggled against technology. Rather, one of its main tasks was consciously to affirm, to fill it inwardly with soul, to discipline it, and to place it in the service of our people and their cultural level. . . . On the contrary, it has discovered a new romanticism in the results of modern inventions and technology" (cited in Herf 1984: 196). It was only a short step from such views to calling the Peenemünde rockets "miracle weapons" (*Wunderwaffen*) during World War II.

The Émigrés: Learning from Persecution

All this stands in stark contrast to scientific changes resulting at least in part from the work of émigré scientists and artists in collaboration with others in their countries of refuge. In order to understand what occurred here, it is necessary to clarify a fundamental issue. It is a common error to suppose that the émigrés' justly famous contributions to the sciences and culture were "losses" to the German-speaking world and "gains" for American or British culture. Such views presuppose a static view of science and of culture, as though the émigrés brought with them finished bits of knowledge, which they then inserted like building blocks into already established cultural constructs elsewhere. This assumes that such research programs or groupings would necessarily have remained in place or continued working as before had their members not been forced to leave their homelands. It also ignores both the fact that forced migration made possible careers that could not have happened in the smaller, more restrictive university and science systems of Central Europe, and the possibility that the need to respond to new circumstances—or, better, the ability to do so—led to innovations that might not have occurred at the same speed or in the same way otherwise (Ash 2003).

The scientific changes that are most relevant here are those initiated during and after the Nazi takeover of power by émigré Jewish scientists and scholars as a result of conscious or unconscious reflection on their own biographies. The causal link with the events of 1933 and after is clear in this case. As stated above, in the years before the Nazi takeover the majority of Jewish scholars and scientists usually did not concentrate on "Jewish" thought and customs or on the psychological and social problems of Jews. Well-known exceptions such as Martin Buber, Gershon Scholem, and Erich Fromm confirm this point. Only after their forced emigration did more than a few such scholars and scientists identify increasingly with Judaism or concern themselves with anti-Semitism. Such moves point to a phenomenon that might be called scientific change through *reflexivity*, that is, the scientific working through of issues presented by radical biographical or political change. The Austrian social psychologist Marie Jahoda formulated this change with admirable clarity when she said, "My Jewishness only became a true identity with Hitler" (Jahoda 1983). This formulation and also the title of an autobiographical essay by Hans Speier, "Not the Emigration, but the Triumph of Hitler Was the Important Experience," suggest a political rather than a religious conception of Jewish identity (Speier 1988). Several examples of such changes in science and scholarship have been analyzed before (see, e.g., Kurzweil 1996; Papcke 1993). The most famous example of such a linkage from the social sciences is the "Authoritarian Personality" study, in which, we should recognize, not only members of the Frankfurt School were involved (Ash 2005). A brief reminder that Arnold Schoenberg, too, reflected increasingly on Jewish themes in his later music deserves mention in this context, even though this process began before 1933.

Conclusion

With this remark I have returned to the starting point of this chapter. It is well-known that all these scientific and cultural innovations were highly controversial at the time, and some of them remain so to this day. Not all the participants agreed that the emancipation of self-referential symbol systems from the tyranny of representationalism was in fact an act of liberation. It is also becoming accepted that a simple, linear ordering or linkage of cultural innovation to progressive politics is no longer possible.

As a tentative conclusion, let me suggest that the synthesis of modern theoretical science and culture, understood as the emancipation of self-referential symbol systems and the victory of instrumental or technologized reason symbolized, for example, in nuclear weapons, is a product of the late twentieth century and should not be regarded as inevitable. In the first third of the twentieth century multiple constructions of modernism lived alongside one another and at times even competed for supremacy in the same discipline. Moreover, as noted above, the widely admired revolutions in urban life resulting from modern technologies such as electrification and the

streetcar had little to do with breakthroughs in modern science such as non-Euclidean geometry or relativity theory; rather, they rested on applications of the very classical mathematics and physics that had supposedly been overcome by those modern developments. Mendelian genetics—which was accepted first at agricultural research stations—Galton's eugenics, and Taylorism and the assembly line, as well as fundamental ideas of socialist thought, in particular the assumption that economy and society could be organized and planned scientifically, can all be interpreted as manifestations of technocratic modernity.

The relationships between these manifestations of technocratic modernity and modernism as the emancipation of self-referential symbol systems remain to be explored in detail. A number of possible answers to this question are imaginable: radical rejection of and reaction against "soulless technology"; equally enthusiastic acceptance, as manifested by the Futurists in Italy; deep reflection on the meaning of the technologization of the lived world for culture, as in the work of Weber and Freud; and finally the use of technology as a resource for artistic creation. As Stephen Kern put it some years ago: "Scientific management, the motion studies of Muybridge and Marey, early cinematography, Cubism and Futurism reflect aspects of each other across the cultural spectrum like images in a funhouse mirror" (Kern 1983: 117).

Perhaps the sense that modernity was in crisis—or the view among cultural conservatives that modernity was itself a symptom of crisis—

was rooted in two states of affairs. The first of these was the already mentioned departures from the cultural conventions of the nineteenth century—for example, the academic conventions of supposedly realistic representationalism in the visual arts or the rules of classical composition in music. At least as important, however, is the lack of clarity about how to find a common link with which to connect these multiple innovations in the sciences and the arts, technology, economy, and society. The aim of these remarks has not been to find a common conceptual denominator, but to offer support for an attitude that accepts the plurality of modernity and modernism without anxiously searching for ways of reducing it to some imagined essence. Though such an approach may seem less satisfying in some respects than the simplifications of postmodernism, it has the advantage of avoiding a needless and uncritical replication of the anxieties and nervousness already evident in a historical era we hope to understand better.

❧

::: **NOTES** :::

1. "Man glaube doch nicht, daß man sich durch das Wort Kontinuum oder das Hinschreiben einer Differentialgleichung auch einen klaren Begriff des Kontinuums verschafft habe! Bei näheren Zusehen ist die Differentialgleichung nur der Ausdruck dafür, daß man zuerst eine endliche Zahl zu denken hat."

::: **WORKS CITED** :::

Ash, Mitchell G. 1995. *Gestalt Psychology in German Culture, 1890–1967: Holism and the Quest for Objectivity.* Cambridge: Cambridge University Press.

———. 1999. "Die Wissenschaften in der Geschichte der Moderne (Antrittsvorlesung am Institut für Geschichte der Universität Wien, 2. April 1998)." *Österreichische Zeitschrift für Geschichtswissenschaften* 10: 105–29.

———. 2000. "Krise der Moderne oder Modernität als Krise? Stimmen aus der Akademie." In Wolfram Fischer, ed., with the assistance of R. Hohlfeld and P. Nötzoldt, *Die Preußische Akademie der Wissenschaften zu Berlin in Krieg und Frieden, in Republik und Diktatur 1914–1945*, 121–42. Berlin: Akademie-Verlag.

———. 2003. "Forced Migration and Scientific Change: Steps Towards a New Overview." In Edward Timms and Jonathan Hughes, eds., *Intellectual Migration and Cultural Transformation: Refugees from National Socialism in the English-Speaking World*, 241–63. Vienna: Springer-Verlag.

———. 2004. "Innovation, Ethnicity, Identity: German-Speaking Jewish Psychologists and Social Scientists in the Interwar Period." *Jahrbuch des Simon Dubnow Instituts/Yearbook of the Simon Dubnow Institute* 3: 241–68.

———. 2005. "Learning from Persecution: Émigré Social Scientists' Studies of Authoritarianism and Anti-Semitism after 1933." In Beate Meyer and Marion Kaplan, ed. *Jüdische Welten: Juden in Deutschland vom 18. Jahrhundert bis in die Gegenwart: Festschrift für Monika Richarz*, 271–94. Göttingen: Wallstein Verlag.

———, and Alfons Söllner, eds. 1996. *Forced Migration and Scientific Change: German-Speaking Scientists and Scholars after 1933.* Cambridge: Cambridge University Press.

Beller, Steven. 1989. *Vienna and the Jews, 1867–1938: A*

Cultural History. Cambridge: Cambridge University Press.

———. 1996. "Patriotism and the National Identity of Habsburg Jewry, 1860–1914." *Leo Baeck Institute Yearbook* 41: 215–38.

Beyerchen, A. D. 1983. "Anti-Intellectualism and the Cultural Decapitation of Germany under the Nazis." In Jarrel C. Jackman and Carla M. Boden, eds., *The Muses Flee Hitler: Cultural Transfer and Adaptation, 1930–1945*, 29–44. Washington, D.C.: Smithsonian Institution Press.

Bialas, Wolfgang. 1996. "Intellektuellengeschichtliche Facetten der Weimarer Republik." In Wolfgang Bialas and Georg Iggers, eds., *Intellektuelle in der Weimarer Republik*, 13–30. Frankfurt am Main: Peter Lang.

Boltzmann, Ludwig. 1905. "Über die Methoden der theoretischen Physik." In *Populäre Schriften*, 1–10. Leipzig: Barth. Orig. publ. 1892.

———. 1905. "Über die Unentbehrlichkeit der Atomistik in der Naturwissenschaft." In *Populäre Schriften*, 141–57. Leipzig: Barth. Orig. publ. 1897.

———. 1905. "Über die Entwicklung der Methoden der theoretischen Physik in neuerer Zeit." In *Populäre Schriften*, 198–227. Leipzig: Barth. Orig. publ. 1899.

vom Bruch, Rüdiger, ed. 1989. *Kultur und Kulturwissenschaft um 1900: Krise der Moderne und Glaube an die Wissenschaft*. Stuttgart: Franz Steiner-Verlag.

Coen, Deborah. 2007. *Vienna in the Age of Uncertainty: Science, Liberalism and Private Life*. Chicago: University of Chicago Press.

Deichmann, Ute. 1996. *Biologists under Hitler*. Trans. by Thomas Dunlap. Cambridge, Mass.: Harvard University Press.

Epple, Moritz. 2002. "Rechnen, Messen, Führen: Kriegsforschung am Kaiser-Wilhelm-Institut für Strömungsforschung, 1937–1945." In *Rüstungsforschung im Nationalsozialismus, Organisation, Mobilisierung und Entgrenzung der Technikwissenschaften*, ed. Helmut Maier, 305–56. Göttingen: Wallstein Verlag.

Epple, Moritz, and Volker Remmert. 2000. "Eine ungeahnte Synthese zwischen reiner und angewandter Mathmatik: Kriegsrelevante mathematische Forschung in Deutschland während des II. Weltkriegs." In *Geschichte der Kaiser-Wilhelm-Gesellschaft im Nationalsozialismus: Bestandsaufnahme und Perspektiven der Forschung*, ed. Doris Kaufmann, 1: 258–95. Göttingen: Wallstein Verlag.

Fischer, Klaus. 1998. "Jüdische Wissenschaftler in Weimar: Marginalität, Identität und Innovation." In Wolfgang Benz, Arnold Paucker, and Peter Pulzer, eds., *Jüdisches Leben in der Weimarer Republik*, 89–116. Tübingen: Mohr.

Fisher, Peter S. 1991. *Fantasy and Politics: Visions of the Future in the Weimar Republic*. Madison: University of Wisconsin Press.

Fischer, Wolfram, Klaus Hierholzer, Michael Hubenstorf, and Peter T. Walter, eds. 1994. *Exodus von Wissenschaften aus Berlin*. Berlin: Duncker & Humblot.

Forman, Paul. 1971. "Weimar Culture, Causality, and Quantum Theory, 1918–1927: Adaptation by German Physicists and Mathematicians to a Hostile Intellectual Environment." *Historical Studies in the Physical Sciences* 3: 1–115.

———. 1974. "The Financial Support and Political Alignment of Physicists in Weimar Germany." *Minerva* 12: 39–66.

———. 2007. "The Primacy of Science in Modernity, of Technology in Postmodernity, and of Ideology in the History of Technology." *History and Technology* 23: 1–152.

Funkenstein, Amos. 1994. "Reform und Geschichte: Die Modernisierung des deutschen Judentums." In Shulamit Volkov, ed., *Deutsche Juden und die Moderne*, 1–8. Munich: Beck.

Galison, Peter L. 2003. *Einstein's Clocks and Poincaré's Maps: Empires of Time*. New York: W. W. Norton.

Gay, Peter. 1969. *Weimar Culture: The Outsider as Insider*. New York: Harper & Row.

Gerstengarbe, Sybille. 1994. "Die erste Entlassungswelle von Hochschullehrern deutscher Hochschulen aufgrund des Gesetzes zur Wiederherstellung des Berufsbeamtentums vom 7.7.1933." *Berichte zur Wis-*

senschaftsgeschichte 17: 17–40.

Giddens, Anthony. 1990. *The Consequences of Modernity*. Stanford, Calif.: Stanford University Press.

Gombrich, Ernst. 1997. *The Visual Arts in Vienna circa 1900: Reflections on the Jewish Catastrophe*. London.

Grüttner, Michael, and Sven Kinas. 2007. "Die Vertreibung von Wissenschaftlern aus den deutschen Universitäten, 1933–1945." *Vierteljahreshefte für Zeitgeschichte* 55: 123–86.

Hacohen, Malachai. 2001. "Popper's Cosmopolitanism: Culture Clash and Jewish Identity." In Steven Beller, ed., *Rethinking Vienna, 1900*, 171–94. New York: Berghahn Books.

Harrington, Anne. 1996. *Holism in German Science from Wilhelm II to Hitler*. Princeton, N.J.: Princeton University Press.

Harwood, Jonathan. 1997. "German Science and Technology under National Socialism." *Perspectives on Science* 5: 128–51.

Helmholtz, Hermann. 1862. *Die Lehre von den Tonempfindungen als physiologische Grundlage für die Theorie der Musik*. Braunschweig: Vieweg.

Hentschel, Klaus, ed. *Physics and National Socialism: An Anthology of Primary Sources*. Basel: Birkhäuser.

Herf, Jeffrey. 1984. *Reactionary Modernism: Technology, Culture and Politics in Weimar and the Third Reich*. Cambridge: Cambridge University Press.

Hoffmann, Christoph. 1997. "*Der Dichter am Apparat*": *Medientechnik, Experimentalpsychologie und Texte Robert Musils, 1899–1942*. Munich: Wilhelm Fink Verlag.

Hoffmann, Christoph, ed. 2001. *Über Schall: Ernst Mach's und Peter Salchers Geschoßfotografien*. Göttingen: Wallstein Verlag.

Jahoda, Marie. 1983. "Für mich ist mein Judentum erst mit Hitler eine wirkliche Identität geworden." *Ästhetik und Kommunikation* 14 (51): 71–89.

Jay, Martin. 1984. *Marxism and Totality*. Berkeley: University of California Press.

Kern, Stephen. 1983. *The Culture of Time and Space, 1880–1918*. Cambridge, Mass.: Harvard University Press.

Kittler, Friedrich. 1995. *Aufschreibesysteme 1800–1900*. 3rd ed. Munich: Wilhelm Fink Verlag.

Kurzweil, Edith. 1996. "Psychoanalytic Science: From Oedipus to Culture." In Ash and Söllner, *Forced Migration and Scientific Change*, 139–55.

Kwiram, Sydney M. 1999. "Tones for Thought: Arnold Schoenberg and the Culture of Scientific Modernism in Fin-de-siècle Vienna." Honors thesis, Harvard University.

Laqueur, Walter. 1974. *Weimar: A Cultural History, 1918–1933*. New York: G. P. Putnam's Sons.

Liste der auf Grund des Gesetzes zur Wiederherstellung des Berufsbeamtentums verabschiedeten Professoren und Privatdozenten. 1934. Submitted by the Reichsministerium für Erziehung, Wissenschaft und Volksbildung to the Foreign Office, 11 December. Politisches Archiv des Auswärtigen Amtes, Bonn.

Mach, Ernst. 1985. *Einleitung in die Helmholtzsche Musiktheorie: Populär für Musiker dargestellt*. Reprint. Vaduz: Sändig. Orig. publ. 1866.

———. 1943. "The Economical Nature of Physical Inquiry." In Mach, *Popular Scientific Lectures*, 186–213. 5th ed. Trans. by Thomas J. McCormack. LaSalle, Ill.: Open Court Press. Orig. publ. 1882.

———. 1910. "Über Erscheinungen an fliegenden Projektilen." In Mach, *Populärwissenschaftliche Vorträge*, 356–83. 4th ed. Leipzig: Barth. Orig. publ. 1897.

———. 1960. *The Science of Mechanics: A Critical and Historical Account of Its Development*. 6th ed. Trans. by Thomas J. McCormack. LaSalle, Ill.: Open Court Press.

Mehrtens, Herbert. 1990a. *Moderne Sprache Mathematik*. Frankfurt am Main: Suhrkamp.

———. 1990b. "Entartete Wissenschaft? Naturwissenschaften im Nationalsozialismus." In Leonore Siegele-Wenschkewitz and Gerda Stuchlik, eds., *Hochschule und Nationalsozialismus: Wissenschaftsgeschichte und Wissenschaftsbetrieb als Thema der Zeitgeschichte*, 113–28. Frankfurt am Main: Haag & Herchen.

Micale, Mark S., ed. 2004. *The Mind of Modernism: Medicine, Psychology, and the Cultural Arts in Europe and America, 1880–1940.* Stanford, Calif.: Stanford University Press.

Mommsen, Hans. 1991. "Nationalsozialismus als vorgetäuschte Modernisierung." In Mommsen, *Der Nationalsozialismus und die deutsche Gesellschaft: Ausgewählte Aufsätze*, 405–27. Reinbek bei Hamburg: Rowohlt.

Münch, Richard. 1993. *Die Kultur der Moderne.* 2 vols. Frankfurt am Main: Suhrkamp.

Multiple Modernities. 2000. Special issue of *Daedalus* 129 (1).

Neufeld, Michael. 1990. "Weimar Culture and Futuristic Technology: The Rocketry and Spaceflight Fad in Germany, 1923–1933." *Technology and Culture* 31: 725–52.

———. 1995. *The Rocket and the Reich: Peenemünde and the Coming of the Ballistic Missile Era.* New York: Free Press.

Nolan, Mary. 1994. *Visions of Modernity: American Business and the Modernization of Germany.* New York: Oxford University Press.

Papcke, Sven. 1993. "'Lernen aus der Barberei': Zur Entwicklung der politischen Soziologie von Franz Leopold Neumann." In Papcke, *Deutsche Soziologen im Exil: Gegenwartsdiagnose und Epochenkritik, 1933–1945*, 77–99. Frankfurt am Main: Campus-Verlag.

Peukert, Detlev J. K. 1989. *Max Webers Diagnose der Moderne.* Göttingen: Vandenhoeck & Ruprecht.

———. 1993. *The Weimar Republic: The Crisis of Classical Modernity.* Trans. by Richard Deveson. New York: Hill & Wang.

Proctor, Robert N. 1999. *The Nazi War against Cancer.* Princeton, N.J.: Princeton University Press.

Rabinbach, Anson. 1992. *The Human Motor: Energy, Fatigue and the Origins of Modernity.* Berkeley: University of California Press.

Radkau, Joachim. 1998. *Das Zeitalter der Nervösität: Deutschland zwischen Bismarck und Hitler.* Munich: Hanser.

Renneberg, Monika, and Mark Walker, eds. 1994. *Science, Technology and National Socialism.* Cambridge: Cambridge University Press.

Ringer, Fritz K. 1969. *The Decline of the German Mandarins: The German Academic Community, 1890–1933.* Cambridge, Mass.: Harvard University Press.

Schivelbusch, Wolfgang. 1995. *Disenchanted Night: The Industrialization of Light in the Nineteenth Century.* Trans. by Angela Davis. Berkeley: University of California Press.

Schoenberg, Arnold. 1978. *Theory of Harmony.* Trans. by Roy E. Carter. Berkeley: University of California Press. Orig. publ. 1911.

———. 1984. "Composition in Twelve Tones." In Schoenberg, *Style and Idea: Selected Writings of Arnold Schoenberg.* Ed. by Leonard Stein. Berkeley: University of California Press.

Sigurdsson, Skuli. 1991. "Hermann Weyl's Mathematics and Physics, 1900–1927." Ph.D. dissertation, Harvard University.

Speier, Hans. 1988. "Nicht die Auswanderung, sondern der Triumph Hitlers war die wichtige Erfahrung: Autobiographische Notizen eines Soziologen." *Exilforschung* 6: 152–73.

Spengler, Oswald. 1977. *Der Untergang des Abendlandes.* Munich: Deutscher Taschenbuchverlag. Orig. publ. 1923.

Stiegler, Bernd. 1998. "Ernst Machs 'Philosophie des Impressionismus' und die Momentphotographie." *Hofmannsthal: Jahrbuch zur europäischen Moderne* 6: 257–80.

Stumpf, Carl. 1883–90. *Tonpsychologie.* 2 vols. Leipzig: Hirzel.

Szöllöszi-Janze, Margit, ed. 2001. *Science in the Third Reich.* Oxford: Berg.

Volkov, Shulamit. 2001. "Jewish Scientists in Imperial Germany (Parts I and II)." *Aleph: Historical Studies in Science and Judaism* 1: 215–49, 250–81. First publ. 1887 and 1997, respectively.

Weikart, Richard. 1999. *Socialist Darwinism: Evolution in German Socialist thought from Marx to Bernstein.* Washington, D.C.: International Scholars.

Weindling, Paul. 1989. *Health, Race and German Politics between National Unification and Nazism*. Cambridge: Cambridge University Press.

Weingart, Peter, Jürgen Kroll, and Kurt Bayertz. 1988. *Rasse, Blut und Gene: Geschichte der Eugenik und Rassenhygiene in Deutschland*. Frankfurt am Main: Suhrkamp.

Wertheimer, Max. 1925. *Über Gestalttheorie*. Erlangen: Verlag der Philosophischen Akademie.

Willet, John. 1978. *Art and Politics in the Weimar Period: The New Sobriety, 1917–1933*. New York: Pantheon Books.

2

Sephardic Fins des Siècles

The Liturgical Music of Vienna's *Türkisch-Israelitische* Community on the Threshold of Modernity

::: EDWIN SEROUSSI

Prologue

Vienna is not a city generally associated with the Sephardic Jews. While drawing the map of Jewish ethnicity along modern Western and Central European perceptions of self and other, Jewish historians rarely mentioned the small enclave of Judeo-Spanish-speaking Jews from Turkey and the Balkans who had settled in the Habsburg capital beginning in the late eighteenth century (see, however, Gelber 1948; Geller 1983; Seroussi 1992a). For Jewish historians of Ashkenazic origins, whose own historiographic imagination manifested itself as decidedly Jewish responses to modernity, the "Orient" or "Levant" had clear geographical, ethnic, and cultural boundaries, and Vienna lay beyond these. Removed from the cognitive horizons of modern Jewish history, the Sephardic Jews of Vienna have remained a footnote within the modern narrative designed to explain how the Jewish people came to occupy the historical present of European modernity. Yet, as modern and postmodern literary criticism has shown, footnotes may well be critical texts that bear a unique quality: They carry in their small fonts what the main text shifts from its center to its peripheries. In Jewish history—and in Jewish music history—the peripheries contain an abundant share of crucial narratives.

Living in one of the urban cradles of European modernity, the Sephardic Jews of Vienna were destined for direct confrontation with the distinctive variants of Jewish modernity in a multicultural metropolis (see Zohar 1993; Stillman 1995). In this chapter I discuss one, if not the main, manifestation of this encounter between a traditional Jewish community of Eastern Mediterranean origins and the emancipatory forces of Western and Central Euopean Judaism that collapsed the old Jewish order, historically distinct because it was marked by religious legislation. This manifestation, the reform of the musical performance of the liturgy in the Sephardic synagogue in Vienna in the last two decades of the nineteenth century, is one of the most important and best-documented episodes in the rather short history of this small community. For the Sephardic community liturgical music became a contested historical text, pulled away from tradition and toward modernity. Modernity, moreover, had multiple meanings in the history of Sephardic liturgical music, for it could mean both Ashkenazic and secular.

The very nature of the liturgical-music documentation with which this research originated marks a turning point in the exposure of the Sephardic Jews of Vienna to Jewish modernity. Orality was one of the markers of the "oriental" Jewish culture that the founders of modern Jewish history recovered and reintroduced into their inclusive narrative. Orality was also the venue of musical transmission among the Sephardim in Vienna. The passage from the realm of the oral to the written medium of liturgical-music transmission symbolizes the transition into modernity. This apparently technical transformation had a profound epistemological dimension because it led to the control of time and space in the synagogue ritual. Reform in liturgical music led to even more profound challenges to the old Jewish

order. The idea of music as an autonomous entity and as the embodiment of a new form of spirituality provided the kernel of the liturgical reforms in Vienna's Sephardic community. The resistance to these transformations by members of the community in the early twentieth century nonetheless came to illustrate a unique reversibility within Jewish modernity, what Stillman (1995: 8) has referred to as "demodernization." Looking at the threshold between tradition and modernity and beyond to the globalization of the twentieth century, we can also understand the transformation that altered Sephardic Viennese history as its centripetal movement toward the local (see Bohlman, introduction to this volume).

As Jewish modernism passes first through the past, an ethnomusicological inquiry into an oral musical culture exposes a set of quandaries. Ethnomusicologists have by no means avoided modernism, but approaching it from the past before establishing the modernity or postmodernity of the ethnographic present has more often than not been counterintuitive. Yet, historical inquiry has made deep inroads into the study of orally transmitted music traditions. One can certainly do "fieldwork in the ethnomusicological past," as Philip Bohlman (1997) has phrased it, and this is precisely how I undertake the study of the Sephardic liturgical music in Vienna here.

I first tackled the liturgical-music reforms of the Sephardic community in Vienna in the framework of study that was explicitly ethnographic (Seroussi 1988). The theoretical trope of that work was the then-common ethnomusicological binary opposition contrasting continuity and change. The present chapter is framed by a totally different theoretical concern—Jewish modernism—and therefore employs a methodological concern for a present that is constantly changing. From the pespective of this concern, my earlier work on Vienna now seems to devolve to the more poignant issue of dissolution and discontinuity, which by extension integrates Sephardic culture in late nineteenth-century Vienna into Sephardic cultural identity in late twentieth-century Israel. In this chapter, with its new historical framework, the Sephardic past, as well as the present, becomes very modern indeed.

Although my earlier work recognized in passing Carl Schorske's famous analyses of *fin-de-siècle* Vienna in his book of the same name (1980), I was at the time unwilling fully to embrace the concept of the "end of centuries." The cycles of time that order our perceptions of history are not only capricious, but also bounded by complex cultural processes. One wonders if the Jews of the year 5760, the Muslims of the year 1322, and the Western European– and American-dominated global culture of the year 2000—"Christians" would be a distortion in this case—are living, in fact, at the same "time" at all. The fin de siècle is, therefore, one of those imaginary constructions of time that preoccupies the West, and, as a result of the global domination of Western culture at the beginning of the third Christian millennium, the fixation with the ends of centuries is no longer practically separable from a preoccupation with the global. One may describe this preoccupation as a communal state of mind that implies either intensified processes of disintegration of established social and cultural orders or the expectations of deep renewal and change. Underlying this Western manner of perceiving time, what Foucault (1972: 148) calls "those confused units that we call 'periods,'" is the pervasive idea of progress, which has dominated Western thinking since at least the Renaissance. From this point of view, each new century has to be more modern than the previous one. The fin de siècle has no choice but to challenge previous ideological and scientific paradigms.

How does the state of mind called fin de siècle apply to the Sephardic Jews? I have come to realize that studying the music of the only Sephardic synagogue in Vienna in the late nineteenth century has become for me far more than interpreting a process that takes place in the dimension of chronological time, when a "traditional" musical past is being transformed into a "modern" musical present. My analysis, moreover, must also include a spatial dimension, the modern Jewish nation-state, where multiple displaced Sephardic identities have been converging throughout the twentieth century and now into the twenty-first. Together these multiple Sephardic dimensions—Vienna at the end of one fin de siècle, Israel at the end of another—form a space, articulated by the ethnomusicological past and the ethnographic present.

Nineteenth-Century Fin de Siècle

In 1889 the small Sephardic community in Vienna published *Schir Hakawod*, a collection of choral arrangements of traditional melodies and other original compositions for the Sabbath, the festivals, and weddings (see fig. 2.1). The book was unique, indeed modern, in Sephardic music history, for it was the first published anthology of Eastern Mediterranean Sephardic music for practical use in the synagogue. *Schir Hakawod*, however, was rapidly forgotten.[1] Only a small number of copies appeared in print, and despite efforts by the publishers to distribute it, the majority of its potential users, the Eastern Mediterranean Sephardim, proved to be indifferent toward it.[2] Moreover, Jewish music scholars who were acquainted with this anthology did not see it as a reflection of an "authentic" tradition (Birnbaum 1889; Idelsohn 1923: 29, n. 4; Avenary 1971: 35). *Schir Hakawod* was further eclipsed by the publication in the twentieth century of comprehensive collections of Sephardic liturgical music, particularly those by Idelsohn (1923), Camhy (1959), and Levy (1964–80).[3] For the scholar interested in the historical and analytical study of Sephardic liturgical music, however, the more recent sources are not more reliable than *Schir Hakawod* because basic information about the circumstances under which

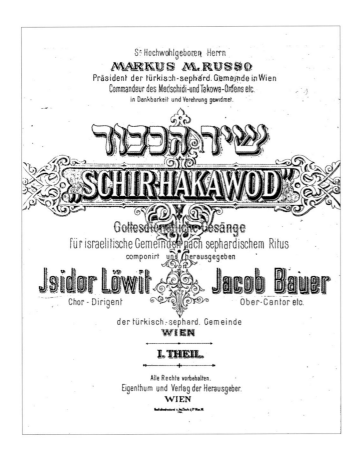

Figure 2.1 Title page of *Schir Hakawod*, 1889

these collections are gathered is obscure, the background of the informants who supplied the music is generally unknown, the skills and goals of the transcribers and/or editors influenced the output, and, finally, the techniques of transcription are unspecified and therefore unreliable.

What can scholars learn from these sources, and what uses do they hold for us today? Are they simply local transformations of tradition, or do they mark an historical moment when Sephardic music becomes modern? The attempt to fix the oral tradition on paper by a number of Sephardic communities since the publication of Aguilar and de Sola's anthology in 1857 is in itself a cultural phenomenon that deserves reflection. The printed collections are tools for elucidating the very concept of liturgical music from the standpoint of the Sephardim and the social and cultural circumstances that led a community to publish a collection of liturgical music, and for analyzing notated sources in the light of present-day oral tradition.

The impact of Western musical notation on Jewish communities whose liturgical music had hitherto been transmitted orally parallels similar phenomena studied by ethnomusicologists and folklorists examining the contact between Western and non-Western music. Albert Lord, in his classic study of the Balkan epic singers, noted: "But there was another world, of those who could read and write, of those who came to think of the written text not as a recording of a moment of the tradition but as *the* song. This was to become the difference between the oral way of thought and the written way" (Lord 1964: 125).

In 1979, ninety years after the publication of *Schir Hakawod* in Vienna, an unusual manuscript attracted my attention while I was cataloging the Birnbaum collection of Jewish music at Hebrew Union College in Cincinnati. Browsing through the manuscript, I found *Aḥot qetannah*, a thirteenth-century *piyyut* (liturgical poem) sung exclusively by the Sephardim for the evening service of Rosh Hashanah (New Year). Because the bulk of the Birnbaum collection comprised materials from Western and Eastern Ashkenazic liturgical music traditions, a manuscript of Sephardic liturgical melodies was highly unusual and demanded an inquiry. After reviewing the music in this manuscript, moreover, I realized that this source was based almost entirely on oral tradition (see fig. 2.2).

Through subsequent research I determined that the manuscript belonged to the Sephardic community in Vienna and included the materials published in *Schir Hakawod* as well as a substantial unpublished sequel that included the music for the High Holidays. In the course of further research in the Birnbaum collection, additional manuscripts and archival information about the music of this Sephardic community came to my attention, and I came to realize that *Schir Hakawod*—both the published volume and the unpublished sequel—is not a conventional collection of Sephardic liturgical music. As research proceeded, the uniqueness of *Schir Hakawod* revealed itself to be related to a process of social change occurring in the Sephardic community in Vienna at the time the collection was being compiled. It was indeed a by-product of a profound transfor-

Figure 2.2 Facsimile of *Ahot getannah*. Birnbaum Collection, Mus. Add. 25, Hebrew Union College, Cincinnati.

mation that took place in this Sephardic community in the late nineteenth century, the very turn toward a modernity that was at once Jewish and Viennese (see the essays in Botstein and Hanak 2004).

The contents of *Schir Hakawod* reveal a new and distinctive approach to the collection, transcription, arrangement, and performance of liturgical music. Thus, the music within the collection has to be considered together with the processes and goals underlying its preparation and the individuals who were involved in its compilation.

A Traditional Liturgy Renewed

By 1870 the religious music of the Sephardic community in Vienna was being reshaped to suit new aesthetic concepts borrowed from the surrounding culture. Manfred Papo, living in the United States but descended from a Viennese Sephardic family, wrote in 1967:

In 1880, the Sephardic synagogue in the Fuhrmanngasse was the only big synagogue in Vienna which did not have a choir. The older generation, used to the Oriental tunes, were quite satisfied to have the prayers recited in the traditonal Eastern way by the Chazan-Minister, but their children, since they came from wealthy homes, had acquired a taste for Western music, exemplified in the operas they went to hear and the concerts they attended. After all, Vienna was the city of music in those days. It was not only the city of Salomon Sulzer, but also of Johann Strauss. (Papo 1967: 322)

Cantor Salomon Sulzer's musical approach to the Jewish liturgy influenced many Ashkenazic communities throughout nineteenth-century Europe. The chief cantor of Vienna and the leading musical force in the city's main synagogue (the Stadttempel), Sulzer initiated the reforms around 1825, and his ideas, implemented in the Stadttempel, became the nucleus of a new practice of Jewish liturgical music. They also affected musical reforms in the Sephardic community of Vienna and in the conception of *Schir Hakawod*. Sulzer's reforms were a compromise between the conservative Viennese Jews and the reformers, led by Isaac Noah Mannheimer, who advocated radical changes in the liturgy such as those adopted by Reform congregations in Berlin and Hamburg (Goldberg 1992). The majority of Vienna's Ashkenazic Jews, nonetheless, adhered to more moderate changes, especially in matters of ritual. The moderate attitudes of the Viennese Ashkenazim can be attributed to the influence of the conservative Catholic Church of the Austro-Hungarian Empire, whereas the more radical positions of the German Reform Jews can be percieved as reflecting the northern German Protestant enviroment.

A. Z. Idelsohn (1929: 247–52) succinctly summarized the reforms Sulzer instituted after 1826:

1. Old tunes and singing modes should be improved, selected, and adjusted to the rules of musical art.
2. This adjustment was intended to cleanse the ancient dignified type of traditional tunes from the later accretions of tasteless embellishments, to bring them back to the original purity, and to reconstruct them in accordance with the text and the rules of harmony.
3. The ideal medium for the performance of the liturgy was a combination of a soloist singing the traditional "cleansed" recitatives and a choir singing in four-part choral arrangements.[4]
4. The use of the organ in the synagogue was favored first implicitly (Sulzer 1865) and then explicitly (Sulzer 1876).
5. The vernacular language was to be used in the synagogue, despite Sulzer's respect for the "sacred sounds of the holy tongue in which our ancestors expressed their joys and pain" (Sulzer 1876, quoted in Idelsohn 1929: 252).
6. Musical improvisation of any type, including biblical cantillation, was to be abolished.
7. Active participation of the congregation in the performance of the liturgy was curtailed, reduced to a few hymns and responses.
8. Original compositions commissioned from Jewish or Gentile composers were introduced into the services.

The musical reforms emerging from Sulzer's concept of synagogue music had a tremendous impact on the modernization of Jewish music throughout Europe. They reached almost every liberal or progressive Jewish community in Eastern and Western Europe during the second part of the nineteenth century (Idelsohn 1929: 256–60; Mandrell 1967; Wohlberg 1970; Werner 1976: 206–19; Zimmermann 2004). Sulzer introduced a style of music that recuperated the sense of "decorum" in Jewish religious ceremonies, which had been lost, he said, by eighteenth-century cantors. He combined structural elements from the traditional styles (e.g., motifs or modes) or performance techniques (e.g., the use of recitative) with new elements, such as original compositions and a four-part choir. For the first time in the history of synagogue music in Europe, the concept of music as art was conspicuously applied to entire services.[5] "Sulzerism" became a cult among Jewish cantors. Prior to Sulzer's transformations in the nineteenth century, synagogue music had been essentially functional; the development of an aesthetic concern for music represented a radical new approach, which elevated the cantor's status closer to that of a professional musician.[6] Improvised participation by the congregation was replaced by a prescribed and controlled performance of the ritual and its music. Once the cantor had turned it into art music, Jewish music became distinctively modern.

The innovations in Jewish liturgical music, both practical and conceptual, both implicit and explicit, provided the background and impetus for the reform of liturgical music in the Sephardic community in Vienna (Avenary 1985: 81). Sulzer, who enjoyed contacts with the local Sephardic community, included an arrangement of a Sep-

hardic melody in the second volume of his anthology for the synagogue, *Schir Zion* (Sulzer 1865, no. 106: *Ygdal*).[7] We know, too, that he attended the services at the Sephardic synagogue. The following note appeared in a Judeo-Spanish journal published in Vienna:

> It is well known that the Turkish Jewish community in Vienna has undertaken an important reform with the introduction of the choral services during the past year. Reform was favorably received in synagogue circles. One casual Friday evening, Papa Sulzer arrived in the synagogue and was cordially received by the leadership. With great interest and apparent approval he followed the unfolding of the service, which primarily contained performances of his own compositions. After the close of the service he warmly congratulated chief cantor Jacob Bauer and the leaders of the community. (*CdV* 2/6, 8/2/1882: [6])

This kind of interaction—and there are many other instances of Sephardic-Ashkenazic crossings of boundaries in late nineteenth-century Vienna, including intermarriage—clearly subverts any essentialist distinction between Sephardic and Ashkenazic Jews constructed on the basis of contemporary perceptions. Although decidedly affiliated and institutionalized on the basis of ethnic allegiance, members of both Jewish groups in Vienna were subjected to the same dilemmas and shared similar attitudes in respect to religious observance and synagogue ritual. In fact, socioeconomic class divisions were as decisive a cultural factor among fin-de-siècle Jews in Vienna as any other social division. And because many distinguished Sephardic families of the city belonged to the upper economic echelon, their adherence to modernizing trends in liturgical matters comes as no surprise. The ascent to community influence of members of these financially empowered Sephardic families was a catalyst for liturgical-music reform in their new, sumptuous *Tempel*.

One crucial event in the history of the Sephardic community in Vienna accelerated the reform of its liturgical music: the election of Markus M. Russo as president of the community in 1881. Russo was a young Sephardi raised in Vienna and cultivated in "modern" manners of social behavior and taste sensibility: "He decided to modernize the services and make them attractive to the younger generation, without upsetting the older members more than absolutely necessary" (Papo 1967: 322). This search for a balance between tradition and modernity was characteristic of Sephardic musical reforms in Vienna. In order to modernize the liturgy, Vienna's Sephardic community leaders took four steps:

1. to contract a "professional" cantor and a choirmaster;
2. to organize a four-voice choir;
3. to install an organ in the synagogue; and
4. to start a project that included the collection, transcription, and arrangement of traditional liturgical music. Such a project had to be directed by the new cantor and the choirmaster.

These steps formed the core of the musical reforms of the Sephardic community in Vienna. Such reforms, nonetheless, were alien to the basic liturgical-music concepts and practices of any Sephardic community in the Ottoman Empire until that time.

Ḥazzan and Choirmaster

The concept of a cantor as a professional functioning independently in the community was foreign to most Sephardic communities (even those in Western Europe), to which the following two assessments apply:

> A Sephardic ḥazzan is not a cantor in the Ashkenazic sense, but rather a reader and a leader of the services. In many Sephardic congregations the hakham or the rabbi also not infrequently acts as a reader. The essence of Sephardic ḥazzanut [cantorial art] is meticulous correctness with no improvisation. (Lopes Cardozo 1960: 40)

> It is among the pious that ḥazzanim were recruited. . . . While occupying themselves with their business or their profession, [they] came in the hours marked by the march of the sun to practice the religion for themselves and for their coreligionists. From their fathers they learned how to recite and to sing their prayers; they taught it to their sons, and in this way this tradition was perpetuated from generation to generation so that its origins could be traced back to the most remote ages of Judaism, keeping for these Jews the oriental pronunciation of Hebrew, the intonation of the reading, and the synagogue chants, whose compositional age is lost

in the night of the centuries. Every person capable of reciting prayers, reading the Torah, and singing the Psalms could ascend to the Tebah and conduct the ritual; the public follows [him] and responds as a choir. There is also no fixed costume for ḥazzanim; they wear the talit under their hat and this was all. (Léon 1893: 301)

Henry Léon and particularly Abraham Lopes Cardozo were surely describing a ḥazzan of the Spanish-Portuguese type characteristic of the Western European Sephardic communities, but their descriptions apply to Eastern Mediterranean Sephardic ḥazzanim as well. The Sephardic ḥazzan was not a "professional," regularly remunerated by the community, or an individual upon whose initiative and musical skills the entire musical life of the synagogue depended. Rather, he was a knowledgeable individual with a good voice who performed in conjunction with the congregation and was paid, if at all, only with symbolic donations. Historically, the contrast between the Sephardic ḥazzan and the Ashkenazic cantor was also one between tradition and modernity. In fin-de-siècle Vienna, though, that contrast would collapse (Frühauf 2004).

In 1880 the Sephardic community of Vienna elected Jacob Bauer as cantor. Born in 1852 in Szenice, Hungary, as a child he sang soprano in the choir of the famous ḥazzan Pessah Feinsinger. Bauer moved to Vienna as a young student, where he took voice-training classes. He was then employed as ḥazzan in Ottakring, then a suburb of Vienna and today the city's sixteenth district. He also held cantorial posts in Szigetvan, Hungary (in 1875), and in Graz, Austria (in 1878), before he was hired by the Sephardic community in Vienna (see Zaludkowsky 1930: 196; Avenary 1972).

The actual process of electing the cantor is not clear. We know only that the community had sought to elect a professional cantor as early as 1870, which is noteworthy because it predates by ten years the advent of the musical reforms and Bauer's appointment. An advertisement published in that year in *El correo de Viena* reads:

> For the Sephardic community community in Vienna is needed a precentor [*sheliaḥ tzibbur*] age 30 up to 40, fearful of God [*yore elokim*] as is proper for this sacred position, and his voice has to be pleasant [*sabroza* in Spanish]. His duty will be to say *shaḥarit, minḥa,* and '*arvit* [morning, afternoon, and evening services] every Monday and Thursday [the days in which the *Torah* is read] and all the prayers of the High Holidays, festivals, and all the days when the Torah scrolls [are read]. His salary will be 800 up to 1,000 *florines* a year, plus the donations [*nedavot*] of the honorable members.

Once he was installed in his new position, Bauer revealed himself as an idiosyncratic personality. Not only was he interested in his work as cantor, but he devoted time to journalism and to union activities among Central European cantors. He founded the journal *Österreichisch-ungarische Cantoren-Zeitung*, which appeared between 1881 and 1899; after 1899 it was incorporated as a supplement into the Viennese journal *Die Wahrheit*. As editor of the *Cantoren-Zeitung*, Bauer was in contact with most of the personalities in Jewish liturgical music circles throughout Europe. His journalistic activities enabled him to enhance and promote his name beyond his actual skills as a cantor.

For the post of choirmaster a rather obscure Viennese musician, Isidor Löwit, was hired. Löwit, born in 1864, sang as a child in the choir of Leopoldstadt Temple (1870–1880). He also sang at the Vienna Comic Opera and studied violin at the Vienna Conservatory. He was hired in 1880 by the Sephardic community in Vienna, where he became a central figure in the musical life of the community until his death during World War II (Friedmann 1927). Like Jacob Bauer, he married a Sephardic woman, Josefine Albachari (*ÖUCZ* 7/38, 24/11/1887: 6).

For the first time in Jewish music history, an Ashkenazic cantor and a Western European choirmaster were simultaneously appointed to serve a Sephardic community and fill the most important positions in the musical life of its congregation. Bauer and Löwit held duties that extended not only to synagogue services and community events, but also to pedagogical tasks. This is demonstrated by the periodic reports of their activities published in *CdV* and *ÖUCZ*. Bauer taught ḥazzanut (*ÖUCZ* 18/24, 11/10/1898: 6), while Löwit taught music to the children of the community's Talmud Torah schools (*ÖUCZ* 17/17, 8/6/1897: 5). Their musical positions reveal that musical life in Vienna's Sephardic community, fully professional by the fin de siècle, had entered a modern era in its history (cf. Bohlman 1994 and Schmidt 1998 for other aspects of the profession-

alization of Viennese Jewish musical life, in both sacred and secular realms).

The Choir

The Viennese Sephardic synagogue organized a choir for its services, an innovation for an Eastern Mediterranean Sephardic community but not for the Spanish-Portuguese region of the Sephardic world. As early as 1818 the Spanish-Portuguese congregation in New York City, Shearith Israel, attempted to organize a choir under the direction of the *ḥazzan* Jacob Seixas. The choir was accepted as a permanent feature of the New York community services only in 1859, albeit with the restriction that it would be limited to boys and men. All the choirmasters of this Spanish-Portuguese community were Ashkenazic. The most prominent among them, Léon M. Kramer (1883–1943), was a student of Lewandowsky in Berlin (de Sola Pool 1955: 152). In the Ottoman Empire choirs were incorporated into synagogue services only after 1880 (see Seroussi 1988). The first advocates of choirs are found in Belgrade (see *CdV* 12, 16 Sivan 5630: 6).

The first formal organization of a choir in a Sephardic community, however, took place in Vienna. The Sephardic choir in Vienna consisted of ten to fifteen boy sopranos and contraltos, trained by Löwit, and four adults: one tenor, two baritones, and one bass (Papo 1967: 322). The adult choir members were professional male singers, mostly Ashkenazic, who sang in the Imperial Court Opera (Hofoper) choir, as the following note attests:

On Sunday, April 10 [1897] Mr. Josef Feldmann, bass singer of the Turkish Temple and member of the Carl Theater's choir, celebrated his twenty-fifth jubilee as singer in the Temple and at the same time his silver wedding anniversary. Mr. Feldman commands a very deep, strong, and today even more resonant bass voice and has been employed since the establishment of the choral services in the Turkish Temple. (*ÖUCZ* 17/11, 11/4/1897: 6)

Jewish professional singers took advantage of a law stating that any member of the Hofoper choir could be excused from his duties if he had to participate in a religious service, regardless of the religious denomination (Papo 1967: 322). The choir played a prominent role in the modernized Sephardic services. A special space for the choir was provided in the new synagogue, inaugurated in 1887 (Papo 1967: 335; see fig. 2.3). Segregation of the sexes in the choir was strictly observed. The absence of women satisfied the orthodox law that forbids listening to the voices of women.

The choir also performed in ceremonies unrelated to the liturgy, such as the celebration of the Turkish sultan's birthday and the anniversary of the coronation of the Austro-Hungarian emperor (*ÖUCZ* 17/2, 11/1/1897: 7). At such public events, the choir performed musical interludes between speeches and orations. A common pattern in the program of these public events would be (1) an instrumental prelude (organ and/or harp), (2) the opening of the Sacred Ark with the choral performance of *Mah tovu* (Numbers 24), (3) a speech, a psalm, or hymn by the choir, (4) a sermon by the rabbi, and (5) the Turkish and Austrian anthems sung by the choir. This ceremonial pattern, frequently found in German synagogues in the second half of the nineteenth century, reflects the influence of Bauer and Löwit on the nonliturgical rituals of the Sephardic community in Vienna.

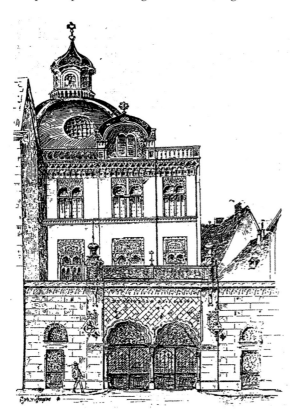

Figure 2.3 Façade of the Turkish synagogue in Vienna, ca. 1890

The use of a choir, moreover, derived from a concern with renewing "decorum" in the synagogue. Beyond this, however, Sephardic liturgical reformers wanted to attract the members of the younger generation. Synagogue rituals, the reformers believed, would be more appealing if they included Western European–oriented musical performances.

The Organ

When the new Sephardic synagogue in Vienna opened its doors in 1887, an organ was installed, thereby as they had been into Central European synagogues throughout the nineteenth century (Frühauf 2005). The instrument, with its twelve registers, was a masterpiece constructed by the Viennese organ builder Franz Strommer (ÖUCZ 7/31, 22/9/1887: 4). Not surprisingly, the installation spawned a dispute between the young leadership and the older congregation members, who had not been consulted about the plans.[8] When the notice of the plans reached the older members, they were assured that the organ was to be used primarily for weddings and festive occasions, not on the Sabbath or any other Jewish holiday for which the playing of musical instruments is forbidden by *halakhah* (religious law).

Having already been deceived once, the elders no longer had faith in the young leadership's assurances. They therefore appointed A. M. Elias, one of the prominent conservative elders of the community, to work out an agreement with the young president of the community, Markus Russo, specifying rules for using the instrument.

Elias offered to Russo "to pay for the whole cost of the organ and its installation, on condition that the committee sign a document before a public notary and deposit it with the High Court, to the effect that the organ donated by A. M. Elias would never . . . be played on any day on which the playing of a musical instrument was forbidden by Orthodox Jewish Law" (Papo 1967: 344).

The Simḥat Torah Festival

Even specific holiday celebrations, such as the traditional *haqqafot* (circling the synagogue holding the Torah scrolls while singing and dancing) during the holiday of Simḥat Torah (Rejoicing in the Torah), were affected by the reforms in Vienna. The *haqqafot*, indeed, turned into a public event. An ordered and picturesque procession was staged instead of the traditionally spontaneous dancing with the scrolls, again crossing the boundaries from traditional ritual into modern spectacle. Papo recalled the transformation:

> The procession was headed by one of the beadles in full livery (complete with Turkish *fez*); he was followed by two choir boys in cap and gown, walking in pairs; behind them came the adult members of the choir, one tenor, two basses, and the choirmaster. A few steps behind them came the Rabbi and the Chief Cantor, and then the bearers of the twenty-five scrolls of the law, led by the *Chatan Torah* [The Groom of the Torah] and the *Chatan Bereshit* [The Groom of Bereshit, the individual who had purchased the right to recite the first portion of the Pentateuch, which is read during Simḥat

Torah, initiating the annual cycle of reading the Scriptures], both in tails and silk hats, and carrying the scrolls wreathed in flowers. At the end of the procession walked a group of schoolboys under *Bar Mitzvah* age [less than thirteen years old], carrying three small *Sifrei Torah* especially provided for the purpose. (Papo 1967: 339)

Papo adds that the Sephardic Simḥat Torah services were so popular in Vienna that the police had to regulate the entrance of the public to the Sephardic synagogue (ibid.).

Musical Reforms in Life-Cycle and Community Events

Musical practices in weddings and funerals most effectively reveal the connection between the new socioeconomic status of the Viennese Sephardic community and the changes in its musical activities. Weddings and wedding music were divided into four categories in accordance with the economic status of the families. At a "first-class" wedding a large choir performed music specially composed for the occasion, accompanied by two harps and the organ. For example, two new compositions, one of them by Joseph Sulzer, the son of Salomon Sulzer, were premiered at the sumptuous wedding of the painter J. Russo (of the prominent Russo family) to the daughter of the wealthy banker A. M. Elias (the donor of the synagogue's organ), which was attended by members of the diplomatic and artistic circles of Vienna and reported in the press (ÖUCZ 2/41, 26/11/1882: 7). At second-class weddings, a small choir with organ

accompaniment performed. At third-class weddings, an unaccompanied male quartet sufficed. At fourth-class weddings, the ceremony was performed just by the rabbi, with the support of the assistant cantor. A similar musical and ceremonial hierarchy came also to characterize funerals (Papo 1967: 340).

The new trend toward modernity, so prominent in the liturgy and in ceremonies such as weddings, spilled over into other community events. One such was the celebration of the Ottoman sultan's birthday. On this kind of occasion a special choral service was performed in which Habsburg, Turkish, and Jewish officials all participated. The 1887 celebration, attended by Habsburg authorities and the Ottoman ambassador, included the following program:

1. Prelude with harp accompaniment for the entrance of the ambassador accompanied by the community authorities
2. *Mah tovu* for ḥazzan, choir, organ, and harp
3. Address by Rabbi M. Papo
4. Opening of the Sacred Ark and exposition of the Law Scrolls by the Honorable Gabr. H. Adutt and M. Danon
5. Festive prayer for the Sultan by Cantor Bauer
6. Festive psalm performed by H. Elias and the choir, conducted by Löwit
7. Turkish anthem
8. At the end of the ceremony the Turkish ambassador greeted the community and thanked members for their patriotism. (ÖUCZ 17/3, 21/1/1897: 4)

At the festive inauguration of the new synagogue in September 1887, the following musical program accompanied the ceremony:

1. Praeludium for organ by Joseph Sulzer from the Court Opera
2. *Le-david mizmor* [Psalm 24] sung by Cantor Bauer with organ accompaniment
3. *Halleluja* by [Louis] Lewandowsky, cantor in Berlin, sung by the choir conducted by Löwit
4. *Mah tovu*, specially composed by Joseph Sulzer for this occasion
5. Prayer in Spanish by Hakham Papo
6. Austrian and Turkish anthems
7. *Mizmor le-david* [Psalm 29] performed by the choir
8. *Yigdal* performed by the choir (ÖUCZ 7/31, 22/9/1887: 4)

The extent to which such Sephardic ceremonies had entered the public sphere by the end of the century is quite striking indeed when we recognize that only one musical work, the concluding hymn "Yigdal," was probably based on a traditional Sephardic melody. The rest of the music was composed by Ashkenazic cantors and the choirmaster, Löwit, who regularly composed new pieces for these special events (Papo 1967: 339).

Reception of the Liturgical and Musical Reforms

The opposition to the musical reforms was muted because of the overwhelming support they were receiving from powerful members of the congregation. It is important, however, to listen to the protests of the more conservative older gen-

eration. As Gelber observes, "The demand for the introduction [of the choir] caused controversies among members of the community" (Gelber 1948: 380). The voice of opposition can be detected in the Judeo-Spanish preface to the printed volume of *Schir Hakawod*: "The congregation responded to liturgical renewal with great enthusiasm. Even if some people look suspiciously at the new forms it has taken, with time they begin to like it. When they recognize that the old melodies of the past now sound anew, they were pleased and happy." A compromise was reached between the views of members of different factions, the reformers and the opposition. This compromise consisted of keeping the traditional melodies while rearranging them for performance by a cantor-soloist, an organized choir without women, and organ accompaniment, with the provision that this would be only on those occasions when Jewish law permitted the use of musical instruments. Liturgical texts were not affected by the reforms. Extant documentation indicates that in Vienna some prayers and hymns were translated to Judeo-Spanish (a common phenomenon in Sephardic prayerbooks since the Middle Ages), but there was no systematic attempt to translate all the Hebrew texts into Judeo-Spanish. The prayers themselves were not changed, paraphrased, or abridged. The reservations of the older members of the community were gradually overcome, ensuring general support for the reforms:

Above all, Markus M. Russo succeeded not only in concieving a sanctified . . . *Kultus*, but he also paved his way with energy, uprooting the old and inappropriate customs that had proved obsolete for the community. [He] proceeded step by step, without hesitation, in the direction of innovation, and all the community followed him. . . . The former presidents already thought that the introduction of a choir was of great benefit for the prayer and the community, but they never put their thoughts into practice, fearing the stormy discord and the opposition that could arise over the slightest insinuation of such an idea. But Markus M. Russo, possessing the necessary energy and the proper wisdom, knew what was needed and indispensable for the well being of the community. The entire community joyfully greeted the reform . . . and not even a single voice was raised against it. (Zemlinsky 1888)

Reforms after World War I

Modernity in Vienna's Sephardic community, however, also had its opponents. Resistance to these changes in the music of the liturgy remained, even though the vast majority of members in the Sephardic congregation seemed to be enthusiastic about reform. After World War I, the opposition finally found support among newer members of the congregation, leading to the abolition of some reforms. During the era of Austria's First Republic many Sephardim migrated from the Balkans and other Jewish communities in the former empire to Vienna. The influx was due in part to a brief postwar economic recovery and the appointment in 1918 of the renowned Nissim Ovadia as rabbi of the Sephardic community of Vienna. For a brief period during the early 1920s, Vienna again became an important Sephardic center.

Papo stresses that the newcomers found the modern services of the Vienna synagogue very strange. The newcomers "began to exert pressure for services to use the premodernized Oriental melodies. More and more laymen joined in reading the services, something which had been strictly prohibited previously" (Papo 1967: 342). Papo's commentary confirms that during Bauer's tenure the role of the congregation in the services had been drastically curtailed. The conservative attitude of the growing majority of immigrants created stress between them and the original Viennese Sephardim. The highly respected Rabbi Ovadia was able to smooth over ideological differences between conservatives and reformers. Most of the original musical reforms were eventually abolished in favor of more "traditional" services. The choir, however, remained intact, and Löwit served in his post as choirmaster until his death during World War II. The choir thus retained its modern role in the community until it was finally destroyed in the Holocaust. The struggle between the advocates and the opponents of musical reform is reflected in an exchange of letters published in the journal *El correo sefaradí* in 1923:

An open letter to the Honorable Administrators of the Community of the Sephardic Rite, Vienna.

Gentlemen Administrators:

One of the principal assets that until today ensured the existence of our people, as you might well know, has been the preservation of all our traditions and customs against threat and persecution. Our community leaders, during the magnificent period of our glorious history, were charged by those who

chose them to protect them in this manner from assimilation, even including the diverse ritual of the
family of [the people of] Israel. In response to the
deviation from tradition followed by our small but
important community, those who sign their names
below . . . seriously ask the administration of our
community to consider the following demand.

As its name indicates, our qehillah [community]
must rely as its foundations on the conservation of
the true Sephardic rite, following the model of the
rite practiced in Turkey. Despite all the measures
taken by Chief Rabbi Nissim Ovadia, our foundations are disintegrating day after day because of the
lack of a cantor who can answer to our needs. This
situation contributes to the dwindling of faithful
community members [from the services], which
has now reached the point that during prayers and
services one see no more than the ten persons paid
by the community, the indispensable number to
form a minyan.

Because our objective is rather more elevated
than maintaining only ten individuals for prayers,
we ask you to hire a ḥazzan able to maintain our
rite and to respect our customs in every way, even if
that risks agreeing to certain sacrifices with which
the contributors will certainly know how to deal.

With the hope that you will give a favorable
reply to the present request we, Gentlemen, want
to thank you, expressing our most distinguished
blessings.

[Signatures]
Vienna, May 25, 1923 (CS 1/7, 1/6/1923: 7)

The community administrators replied in part:

Having never distanced [ourselves] from the
beautiful Oriental melodies—a heritage from our
grandfathers—we desire at any rate to enhance the
solemnity of our Holy Service [Santa Avoda] by add-
ing something from the European-Jewish chants,
especially for Festival days, and on the occasion of
weddings, funerals, etc.

We are convinced that by finding a good Turkish ḥazzan we can satisfy both requirements. Surely
this will be possible only with great sacrifices, and
it is for us a pleasure that the undersigned Gentlemen declare themselves ready to contribute in
facing these heavy sacrifices, even though among
the 34 yeḥidim [heads of families] who signed the
open letter under question we find that only eleven
Gentlemen have already paid their synagogue duties for 1923 while the other twenty-three are today,
already at mid-year, behind in their payments.

The synagogue committee does not agree with
the honorable Gentlemen on one point: They assume that the lack of a Turkish ḥazzan is the reason that the yeḥidim do not attend the prayers. No,
Gentlemen! That diagnosis is not entirely true! The
real reason is the disease of religious indifference
that reigns among us. On erev shabbat [Friday evening services] it is possible to count 80 yeḥidim who
come to the community, and they are all happy with
the solemn prayers. But in shaḥarit of the shabbat,
the eight to ten yeḥidim who are never absent feel
an indescribable pain when they see that this magnificent Temple, so unique in its beauty, remains
empty, entirely empty. . . . Some members do not
want to be roused from their comfort to attend services, or they may have the pretext that they dwell

far away; others excuse themselves, claiming they must work, and this in turn does not allow them to attend services.

Receive, Gentlemen, the expression of our great esteem, with fraternal grettings,
The Communal Council

Lazar H. Susin (*CS* 1/8, 1/7/1923: 9)

Cantor Bauer retired during World War I and was succeeded by his young assistant, Isaac Kalmi Altarac (1890–1941). Altaras was a young Sephardi from Sarajevo who had studied music at the Vienna Conservatory (Papo 1967: 338; Petrovic 1982: 46–47). He was very popular with the community in Vienna, partly because he was Sephardic, but he left Vienna soon after the war to become chief cantor of the Great Synagogue in Sarajevo, where, in a previously traditional Sephardic center, he successfully introduced the Vienna-style choral services. When the newly built synagogue of Sarajevo opened its gates in 1930, a special space for a choir and an organ was provided.[9] If Vienna Sephardim entered a conservative period between the world wars, they had nonetheless succeeded in exporting their modern liturgical tradition to one of the great centers of Sephardic tradition in the Balkans.

Altarac was briefly followed as cantor in Vienna by A. Manda, about whom we know nothing. Manda was succeeded by Isaac Asseo from Belgrade, who remained in the post until the dissolution of the congregation in 1938 at the time of the *Anschluss*. Asseo managed to survive the Holocaust, escaping Vienna in 1938 and immigrating to the United States (Papo 1967: 342).

Evaluating the Musical Reforms

The liturgical-music reforms in the Sephardic community in Vienna have to be interpreted within the context of the cultural changes occurring in the Sephardic communities of the disintegrating Ottoman Empire. The reforms spread from Vienna to other communities such as Sarajevo (Friedenreich 1979; Petrovic 1982: 47), Sofia, and Bucharest (Geller 1983: 17–18, 35–36). The transformation of religious music is an integral aspect of the internal struggle of these communities to respond to the challenges of modernity during the late nineteenth and early twentieth centuries (see Seroussi 1988; Benbassa and Rodrigue 2000: chaps. 3 and 4). These were the same challenges that had affected the European Jewry since the early nineteenth century and had produced diverse responses, such as the rise of the Reform movement, the establishment of modern Jewish institutions such as the Alliance Israélite Universelle (Rodrigue 1993), and Jewish nationalism, that is, Zionism (Faur 1977; Faur 1982). In the specific case of the Sephardic community in Vienna, the liturgical-music reforms reflected the immediate influence of the Sulzer model, the *Wiener Ritus*. The implementation of this model resulted in changes in the performance and content of the music of the internal (liturgical and nonliturgical) events in the community.

Modernity entered Sephardic traditions much later, and modernism developed within Sephardic music at the encounter between Jewish traditions—Ashkenazic and Sephardic, but to some extent also Eastern—in the cosmopolitan cities of Jewish Europe. Despite the growing conflict between the Habsburg and Ottoman empires in the late nineteenth century, the cosmopolitan Sephardic community of Vienna was an oasis of cohabitation between the Western and Eastern cultural paradigms. The Ottoman and Austrian flags that adorned the entrance to the Sephardic synagogue in Vienna on holidays and festive occasions were emblematic of a duality whose representation in the field of liturgical music created an apparent generational rupture.

Was the modernization of Sephardic traditions in Vienna, however, really a struggle between generations, or do I project in my analysis of this case study a binary model of oral/traditional versus written/innovative liturgical music, when in fact the two options were not necessarily perceived as dichotomous? Perhaps the community members' recognition during the ritual performances of the traditional melodies in new versions distilled by Bauer from the music of the elders was more relevant than their manner of preservation (musical notation) and transmission (Western European choral performance). Perhaps this recognition was a process of fulfillment meant to reproduce a sense of the self as Sephardic and to reinforce tradition. Modernity, as the retreat from liturgical reform between the world wars surely demonstrates, was not irreversible.

Twentieth-Century Fin de Siècle

During a recording session at the Sinai synagogue in Jaffa on the occasion of the Jewish New Year of 1987, a minor event challenged my earlier views on fin-de-siècle Vienna. The Sinai synagogue, a congregation of Bulgarian Sephardic Jews, is located on the main commercial street of Jaffa. It is a very small building flanked by fresh fruit and vegetable stands and a sporting-goods store. The leader of the congregation was Rabbi Abraham Bakhar, known as the "Rabbi of Maccabi Jaffa" owing to his long-standing support for and blessing from the local soccer team. The synagogue was a remnant of a Sephardic Judaism characterized by a lenient approach to orthodoxy, and its music reflected that attitude. In fact, the synagogue was a link to the post–World War I Sephardic community in Vienna, a community that favored a return to tradition but could not refrain from keeping the reformed liturgical melodies of the previous era in its musical memory.

During the Torah service of the *shaḥarit* (morning) service for Rosh Hashanah a certain song captured my attention: *Tzena u-re'ena* ("O Maidens of Zion, Go Forth and Gaze upon King Solomon," Song of Songs 3:11), a short biblical insertion of the Eastern Sephardic liturgy performed in a manner that clearly recalled the choral arrangement of the text Bauer and Löwit had written a century earlier in Vienna. The arrangement was preserved in oral tradition by Sephardic Jews from Bulgaria who in their youth had sung this piece or heard it performed by the choir of the great Sephardic synagogue in Sofia.

Liturgical-music memory proved itself remarkably resistant to the challenges posed by change in time and space. The sounds heard at the synagogue in Große Fuhrmanngasse 401 (later renamed Zirkusgasse 22) in Vienna, at a time when the old Brahms and the young Mahler walked on adjacent streets, were perpetuated in a disintegrated version on a hot, humid September morning in the remote Middle Eastern port of Jaffa. The performance in Israel was the swan song of another swan song, but in its remembrance of a dying tradition it also reminds us of the renewal of tradition, the modernity of pastness. The Viennese Sephardic culture that slowly disintegrated toward the end of the nineteenth century and eventually disappeared in the aftermath of World War I was echoed in a location where the same Sephardic culture was passing through transformations under very different circumstances. The claims of age and timelessness made by the Sephardic liturgical repertory, which provided it with authority in the Viennese setting, were being replaced by other musical realities in Israel's modern and postmodern fins des siècles, its passage from the twentieth to the twenty-first century.

The representation of Sephardiness in liturgical music within the contemporary Israeli context is based on contemporary Arabic music aesthetics, especially on the use of the *maqām* principle, the classical Arabic modal framework, which supplanted the Judeo-Spanish Ottoman tradition. This substitution is one of the many paradoxes of modern Israeli society, for this is the music of cultures opposed to the new nation of Israel into which the Sephardim, sometimes reluctantly, were "absorbed" (to use the Israeli euphemism for the reception of new immigrants).

Entering this paradox as an ethnomusicologist with Sephardic origins—origins that my surname signifies in Israel, whatever my actual ethnic ori-

gins are—I was called in the early 1990s by the director of a new school of Sephardic cantors established in Tel Aviv. The school was an initiative of Shas, the political and social movement that revolutionized Sephardism in Israel, transforming it into an unprecedented mutation of ultra-orthodox Lithuanian Ashkenaziness (see Dayan 1999). The idea of a Sephardic school of cantors emerged as a reaction to the well-established Ashkenazic school of cantors in Tel Aviv, which was heavily sponsored by the former mayor of Tel Aviv, Shlomo Lahat, an avid consumer of Ashkenazic *ḥazzanut*. My task as a "Sephardic professor of music" was to propose a curriculum for the school and, moreover, to transcribe the modes, the *maqāmāt*, "*be-tavim*" (literally "into [musical] notes") and devise a system for learning the Arabic musical modes and new melodies using Western musical notation. So imposing was the authority of written music and of "systematic" Western music pedagogy in Israeli culture that they made up the platform for this new school of cantors.

Was I about to become, through some poignant act of destiny, the Jacob Bauer of Sephardic liturgical music in yet another stormy Sephardic fin de siècle? Was my refusal to carry out this job, on the basis of the argument that an oral system of learning that had worked so well for so many centuries should not be changed, a fair response to a legitimate demand? Was I unconsciously interested in the perpetuation of the oral tradition in order to secure my own professional interests or even future positions for my students of ethnomusicology?

Epilogue

I close by recapitulating my initial meditations about the concept of the ends of centuries. Sephardic liturgical music shows us that conceptual frameworks for the interpretation of the past as a unilinear development are an arbitrary construction. The reform of Sephardic liturgical music in fin-de-siècle Vienna was not an attempt to modernize an old-fashioned musical style, but rather a desperate strategy to attract the young, whose Jewish identity was eroding rapidly. The capitulation to musical otherness in a cosmopolitan Vienna—the Salomon Sulzer of an Ashkenazic modernity, the Richard Strauss or Arnold Schoenberg of a Viennese modernism—failed, however, to effect a transformation from modernity to modernism, that is, to replace Sephardic tradition with Jewish modernism. After World War I, musical orthodoxy made a comeback in Sephardic Vienna, and the "oriental" style was reinstated for a short time. The Sephardic community in Vienna slowly disappeared from the stage of history in the late 1920s, and after the Austrian *Anschluss* and *Kristallnacht* it vanished forever. Only the musical manuscripts remained as a silent witness, not only to the community's existence but also to its failed attempt to save the identity of the Viennese-born fin-de-siècle generation.

In fin-de-siècle twentieth-century Israel we witness another shift in Sephardic history. As religious fundamentalism of Ashkenazic origin makes inroads into the pan-Sephardic public, a new musical orthodoxy, the Arabic one, becomes a tool in the forging of Sephardic identity in the unprecedented situation of a modern Jewish nation-state. Singing in *maqāmāt* or adopting prayers to the tunes of the Egyptian popular-music stars Umm Kulthum or Muhammad Abd el-Wahab is therefore one of the major components in the strategy of resistance to Ashkenazic hegemony and in the re-creation of the Sephardic past in the lands of Islam. Historically shaped by its encounter with Islam, from the Middle Ages in Andalusia to the Sephardic Diaspora that stretched across the Mediterranean, Sephardic liturgical music in twenty-first-century Israel makes tradition modern by turning to its past in search of survival.

::: **NOTES** :::

1. A few other publications of Sephardic liturgical music appeared before 1889, most notably Aguilar and de Sola (1857; see Seroussi 1992b). It includes seventy items but its scope is rather limited; these seventy items cover the entire annual liturgical cycle. The Aguilar–de Sola collection, which represents the Western Sephardic liturgical tradition, includes only eleven items from the High Holidays as compared with twenty-five items included in *Schir Hakawod*. The Spanish-Portuguese community of Paris, also, was active in the early publication of liturgical music (see Jonas 1854; Villers 1872).

2. Throughout this essay, the terms "Sephardi" (pl. "Sephardim") and "Sephardic community" are employed to denote Jews and Jewish communities with the following geographic and linguistic criteria: (a) Jews of Spanish descent who established themselves after the fifteenth century in the territory of the Ottoman Empire and their descendants who settled in other parts of the world (e.g., Vienna or the Americas); (b) Jews who use Judeo-Spanish dialects, variously named "Ladino," "Djudesmo," "Djudio," or "Espaniol." When referring to the "Sephardim," therefore, I do not include the Spanish-Portuguese or "Western Sephardim" who settled in Western Europe and the United States, nor do I include the Arabic-speaking Jews of the Near East and North Africa who, under today's influence of demographic, social, and cultural processes in the state of Israel, are also called "Sephardim." When I refer to other groups that use the denomination "Sephardim" to identify themselves in contemporary Israel, they are labeled specifically according to land of origin, for example, "Syrian Jews."

3. Besides the first five volumes of A. Z. Idelsohn's *Hebräisch-orientalischer Melodienschatz*, other collections of Sephardic liturgical music of local character published by the end of the nineteenth century and in the twentieth century include: Rosenspier (1888) for the Bulgarian tradition; Consolo (1892) and Piatelli (1992) for the Italian Sephardic tradition (Livorno and Florence); Cohen Linaru (1910) and Cauly (1936) for the Bucharest (Romanian) tradition; Gaster (1901–5) for

the London Spanish-Portuguese tradition; Foy (1928) and Benharoche (1961) for the Bayonne (southwestern France) tradition; Lopes Cardozo (1987 and 1991) for the Amsterdam and New York Spanish-Portuguese tradition; Sabbah (1991) for the Moroccan tradition; Behar (1992) for the Sephardic tradition in Los Angeles based on the author's tradition from Bulgaria. For an annotated review and a bibliography on this subject, see Seroussi 1993.

4. Chronologically, the introduction of four-part choirs to the synagogue has to be attributed to the cantor Israel Lovy, who used four-voice choirs in his synagogue in Paris as early as 1822 (Idelsohn 1929: 228).

5. For a discussion of the concept of "art" on synagogue music with reference to Sulzer, see Adler 1966: 1–4.

6. The establishment of cantorial schools and unions also reflects transformations in the social status of the ḥazzan during the nineteenth century, especially in Germany and the Austro-Hungarian Empire (see Goldberg 2002). However, the transformation of the ḥazzan's status in Ashkenazic communities started in the medieval period (see Landman 1972: 174–76).

7. Sulzer's son Joseph seems to have also been an influential figure in the musical life of the Sephardic synagogue in Vienna. Like his father, he was awarded a medal by the Ottoman Sultan for a hymn he wrote in honor of the Turkish monarch (*ÖUCZ* 8/22, 29/6/1889: 6).

8. Papo (1967) is the only source for details about the organ controversy and the final settlement of this case in the Sephardic community of Vienna. Because Papo's father was directly involved in this discussion, it seems entirely plausible to me that the information quoted here is reliable. The controversy reflects similar debates following the installation of organs in Ashkenazic synagogues (Frühauf 2004).

9. It is notable that Altarac was not the first rabbi in Serbia to introduce reformed services. As early as 1903, Rabbi Abraham Kapon (1853–1930, from Bulgaria) held "modern services" in the new Jewish school of Sarajevo (Petrovic 1982: 46). Kapon seated men and women

together and used a choir in the synagogue. The passive role of the congregation in Kapon's synagogue sparked his opponents to give it the nickname "El Qahal de los Mudos" (the congregation of mutes; Friedenreich 1979: 897). A photograph of Altarac with the boys' choir of the Sarajevo synagogue appears in Petrovic (1982: 47). The tallit and hat worn by the cantor are identical to those of Central European Ashkenazic cantors and demonstrate the influence of the Ashkenazic ideal of a cantor in the Sephardic congregations influenced by reforms, such as the Jewish communities of Vienna and Sarajevo. Because Altarac used the Viennese model in the Sarajevo services, this photograph gives us an idea how the Sephardic choir in Vienna might have looked.

::: WORKS CITED :::

Abbreviations

CdV   *El correo de Viena*
CS   *El correo sefaradí*
ÖUCZ   *Österreichisch-ungarische Cantoren-Zeitung*

Adler, Israel. 1966. *La pratique musicale savante dans quelques communautés juives en Europe aux XVIIe–XVIIIe siècles.* 2 vols. Paris: La Haye.

Aguilar, Emanuel, and David Aharon de Sola. 1857. *The Ancient Melodies of the Liturgy of the Spanish and Portuguese Jews.* London: Vallentine.

Avenary, Hanoch. 1971. *Hebrew Hymn Tunes: The Rise and Development of a Musical Tradition.* Tel Aviv: Israel Music Institute.

———. 1972. "Bauer, Jacob." *Encyclopaedia Judaica.* 16 vols. 4: 330–31. Jerusalem: Keter.

———. 1985. *Kantor Salomon Sulzer und seine Zeit: Eine Dokumentation.* Sigmaringen: Thornbecke.

Behar, Isaac. 1992. *Sephardic Sabbath Chants.* New York: Tara.

Benbassa, Esther, and Aron Rodrigue. 2000. *Sephardic Jewry: A History of the Judeo-Spanish Community, 14th–20th Centuries.* Berkeley: University of California Press.

Benharoche-Baralia, Maurice J. 1961. *Chants traditionnels en usage dans la communauté sephardic de Bayonne.* Biarritz: The author.

Birnbaum, Eduard. 1889. *Gottesdienstliche Gesänge für israelitische Gemeinden nach sephardischem Ritus.* Composed and edited by Isidor Löwit and Jacob Bauer. Part 1. Vienna 1889. *Jüdisches Literaturblatt* 18 (39) (26 September): 155–56; 18 (41–42) (3 October): 165–66.

Bohlman, Philip V. 1994. "Auf der Bima—Auf der Bühne: Zur Emanzipation der jüdischen Popularmusik um die Jahrhundertwende in Wien." In Elisabeth T. Hilscher and Theophil Antonicek, eds., *Vergleichend-systematische Musikwissenschaft: Beiträge zu Methode und Problematik der systematischen, ethnologischen und historischen Musikwissenschaft: Franz Födermayr zum 60. Geburtstag,* 417–49. Tutzing: Hans Schneider.

———. 1997. "Fieldwork in the Ethnomusicological Past." In Gregory F. Barz and Timothy J. Cooley, eds., *Shadows in the Field: New Perspectives for Fieldwork in Ethnomusicology,* 139–62. New York: Oxford University Press.

Botstein, Leon, and Werner Hanak, eds. 2004. *Vienna: Jews and the City of Music, 1870–1938.* Annandale-on-Hudson, N.Y.: Bard College; Vienna: Wolke Verlag.

Camhy, Ovadiah, ed. 1959. *Liturgie séphardie.* London: World Sephardic Federation.

Cauly, Isaac. 1936. *Culegere de melodii religioase traditionale.* Bucharest: Comitelur Templelor Comunitati Israelitilor de Rit Spaniol din Bucaresti.

Cohen-Linaru, Maurice. 1910. *Tehillot Israel.* 2 vols. Paris: Durlacher.

Consolo, Federico. 1892. *Libro dei Canti d'Israele: Antichi canti liturgici del rito degli Ebrei Spagnoli.* Florence: Brattie.

Dayan, Arye. 1999. *The Story of Shas.* Jerusalem: Keter. (In Hebrew)

de Sola Pool, David, and Tamar de Sola Pool. 1955. *An Old Faith in the New World: Portrait of Shearith Israel, 1654–1954.* New York: Columbia University Press.

Faur, José. 1977. "Sephardim in the 19th Century: New

Dimensions and Old Values." *Proceedings of the American Academy for Jewish Research* 44: 29–52.

———. 1982. "Modern Sephardic Thought: Religious Humanism and Zionism." In I. Ben-Ami, ed., *The Sephardic and Oriental Jewish Heritage: Studies*, 325–49. Jerusalem: Magnes Press of the Hebrew University.

Foucault, Michel. 1972. *The Archeology of Knowledge.* Trans. by A. M. Sheridan Smith. London: Routledge.

Fraenkel, Joseph, ed. 1967. *The Jews of Austria: Essays on Their Life, History and Destruction.* London: Vallentine.

Foy, Salomon. 1928. *Recueil des chantes hebräiques anciennes et modernes du rite Sefardi dit Portugais en usage dans le communauté de Bordeaux.* Bordeaux: Consistoire Israelite de la Gironde.

Freidenreich, Harriet Pass. 1979. *The Jews of Yugoslavia: A Quest for Community.* Philadelphia: Jewish Publication Society of America.

Friedmann, Aron. 1927. "Löwit, Isidor." In *Lebensbilder berühmter Kantoren.* 3 vols. 3: 61–62. Berlin: Rochelson.

Frühauf, Tina. 2004. "Jewish Liturgical Music in Vienna: A Mirror of Cultural Diversity." In Botstein and Hanak, *Vienna,* 43–64.

———. 2005. *Orgel und Orgelmusik in deutsch-jüdischer Kultur.* Hildesheim: Georg Olms Verlag. (Netiva: Wege deutsch-jüdischer Geschichte, 6)

Gaster, Moses, ed. 1901–5. *The Book of Prayer and Order of the Service According to the Custom of the Spanish and Portuguese Jews.* 5 vols. Oxford.

Gelber, N. M. 1948. "The Sephardic Community in Vienna." *Jewish Social Studies* 10 (4): 359–96.

Geller, Jacob. 1983. *The Sephardic Jews in Rumania: The Rise and Decline of the Sephardic Jewish Community in Bucharest.* Tel Aviv: Tel Aviv University. (Publications of the Diaspora Research Institute, 53) (In Hebrew)

Goldberg, Geoffrey. 1992. "Jewish Liturgical Music in the Wake of Nineteenth-Century Reform." In Lawrence A. Hoffman and Janet R. Walton, eds., *Sacred Sound and Social Change: Liturgical Music in Jewish and Christian Experience,* 59–83. Notre Dame: University of Notre Dame Press.

———. 2002. "The Training of 'Ḥazzanim' in Nineteenth-Century Germany." In Eliyahu Schleifer and Edwin Seroussi, eds., *Yuval 7: Studies in Honour of Israel Adler,* 299–367. Jerusalem: Magnes Press of the Hebrew University.

Idelsohn, Abraham Zvi. 1923. *Gesänge der orientalischen Sefardim.* Jerusalem: Benjamin Harz. (Hebräisch-orientalischer Melodienschatz, 4)

———. 1929. *Jewish Music in Its Historical Development.* New York: Holt, Rinehart & Winston.

Jonas, Emile. 1854. *Recueil des chants hebraïques anciens et modernes (Shirot Yisrael), executés au Temple du Rit Portugais de Paris.* Paris: Temple Israélite de Paris.

Kramer, L. M., and O. Gutman. 1942. *Kol Sheherit Israel: Synagogal Melodies.* New York: Transatlantic.

Krieg, H. M., ed. 1952. *Eighteen Spanish Liturgical Melodies of the Portuguese Israelitish Community [of] Amsterdam, recorded by J. H. Pimentel.* Amsterdam.

———. 1954. *Spanish Liturgical Melodies of the Portuguese Israelitish Community [of] Amsterdam.* Amsterdam.

Landman, Leo. 1972. *The Cantor: An Historical Perspective.* New York: Yeshiva University.

Léon, Henry. 1893. *Historie des juifs de Bayonne.* Paris. Reprint: Marseille: Laffitte Reprints, 1976.

Levy, Isaac. 1964–80. *Antología de la litúrgia judeo-española.* 10 vols. Jerusalem: The author.

Lopes Cardozo, Abraham. 1960. "The Music of the Sephardim." *The World of the Sephardim* (Herzl Pamphlet XV), 37–71. New York.

———. 1987. *Sephardic Songs of Praise According to the Spanish-Portuguese Tradition as Sung in the Synagogue and at Home.* New York: Tara.

———. 1991. *Selected Sephardic Chants.* New York: Tara.

Lord, Albert B. 1964. *The Singer of Tales.* Cambridge, Mass.: Harvard University Press.

Mandrell, Eric. 1967. "Salomon Sulzer, 1804–1890." In Fraenkel, *The Jews of Austria,* 221–29.

Papo, Manfred. 1967. "The Sephardic Community in Vienna." In Fraenkel, *The Jews of Austria,* 327–46.

Petrovic, Ankica. 1982. "Sacred Sephardic Chants in Bosnia." *World of Music* 24 (3): 35–48.

Piatelli, Elio. 1992. *Canti liturgici di rito spagnolo del Tempio Israelitico di Firenze*. Florence: Giuntina.

Rodrigue, Aron. 1993. *Images of Sephardic and Eastern Jewries in Transition: The Teachers of the Alliance Israélite Universelle, 1860–1939*. Seattle: University of Washington Press.

Rosenspier, Maurice J. 1888. *Chir Akavod: Album de chants religieux chez les Israëlites du rite Espagnol*. Varna: Meir Gadol.

Sabbah, Dinah. 1991. *Ne'im zemirot: 102 Selections of Sephardic Jewish Music*. Montréal: Centre communautaire juif.

Schmidt, Esther. 1998. "Die Idee von Professionalismus in der musikalischen Welt des Judentums: Wien im neunzehnten Jahrhundert und die Gründung der *Österreichisch-ungarischen Cantoren-Zeitung*." Master's thesis, University of Vienna.

Schorske, Carl E. 1980. *Fin-de-siècle Vienna*. New York: Knopf.

Seroussi, Edwin. 1988. "Sacred Song in an Era of Change: Musical Reforms in Sephardic Synagogues in Austria and the Balkan States." *Pe'amim* 34: 84–109. (In Hebrew)

———. 1992a. "Die Sephardische Gemeinde in Wien: Geschichte einer orientalisch-jüdischen Enklave in Mitteleuropa." In Felicitas Heimann-Jelineck and Kurt Schubert, eds., *Sephardim Spaniolen: Die Juden in Spanien: Die sephardische Diaspora*. Special issue of *Studia Judaica Austriaca* 13: 145–53. Eisenstadt: Edition Roetzer.

———. 1992b. "The Ancient Melodies: On the Antiquity of Music in the Sephardic Liturgy." *Pe'amim* 50:

99–131. (In Hebrew)

———. 1993. "Sephardic Music: A Bibliographical Guide with a Checklist of Notated Sources." *Jewish Folklore and Ethnology Review* 15 (2): 56–61.

Stillman, Norman A. 1995. *Sephardic Religious Responses to Modernity*. Luxemburg: Harwood Academic.

Sulzer, Salomon. 1865. "Preface." In Sulzer, *Schir Zion*. 2nd ed. 2 vols. Vol. 2. Leipzig: M. W. Kaufmann.

———. 1876. *Denkschrift an die hochgeehrte Wiener israelitische Cultus-Gemeinde*. Vienna: Brüder Winter.

Villers, Alphonse de. 1872. *Offices hebraïques: Rit Oriental appelé communement Rit Portugais; Recueil des chants traditionnels et liturgiques composant du rit oriental (portugais) notes pour la première fois depuis la creation des Tagnamim au IVe siècle*. Paris: Saint Seans.

Werner, Eric. 1976. *A Voice Still Heard . . . : The Sacred Songs of the Ashkenazic Jews*. University Park: Pennsylvania State University Press.

Wohlberg, Max. 1970. "Salomon Sulzer and the Seitenstettengasse Temple." *Journal of Synagogue Music* 2 (4): 19–24.

Zaludkowsky, Eliyahu. 1930. *Kulturträger von der jüdischen Liturgie*. Poland: The author. (In Yiddish)

Zemlinsky, Adolf von. 1888. *Geschichte der Türkisch-Israelitischen Gemeinde zu Wien*. Vienna: Papo Verlag.

Zimmermann, Heidy. 2004. "Schir Zion: Musik und Gesang in der Synagoge." In John Eckhard and Heidy Zimmermann eds., *Jüdische Musik? Fremdbilde—Eigenbilder*, 53–75. Cologne: Böhlau Verlag.

Zohar, Zvi. 1993. *Tradition and Change: Halachik Responses of Middle Eastern Rabbis to Legal and Technological Change (Egypt and Syria, 1880–1920)*. Jerusalem: Ben Zvi Institute. (In Hebrew)

3

Jewish Music and German Science

::: PAMELA M. POTTER

In an essay on Germans and Jews from his book entitled simply *The Germans*, the historian Gordon Craig cites Edgar Allen Poe's story "William Wilson," in which a character finds himself plagued throughout his life by a schoolmate who shares the same name, same date of birth, and similar appearance (Craig 1982: 126–27). At first the character feels "petulant animosity, which was not yet hatred, some esteem, more respect, much fear, with a world of uneasy curiosity" that gradually turns into "the feeling of vexation . . . stronger with every circumstance tending to show resemblance, moral or physical, between my rival and myself." As the schoolmate reappears at various times throughout his life, this vexation grows into a hatred and drives him to kill his perceived rival.

Craig compares this growing obsession to the sentiments in Germany toward its Jewish citizens, which gained momentum from the time of Jewish emancipation to the tragic conclusions of the Holocaust. He points out that many Germans regarded the Jews in their midst as inexplicably different, but also disturbingly familiar. Not only were German Jews indistinguishable from any other Germans in their outward appearance, but they also could draw on their heritage to find ideals similar to those attributed to Germans: a profound reverence for the printed word is common to both the Jewish "people of the Book" and the German nation of "poets and thinkers"; an intellectual drive to solve the mysteries of the universe rather than focus on utilitarian goals characterizes both German metaphysicians as well as Jewish cabalists; and even the negative traits of business-mindedness, obsession with detail, and a certain arrogance have been attributed to both groups by their detractors (Craig 1982: 126–27).

As a plethora of literature on German Jewish relations shows, one can add many more similarities to Craig's list from the time of the Enlightenment, at which point German Jews privately held on to their identification with the Jewish community but publicly set out to make themselves indistinguishable from their compatriots. German Jews could be just as patriotic as any other Germans, and German Jews proved capable of enriching two of Germany's most cherished cultural achievements: music and scholarship. As Jewish emancipation became a reality early in the nineteenth century, Jews found it far easier to advance in the arts and sciences than in public service and other more exclusive professions, and conversion made their entrée even smoother. In the arts, and especially music, a significant component of Germany's rise to cultural prominence came from the contribution of Jews—as composers, music educators, concert artists, scholars, and conductors (Katz 1984; Mendelsohn 1993). The same was true for the sciences. University teaching had provided more openings for Jews than other professions because hiring of faculty was based more on an individual's qualifications and was presumably less vulnerable to nepotism and prejudice (Pulzer 1992: 108–11), and the list of prominent Jews contributing to Germany's leading role in scholarship is long and impressive.

In the late nineteenth century there arose a new activity that could have offered a tremendous opportunity for German Jews to combine these acquired strengths in both music and scholarship. Musicology, the scientific study of music, aptly designated by the German term *Musikwissenschaft* ("music-science"), was developing out of a strengthened sense of Germany's musical superiority and a desire to marry that excellence with Germans' high standards of learning. Musicology derived its methods from the well-established disciplines of philology, physics, and other sciences. German pioneers in the field established university departments, scholarly journals, academic societies, and research facilities and led the way in introducing new research methods, designing and publishing large-scale research initiatives with generous aid from the German government, and launching international organizations and publications (Potter 1998: 32).

German-speaking Central Europe—Germany and Austria—was the birthplace of modern musicology, and scholars ostensibly cast their net wide, aiming to gain a comprehensive understanding of as many Western, as well as non-Western, musical traditions as possible. Yet there is a glaring gap when it comes to Jewish music. Even German Jewish musicologists failed to show interest in it, not only within the context of studying European music but also in the nascent field of comparative musicology, in which a wide range of aspects of ancient and non-Western music was examined. The Jewish component was largely ignored even in the heyday of German musicological growth. When German and German-trained scholars did take an interest in Jewish music, they did so only after they had left Germany for good.

In this chapter I attempt to understand how this curious lacuna came to be and how its effects have been felt recently in Germany. Although circumstances changed, the things that made Germans and Jews so similar—the complexities of defining their identities—as well as the things that make them so different seem constantly to inhibit a serious study of Jewish music within the hallowed halls of German science.

The "German Music" Problem and the "Jewish Music" Problem

Jews and Germans are similar not only in their respective reputations as musical peoples, but also in the difficulties they face in confronting their identity through music. Just as German music defies definition, so does Jewish music, and for similar reasons. Trying to define German or Jewish music offers more questions than answers. Does German music comprise all music in Germany, or just music by German composers, or music performed by Germans, or music tied to German texts and German practices? Similarly, are we to understand Jewish music as the music of the Jewish religion only, or the music of Jewish communities, or the music of the Jewish state of Israel, or the music composed and performed by any Jews anywhere in the world? Is the pop singer Nina just as German as the Beastie Boys are Jewish? And who are the Germans? Do they include all German-speaking populations, including Austrians, Swiss Germans, and the small enclaves of ethnic Germans that the Nazis hoped to resettle within the expanding Reich? Or are Germans an amorphous group of populations that would sooner identify themselves as Bavarians, or Berliners, or even Europeans, than as Germans (see also the essays in Applegate and Potter 2002)? Similarly, who are the Jews? Those born into Jewish families, or only those who practice Judaism, or anyone who chooses to identify with any manifestations of a Jewish community? Do American Jews think of themselves first as Americans and then as Jews, or vice versa?

A more focused examination of these similarities reveals that there are also significant differences between the problems in grasping the totality of German music and those involved in confronting Jewish music. In a way, the German musical complex and the Jewish musical complex represent mirror images of one another. This opposition centers on the connection of each to geographic space. Germany's central location and its long history as a European cultural crossroads made it one of the most cosmopolitan musical landscapes on the continent. Their geographic, political, and cultural situation allowed Germans to act like sponges, absorbing the musical innovations of the Franco-Flemish, the Italians, the Czechs, and the Bohemians. This phenomenon probably accounted for Germany's musical strengths over the centuries, but it was also an obstacle to anyone hoping to define Germanness through German music. The path toward defining "German music" is slippery because one has to consider where to draw the boundaries circumscribing both a national-political German entity and a cultural-musical German entity. The fact, nevertheless, that "Germans"—no matter how one defines them—live side by side generates a discussion that can focus on a pragmatic agenda of inclusion. The concentric placement of a core of Reich Germans surrounded by various groups of German speakers and circumscribed at its edges by "Germanic" peoples such as the Dutch, Belgians, and Scandinavians can serve as a point of departure for the debates about who is a German and what German music comprises.

The situation of the Jews is, in this regard, just the opposite. The Jewish Diaspora by definition lacked a physical geographic center, and Jews throughout the world hinged much of their identification on their hopes of returning to Zion and on their common religion. Despite the continued presence of small Jewish communities in the Holy Land, the geographic center of Judaism was an ideal rather than a tangible locus. Furthermore, unlike the Germans' mostly unconscious absorption of cultural and especially musical influences from surrounding areas, the ghettoization of Jewish communities in the Diaspora subtly encouraged them to develop a distinct cultural identity. Jewish communities inevitably absorbed cultural influences from their surroundings, but their exclusion from the cultural mainstream fostered both real and imagined differences. These differences were, incidentally, highlighted primarily by outside observers as a justification for the separation and exclusion of Jews.

In any event, concerns about defining German music and Jewish music arose simultaneously in the late nineteenth century as notions of national sovereignty forced groups to think of themselves—often for the first time—as national entities. Unification in 1871 urged Germans to stop regarding themselves as Bavarians, Swabians, and Rhinelanders and to start identifying themselves as Germans. Zionism similarly urged Jews to seek out similarities among the multitude of Jewish communities scattered across the globe with a view toward conceptualizing nationhood to replace religion as the Jewish common denominator. However, whereas the German agenda set for itself the pragmatic goals of embracing surrounding communities under the German rubric, the Jewish agenda had to set the much more imaginative and abstract goals of bringing Jews together culturally if not geographically.

Conceptualizing Jewish music was already challenging because of the physical separation of Jewish communities. But the intervening processes of Jewish emancipation and assimilation complicated the issue even more. The breakdown of physical as well as cultural barriers surrounding Jewish communities was a welcome sign of progress, but the participation of Jews in German musical life made the later task of identifying Jewish music all the more difficult. In the end, when the need to know more about Jewish music arose—whether to serve Zionist aims, to serve the pernicious campaigns of exclusion and annihilation in the Third Reich, or to serve more idealistic aims of the recent Jewish renaissance in Germany—an utter lack of understanding of Jewish music became painfully obvious, and scholars had to scramble clumsily to meet these needs. Ironically, often the only tangible sources to which they could turn were the writings of anti-Semitic polemicists. Even if for the wrong reasons, such writings sometimes offered the only guidelines for characterizing Jewish music as a distinct entity. Yet these sources were problematic not only because they contained vitriolic language and destructive intent, but also because they emerged as a negative reaction to the products of assimilation and came too late to offer any insights into drawing real distinctions that may have once existed between Jews and non-Jews. As Jews began to share in and contribute to German musical culture, anti-Semites found it increasingly difficult to single out the Jewish from the non-Jewish. Accordingly, they perceived a need to call attention to and exaggerate alleged Jewish differences, primarily because such differences were far from obvious and quite probably nonexistent.

From Jewish Emancipation to the Rise of Musicology

As many have noted, the emancipated Jews of Germany led something of a dual existence in the eighteenth and early nineteenth centuries, embracing German culture and secularizing their lifestyle without entirely abandoning their identification with the Jewish community. Thus those excelling in scholarship and the arts had focused all their interests on mainstream culture rather than on any cultural components of their own religion. By the late nineteenth century, however, the forces of German nationalism placed them in an unstable position. The desire to define Germanness acquired a sense of urgency with German unification in 1871, and the growing forces of German nationalism had set all Germans off

on the difficult mission of defining what the German nation was all about. For some this meant distinguishing groups in their midst that could be regarded as foreign and that needed to be suppressed if Germanness were to thrive. The influx of Eastern European Jews into Germany, with their distinctive language, dress, and mannerisms, turned attention to this group of outsiders and prompted attacks against them as well as their assimilated brethren. Particularly after World War I, this stigmatization of "alien" groups intensified. Along with the Jews, the main targets suspected of infiltrating German culture were the custodians of the Versailles Treaty—the Americans, French, and British—as well as the Bolsheviks. These so-called enemies were accused of watering down German culture with banalities, sarcasm, superficial rationalism, commercialization, and internationalism.

Music was believed to be particularly vulnerable to these influences. Music had come to be regarded as Germany's greatest cultural achievement over the previous few centuries, and the purest means for expressing the essence of the German soul. One argued that Germany had unfortunately opened its doors to the cheap spectacle of French grand opera, the superficiality of Italian vocal and instrumental virtuosity, the barbarity of American jazz, the salaciousness of French- and Russian-inspired cabaret, and the countless destructive effects of cosmopolitanism manifested in modern compositional trends. Furthermore, the growing workers' movement fostered its own culture, and while one would be hard-pressed to find any identifiable "Bolshevik" trends in German music, the fear loomed large that lofty German music would be dragged down to the level of the proletariat and tainted by internationalism. With regard to the demonization of the Jews as enemies of German music, however, the picture was consistently murky. The German musical legacy counted not a few Jews among its luminaries, and one could not isolate Jewish music without compromising the reputations of some of the more revered figures in German music. Richard Wagner's 1850 essay "Judaism in Music" had presented some food for thought by proposing ways of detecting supposed Jewish musical traits, but most of his observations could apply only to specific works of his Jewish contemporaries (Katz 1980: 189; Wagner 1995).

After Wagner's time, the growing influence of social Darwinism and the development of race theories fueled anti-Semitism by suggesting that Jews were a distinct race, with specific physical, mental, and character traits. Mere conversion could no longer erase this stigma, attempts at assimilation were deemed futile, and intermarriage guaranteed release from "Jewishness" only after several generations. Anti-Jewish sentiments, many believed, could now be supported with scientific evidence. Yet some of the most widely read anti-Semitic literature was the work of dilettantes who cloaked their rhetoric in scientific guise. Theodor Fritsch's *Handbook of Anti-Semitism*, published first in 1894 and including a chapter on music, appealed to an educated readership by quoting extensively from allegedly authoritative sources that all disparaged Judaism (see Fritsch 1933). Houston Stewart Chamber-

lain's widely read *Foundations of the Nineteenth Century* similarly drew broadly from historical and scientific data but still aimed primarily to denigrate the Jews (Chamberlain 1911). German racial theorists in the 1920s also tried to portray their musings as "scientific" but moved even farther away from data and physical anthropology and deeper into the metaphysical realm of the "racial soul" (*Rassenseele*) (Mosse 1964: 302–4; Katz 1980: 303–11).

In the midst of these developments, musicology was starting to emerge as a serious academic pursuit, with the center of its activity in Germany and Austria. The first appearance of musicology as a distinct discipline in the German-speaking realm can be traced roughly to the last decades of the nineteenth century; thus, it was born and raised in an era of increasingly strident nationalist rhetoric and of popularization and "scientification" of anti-Semitism. Initially, musicology's primary goal was to demonstrate its scholarly pedigree and to present itself as growing out of classical philology rather than music performance. Trying to distance themselves from the existing tradition of university music directors and carve out a scholarly niche that would earn the respect of other academicians, musicologists strove to portray the foundations of their pursuits. It seemed in their best interest, at least in the early stages, to stay clear of ideologically charged or methodologically shaky investigations.

As a result, serious musicologists largely avoided making any authoritative statements on modern music, popular entertainment, or Jewish music. As the discipline developed, scholars not only ventured further into the past of European music, but also advanced into the realms of European folk music and non-Western music traditions; their choices, however, displayed a seemingly conscious avoidance of Jewish music. Entire subdisciplines dedicated to Catholic and Protestant church music rapidly grew, while Jewish liturgical music received no attention at all. The collection and study of European folk music largely ignored the Yiddish-texted repertories and music for Jewish ceremonies and festivals. Even in the nascent discipline of comparative musicology, in which scholars applied new methodologies from anthropology and acoustics to learn as much as possible about the music of antiquity and of other cultures, a similar tendency to overlook ancient Jewish music and Eastern Jewish musical traditions prevailed.

This is not to say that there was no scholarly interest in Jewish music anywhere. Around the turn of the century, the Polish watchmaker Judah Loeb Cahan began collecting and publishing Jewish folk songs (e.g., Cahan 1952), and the Russian scholars Shaul Ginsburg and Pesach Marek and the composer Joel Engel—later joined by the St. Petersburg Society for Jewish Folk Music and the Jewish Historical-Ethnographic Society—launched large-scale projects to collect and preserve Jewish folk music by transcribing and recording examples found throughout the countryside (see, e.g., Ginsburg and Marek 1901). An outgrowth of the discovery of this untapped musical resource was a flurry of Jewish-inspired compositions by Russian-Jewish composers who were encouraged to seek out their national heri-

tage (Avenary, Bayer, and Boehm 1971: columns 656–60). In Austria, too, the highly respected cantorial tradition, established by Salomon Sulzer and known as the "Viennese Rite" (*Wiener Ritus*), inspired cantors to pursue serious scholarship on Jewish music (see Seroussi, this volume). Sulzer's younger contemporary Eduard Birnbaum compiled a thematic catalogue of Jewish liturgical melodies and acquired an extensive collection of Hebrew manuscripts (see Birnbaum 1893); A. Z. Idelsohn, a Latvian-born cantor who settled in Palestine in 1906, carried out research in Jewish music with the assistance of the Austrian Academy of Sciences (see, e.g., Idelsohn 1917; Lechleitner 2005); and even after World War II Vienna remained a site of research in Jewish music, producing such works as a dissertation by the Israeli composer Joel Walbe (see Walbe 1975).

In the hallowed halls of German and Austrian universities, Jewish music as a subject of scholarly inquiry, nonetheless, remained off-limits. Even in Vienna, where cantors launched their pioneering work in Jewish music scholarship, the resident musicologists never showed an interest in Jewish music, even though a significant number of them were Jews. Since 1898, Vienna's renowned musicology faculty had been under the direction of a Jew, Guido Adler, who had succeeded Eduard Hanslick, also Jewish. By the time Adler retired in 1927, the five-member faculty included two other Jews, Egon Wellesz and Wilhelm Fischer. The faculty at one point considered recruiting Erich von Hornbostel because he was "Austrian-born," ignoring his Judaism and generally favoring Austrians over German nationals (Potter 1998: 98).

But these musicologists showed no interest in the study of Jewish music throughout their years in Vienna. Other German Jewish musicologists also followed these tendencies while working in German academe. With the exception of Eric Werner, who studied Jewish and early Christian music for his dissertation in Strasbourg and settled in the United States in 1939, any Jewish musicologists who engaged intensively in Jewish music did so only after being forced out of Germany during the Nazi regime, and then usually only if he or she settled in Israel. One of the foremost scholars of Jewish music, Peter Gradenwitz, was born in Berlin, studied in Freiburg im Breisgau, Berlin, and Prague, and specialized at first in the music of Johann Stamitz. He published his comprehensive survey of the music of Israel only after having settled in Palestine (Gradenwitz 1949). Robert Lachmann had investigated Jewish music only in the much broader context of music of the Orient while in Germany, but after immigrating to Palestine in the 1930s he started to focus more of his attention on Jewish music (e.g., Lachmann 1976; see Katz 2003). The same was true for Edith Gerson-Kiwi, who studied the Italian canzonetta for her doctoral work in Germany. Only later, while working with Lachmann after she had settled in Palestine, did she begin to specialize in the music of Jews in the Middle East (see, e.g., Gerson-Kiwi 1938). By contrast, most German Jewish musicologists who came to the United States rarely, if ever, showed any scholarly interest in Jewish music, and some even continued to adhere fervently to the idea of German superiority in both music and scholarship, deriving their inspiration from

Germany's great achievements prior to Hitler's accession and seeing the Nazi phenomenon as an historical aberration.

German Jewish musicologists' avoidance of Jewish topics was clearly a response to emancipation and its assimilationist encouragement to merge into the mainstream. For a long time, this arrangement worked. Jews confined their activities within the established parameters of musicology, even immersing themselves in the study of Christian liturgy, and made names for themselves as experts on a wide range of conventional musicological topics. But the clash of German Jewish assimilation with a form of German nationalism tinged by anti-Semitism was inevitable, and eventually it could be felt personally. In 1929 the German Jewish musicologist Alfred Einstein was excluded from contributing a chapter on J. S. Bach's church music to a volume edited by Hermann von Waltershausen. Waltershausen explained the reasons for Einstein's exclusion not as anti-Semitism per se, even though he had never made a secret of his feelings regarding the "dangers and limitations" of Jews in German culture. Rather, Waltershausen claimed that this particular work was directed toward a general public, and that Bach held a special significance for devout Protestants. All of a sudden, a Jew contributing to studies on Bach was deemed just as inappropriate as a Protestant trying to deal with central questions in Catholic church music, or a non-Jew presenting scholarly findings on essential elements of Jewish ritual. Waltershausen drew this questionable analogy even after Einstein had pointed out the absurdity of reserving Protestant music scholarship for Protestants and of limiting his own work to "Jewish music history, to Mendelssohn and Meyerbeer" (Potter 1999: 304).

Einstein's reaction was telling, revealing not only his limited perception of Jewish music as something best represented by Mendelssohn and Meyerbeer—the main targets, in fact, of Richard Wagner's anti-Semitic polemics—but also the extent of his integration into the mainstream of the profession, despite his own painful awareness of how far anti-Semitism had seeped into the intellectual ranks. He had by this time established himself as the foremost scholar of both the Italian madrigal and the music of Mozart and had served as the editor of the premier German musicological scholarly journal, the *Zeitschrift für Musikwissenschaft*. Yet Einstein was no stranger to anti-Semitic policies, having been systematically excluded from any university posts since receiving his doctorate, the reasons for which could always be traced to an institutionalized form of anti-Semitism at work in German universities.

Einstein and his Jewish colleagues undoubtedly avoided any engagement with Jewish music in order to blend in and not draw undue attention to their Jewishness. This did not, however, always help them circumvent some very real discriminatory policies. Musicology faculties were hardly free of anti-Semitism and may have even surpassed others in their discrimination against Jewish colleagues. Like other disciplines prone to ideological and nationalist exploitation, musicology offered far fewer opportunities to Jews than, for example, mathematics, medicine, and other "objective" sciences (Pulzer 1992: 109). When

Jewish musicologists started to leave Germany in droves after 1933, only 2 out of the entire group of approximately 150 (Brinkmann and Wolff 1999: 341–44), Curt Sachs and Erich von Hornbostel, had positions as university professors in Germany, and that was only because they were working in "value-free" (*wertfrei*) subspecialties. Neither one would have achieved even these successes had he not excelled in new, "objective," "scientific" areas of musicology: acoustics, music psychology, and comparative musicology.

Anti-Semitic Parameters for Defining Jewish Music

With the rise of nationalist sentiment following Germany's defeat in World War I, German musicologists paid unprecedented attention to praising Germany's rich musical heritage while denigrating Jewish music in the form of anti-Semitic literature. In the end, however, neither project led to satisfactory conclusions. In addressing musical Germanness, they were in the end capable only of invoking popularized notions that attributed to the Germans more "depth" and "seriousness" than musicians of any other nations and of asserting that German music was universally understood and accepted as superior. Their understanding of Jewish music was equally vague, informed primarily by Wagner and by rumors proliferating in a climate of growing anti-Semitism. Wagner portrayed German music as an endangered species under attack from alien influences, and he concentrated his discussion of Jewish music and his "definition" of its characteristics on the works of his contemporary Jewish rivals, especially Meyerbeer. One could mimic Wagner's fears and prejudices and claim to detect such "dangers" up to the present, but few succeeded at furthering or deepening any understanding of the nature of either German or Jewish music (see Wagner 1995). The period between 1918 and 1945, nevertheless, witnessed some of the first attempts in German musicological scholarship to confront Jewish music systematically and "musicologically," even if these attempts were all in the name of anti-Semitism and rested on some very shaky methodological foundations.

Reiterating the warnings of Wagner, music scholars and critics in the early 1920s vented their fears that German music was on the brink of extinction, blamed bourgeois individualism and "art for art's sake" for creating an ever-increasing gulf between musicians and the public, and held Jews partly accountable for the perceived crisis by virtue of their historical role in German musical life as conductors, composers, and virtuosi. In the most comprehensive scholarly study of German music to that date, Hans Joachim Moser revealed his internalization of the anti-Semitic thinking of the time, reinforcing Wagner's claims against his Jewish contemporaries and carrying out similar attacks on succeeding generations of Jewish musical luminaries. Moser portrayed Mendelssohn as a "unique product of the rare combination of foreign origins with cultivated traits of the German bourgeoisie," and he pointed to Mendelssohn's Jewish heritage as the reason for his supposed lack of German passion and trite use of rhythm and meter. Moser also referred to the conductor Leo Blech's "clever consciousness of his tribe" in knowing the limits of his talents, denigrated Mahler as a Jewish farce, and indulged in contrived anti-Semitic interpretations of the songs of Mahler, Schreker, and Schoenberg, linking them to Asia or Africa but not to Germany (Moser 1924: 153, 390, 404–8).

Even after the Nazis came to power, little progress beyond Wagner's generalizations could be discerned in the attempts to understand either German or Jewish music. A host of German musicologists offered their services to the new regime, stating their intentions to serve the "people's community" and deepen Germans' understanding of both the positive traits of German music and the negative traits of Jewish music. At the same time, pressure came from the authorities for scholars in all fields to apply racial theories to their investigations. For musicology, the goal of such racial applications was to demonstrate German musical superiority as well as Jewish musical inferiority by identifying certain "racial" characteristics of music that remained constant over the centuries and therefore could be labeled as hereditary. In terms of serious scholarly investigation, however, the "racial question" in musicology had already been answered, negatively, by Robert Lach in 1923. Hoping to put an end to dilettantish digressions on race and music, Lach declared that the serious musicologist was simply incapable of determining a correspondence between music and race through the scientific means available (Lach 1923). After that, musicologists largely abandoned the racial approach. Thus, when Nazi officials imposed these new demands on scholars around 1933, the only existing comprehensive exposé on race and music was the work of the dilettante Richard Eichenauer.

Eichenauer's aim was to isolate the racial features of a composer's soul by looking at physical characteristics and biographical data, albeit primarily by looking at the composer's works. Tracing the roots of the German "Nordic racial soul" back to India, Persia, and especially ancient Greece, Eichenauer attributed the origins of polyphony and the triad to the Nordic race. When it came to tracing the negative traits of the Jews, however, Eichenauer primarily targeted the very same individuals Wagner and Moser had attacked. Although he proposed that Gregorian chant, of Jewish origins and therefore essentially un-German, should not be condemned out of anti-Semitic blindness, he maintained that nineteenth-century Jews constituted an entirely separate group. Both Meyerbeer and Offenbach had abused their musical abilities, and Mahler was frustrated by the conflict between his love for German folk song and his racial limitations. Finally, Schoenberg and all other Jewish progressives "are obeying a law of their race when they seek to destroy harmonic polyphony, which is totally foreign to them" (Eichenauer 1932: 16–42, 55, 59–112, 302).

In the course of the Third Reich, musicologists proved noticeably reticent to make pronouncements about the so-called Jewish problem. Pseudo-scientific writings that promoted racial anti-Semitism had continued to gain currency, but their complete lack of scholarly rigor indicated that any application to a discipline such as musicology would be far too risky, especially when the field was still determined to demonstrate its validity as a science. Signs of heightened awareness came in 1938, the year that not only culminated in the watershed anti-Jewish pogroms of November 9, but also witnessed a renewed attack on "musical Judaism" with the landmark "Degenerate Music" exhibit of May 22–28. Thus pressure resumed, at least momentarily, from within the field, when the Wagner scholar Alfred Lorenz appealed to younger colleagues to pay more serious attention to the "Jewish question." He expressed the need to update Wagner's analysis and to distinguish between real Jewish music (i.e., emanating from the "racial soul") and imitations of non-Jewish music, because the Jews supposedly had no originality (Lorenz 1938). Yet for all of the encouragement and attention it received, this area generally failed to capture the interest of musicologists at all, with only a few exceptions. Under the auspices of Alfred Rosenberg's office for overseeing ideological purity, the musicologist Herbert Gerigk compiled a comprehensive directory of Jews active in music primarily in Germany. This *Lexicon of Jews in Music* was intended as a practical guide for German musicians, providing them with up-to-date information on Jews in their midst to ensure that no one would inadvertently associate with them (Gerigk and Stengel 1940). Karl Blessinger then produced a monograph that claimed to be a more serious musicological confrontation with musical Judaism. The book, entitled *Mendelssohn, Meyerbeer, Mahler: Three Chapters of Judaism in Music as a Key to the History of Music in the Nineteenth Century* (Blessinger 1938), appeared first in 1938 and was reissued in 1944 with the more Wagneresque title *Judaism in Music*.

Following from Eichenauer's claim that it was only the nineteenth-century Jews who had exerted a destructive influence, Blessinger focused almost exclusively on that period, despite the inconsistency of extending the positive racial traits of the Germans back into prehistoric times while limiting Jewish "racial" destructiveness to the nineteenth and twentieth centuries. Once again, this focus on Jewish composers of the nineteenth century obviously took its cue from Wagner's polemics. Blessinger's vindictive tone, surpassing even that of Wagner or Eichenauer, exploited colorful biological metaphors, and although his approach made no attempt to apply racial "science" in any systematic way, he nevertheless tried to establish classifications for and identify stylistic tendencies of "Jewish" music. Blessinger labeled the Jew a "cultural parasite" that attacked its "host" in three stages: the "atomization" of European culture into small components that had lost their inner connection ("the Mendelssohn era"); the mixing of elements of various origins into a "colorful patchwork" ("the Meyerbeer era"); and the false posing of "Talmudic sophistry" as the highest achievement of Nordic philosophy in order to steer development toward Jewish goals ("the Mahler era"). These three composers also came to represent three distinct Jewish "types": Mendelssohn was the "assimilation Jew," Meyerbeer the "unscrupulous business Jew," and Mahler the fanatic type of "Eastern Jewish rabbi." Blessinger cast his net wide to find the final Jewish onslaught on German music in the Jew's use of the exotic to entice the public: the use of Eastern rhythms, jazz, quartal harmonies, and "oriental scales" (Mahler), along with such perversities as a fascination with hermaphrodites (in the films of "the Jew Chaplin" and the odd gestures of Jewish conductors) and the exhausting and narcotic effects of "Jewish rhythm" in jazz and dance music (Blessinger 1938: 16–17, 120–28).

Beyond Blessinger, however, musicologists were generally reluctant to take on the Jewish question. First, one could and did use the excuse that, thanks to Hitler, the Jewish threat had been removed (Blessinger 1941: 80); hence, the discussion was outdated. Attempts to define any race, including a Jewish race, furthermore proved impossible, and characterizing Jewish music was even trickier, as Wagner had already discovered (Katz 1980: 192–93). The musicologist Walther Vetter complained about the insufficient attention to the Jewish question, wanting to see more studies following Blessinger's model and demonstrating how German composers triumphantly "drowned out" Jewish voices (Vetter 1939–40: 106–7). Yet after the initial excitement, some musicologists even quietly reintegrated prominent Jewish figures into their histories of German music. Moser did so in his 1938 *Short History of German Music* by redeeming Mendelssohn and the violinist Joseph Joachim (his own godfather), explaining their excision from the repertory since 1933 as a matter of politics rather than a sound judgment of their contributions to German music (Moser 1938: 244–47, 296–97, 313).

Although these anti-Semitic attempts at approaching Jewish music "scientifically" were few and far between, the interwar years ironically proved to be the most fruitful period for the appearance of German-language publications on Jewish music. For many years thereafter, these works remained the only attempts of German musicologists and their associates to confront the issue of Jewish music. In the 1996 edition of the most authoritative German-language music reference work, *Die Musik in Geschichte und Gegenwart* (*MGG*), the entry on Jewish music attests to this curious lacuna. In the bibliography that follows the entry, aside from the work of Idelsohn, Lachmann, and Leonid Sabanejew, works on Jewish music published in Germany and Austria from 1900 all the way up to 1962 consist exclusively of those devoted all or in part to denigrating the Jews: Hans Pfitzner's 1920 attack on modernism (*The New Aesthetic of Musical Impotence*), Eichenauer's *Music and Race*, E. H. Müller's chapter in Fritsch's *Handbook of Anti-Semitism*, Gerigk and Stengel's *Lexicon*, and Hans Severus Ziegler's catalog for the 1938 "Degenerate Music" exhibit. A long respite thereafter is interrupted only by Hans Hickmann's 1962 volume of musical iconography in Egypt, Joseph Wulf's 1963 compendium of documents on music in the Third Reich (a concentration-camp survivor and member of the Jewish resistance, Wulf revealed scandalous details about the complicity of leading West German cultural figures under the Nazi system and was so hounded by the cultural establishment that he ended up taking his own life in 1974), Joel Walbe's 1975 dissertation, and a 1982 study on music and early Jewish theology by Karl E. Grözinger (Grözinger 1982; Braun, Cohen, Gerson-Kiwi,

and Avernary. 1996: cols. 1564–66). Blessinger is noticeably absent from the list; nevertheless, this group of reactionary and anti-Semitic works published in the first half of the twentieth century— some of them only marginally concerned with Jewish music—stand as the only examples of serious and systematic theoretical engagements with Jewish music from German intellectuals and apparently for that reason warrant inclusion in an otherwise selective bibliography of research on Jewish music. German musicology remained at the forefront of the discipline even after World War II and beyond, yet it never opened its doors to the field of Jewish music research flourishing elsewhere in the world.

From Holocaust to "Renaissance"

If musicologists failed to make pronouncements on Jewish music or provide guidance for ideologues, practical questions nevertheless had to be addressed once Jews were deemed enemies of the state. As German Jews gradually lost their human rights and started disappearing from their homes, policy decisions had to be reached with regard to determining the nature of Jewish culture. Nazi officials organized the Jewish Culture League (Jüdischer Kulturbund) to isolate Jews from participation in German cultural life, setting up theaters, musical groups, lecture series, and other cultural outlets for Jewish performers and Jewish audiences exclusively. Those overseeing the Kulturbund placed restrictions on the performance of German works but encouraged works by Jews and foreigners as long as their content was not anti-German. The Jewish participants and Nazi censors alike nevertheless ran into difficulties in determining which music was Jewish. On one occasion censors rejected the Kulturbund's request to perform Mahler because an inexperienced Nazi subordinate insisted that the composer of *Songs of a Wayfarer* must have been Aryan.

At a national Jüdischer Kulturbund conference in 1936, musicians, critics, educators, and scholars debated the parameters for defining Jewish music. They reached a consensus that synagogue cantillation and Jewish folk music were unequivocally Jewish; but as cultured, bourgeois Germans, the Jews in the Kulturbund felt that such music did not belong in the concert hall. In the end, the Kulturbund's programs consisted mostly of art music from the nineteenth century, allowing for many hearings of the "racially" Jewish Mendelssohn, Meyerbeer, Offenbach, and Mahler, with some attention also to contemporary Jewish composers (Sponheuer 1994: 115–31).

One further pragmatic inquiry into Jewish music, or at least into Jewish themes in German music, raised its ugly head in debates shortly thereafter and led to some frightening observations about the destiny of the Jews. The Nazi authorities had given express permission to choral groups to continue to perform all of Handel's oratorios even if they were based on Old Testament texts that seemed to glorify the Jews. After the Nuremberg Laws and the 1938 pogroms euphemistically known as *Kristallnacht*, however, this inconsistency troubled ardent Nazi ideologues. Eichenauer, himself an SS man, expressed his discomfort with the hypocrisy of singing the praises

of the Hebrews while internalizing the belief that the Jews were the enemy (Eichenauer 1941). How, he complained, can one continue to rejoice in David's slaying of Goliath when every Hitler Youth member has learned that the Philistines are the Germans' racial kin? Moser, too, offered his views on the controversy, but he also hoped that once "we Germans have the Jewish problem far behind us," the oratorios glorifying the Jews could be revived as something "neutralized" to the point of being regarded as "exotic" and "ancient" (Moser 1941: 52; Potter 2001).

Moser's chilling prophecy was, of course, fulfilled: just like the ancient civilizations of the Near East, Jews became extinct in Germany, leaving behind only artifacts that attested to their once-vibrant existence. The Jews of Germany and their music would indeed become an object of interest for their "exotic" nature before century's end, but only after a long and uncomfortable period of silence. Moser would come to learn directly that a respectable amount of time would have to pass before anyone in Germany could talk about the music of the Jews. In his 1,000-page book *The Music of the German Tribes*, which appeared in 1957, Moser referred injudiciously to "Berlin Israelites," "Rhenish Jewry," the "emphatically Jewish Arnold Schoenberg," the "Jewish master Gustav Mahler," and the "three-quarter Israelite Arnold Mendelssohn," a reference to the second cousin of Felix Mendelssohn. In some places Moser even held on to the Nazi-era practice of placing names of Jews in square brackets (Moser 1957). Even though Moser tried to argue that his presentation was meant to embrace German Jews as contributors to German musical culture and to write them into a history from which they had been excluded, he was publicly denounced for his indiscretions. The German musicological society refused to publish a review of the book in its journal, and Moser was forced to withdraw from a number of international organization and projects.

The silence persisted into the next decades, and not only out of embarrassment or discomfort, but possibly also owing to the lack of any Jewish presence in postwar German musicology. With the exception of a few Jewish émigré musicologists who had left Germany as communists and received a hero's welcome in East Germany, there appear to have been no attempts whatsoever to invite other émigrés back to fill positions vacated by colleagues killed in action or banned for their Nazi sympathies, or to fill positions at newly created universities.

Jewish music did eventually experience a renaissance in Germany, but scholars approached their limited engagement with it very cautiously, taking care not to overreach the boundaries of "strict" musicology. The German counterpart of the student rebellions of the 1960s was motivated not only by a desire for social change, but also by a need to break the silence about the entire twelve-year Nazi period that the parents of this generation had so vigilantly guarded. This led to intense involvement in pursuing the truth, and in the musicological realm and elsewhere it translated into a fascination with the victims of National Socialism. The safest and least unpleasant confrontation with Jewish music came initially in the form of so-called exile studies, which al-

lowed musicologists to remain within their traditional parameters by rediscovering German composers of art music who had in some way been "victimized" by the Nazi regime (including such problematic cases as Paul Hindemith, who remained ambivalent about his departure from Germany, and Anton Webern, who had openly declared his support for Nazi policies) (see Kater 1997: 72–74; 2000: 31–56). In the 1980s entire task forces labored to reacquaint themselves with composers who had left Germany, some of them Jewish and some not, and produced a number of monographs, conference proceedings, recordings, and archival projects. This was followed by a bolder confrontation in the late 1980s and early 1990s with musical activities in the concentration camps, with most attention focused on art-music composers such as Viktor Ullmann and Pavel Haas. There one came closest to investigating music of a truly Jewish nature: many of the condemned composers discovered Jewish music for themselves for the first time and incorporated Yiddish and Hebrew themes into their works (see, e.g., John 1991).

Was this approach as a whole, however, really bringing German scholars closer to knowing something about Jewish music? Or was this just the path of least resistance, studying the victims of Nazism, some Jewish, some not, but all producers of concert-hall music? Some of these objects of curiosity may have been Jewish by heritage, or indeed only by the "racial" designation imposed on them by the Nazis, but most of their music was generally indistinguishable from that of their non-Jewish contemporaries. Still, it seemed safer from a musicological standpoint to take an interest in Jewish composers who perpetuated some form of the noble tradition of high German art than to learn about those who wrote Jewish liturgical music or even those who went on to succeed on Broadway or in Hollywood, or to engage in any forays into Jewish folk music or the music of ancient Israel. Jewish music was initially approachable only if it accommodated familiar parameters and did not challenge German musicologists' preconceived notions of high art and established areas of research. When the German scholar Walter Salmen did try in 1991 to conceive of a more comprehensive history of Jewish music and musicians to fill gaps in the knowledge, his study was criticized for being mile-wide and inch-deep (Rubin 1993–94). In little more than 100 pages, Salmen attempted to compile a survey of Jewish musicians and dance troupes in Europe from the thirteenth through the twentieth centuries. This was a start, to be sure, but Salmen was criticized for failing to grasp the enormity of the project and the complexity of the subject (Salmen 1991).

If German musicology has been slow to embrace the study of Jewish music, a grass-roots interest in Jewish music has nevertheless made itself known. Following the "Jewish chic" trend taking hold in Germany, a 1998 issue of the well-known music journal *Neue Zeitschrift für Musik* took up the theme of "Klezmorim and Others" and included articles on klezmer groups in Europe and the United States, on Israeli composers, and on biblical music. However, this issue also reiterated more familiar and even subtly disturbing themes: articles on the Jewish exile art-music composers

Stefan Wolpe and Josef Tal, contributions on Paul Hindemith's alleged musical reaction to the Holocaust, and another article whose relationship to the rest of the issue is not explicitly stated— an item on Felix and Fanny Mendelssohn. Thus, while this issue paid unprecedented attention to a genre of music recently popularized as Jewish (klezmer) and explored other aspects of Jewish music, it also fell back on familiar themes: "good Germans" such as Hindemith, Jewish art-music composers such as Wolpe, and even some of Wagner's "reprehensible Jews," the Mendelssohns, who had in fact converted to Christianity.

In a perhaps more earnest vein, a Web site has been set up by students at the University of Duisburg that offers a basic introduction to Jewish music and strives to promote interest and initiate research projects. This modest site of the Nigun Society for the Encouragement and Research of Jewish Music, founded in 1995, offers a thumbnail sketch of the varieties of Jewish music; peddles a CD of synagogue cantillation by Hungarian cantors; describes plans to build a library and archive and conduct an oral history project to record and transcribe *piyyutim* (paraliturgical songs) in collaboration with American scholars; and advertises a competition for the performance of Jewish music, with all concert proceeds going to the building of a new synagogue in Duisburg. The stated reasons for the competition are a poignant expression of a deep sense of loss: "The competition will serve to sharpen [music] students' awareness of the loss. . . . In addition to the immeasurable sorrow, Jewish culture suffered great damages. The competition should offer the challenge to assume the heritage of Jewish composers and respond to their eradication with new life" (*Nigun Verein* 1995).

This brings us back to Gordon Craig's identification of the Jewish-German kinship. It would be interesting to know what happened to Poe's character after he killed his alter ego. We can speculate that he might have spent the rest of his life tortured by guilt. We can also imagine that this character experienced the loss similar to what we hear about when twins are separated at birth. The responses such experiences generate all attest to an inexplicable sense of incompleteness throughout the lives of separated twins, even if they were never told that they had a twin. They are inevitably amazed at the similar habits and behaviors they share once they are reunited. This visceral need to know more about the Jews and their culture overshadows even the recent criticisms leveled against the "Holocaust industry." Prompted by Daniel Goldhagen's controversial book (Goldhagen 1996), by the debates about Holocaust memorials (e.g., Young 1993), by the growing number of interdisciplinary conferences devoted to Jewish music and musicians in Central Europe (see, e.g., John and Zimmermann 2004 for the proceedings from two of these), and by the renewed demands for compensation to victims of Nazism from Swiss banks and German industries, critics in Germany have begun to question the emphasis on the fate of the Jews in the Holocaust. The speech by Martin Walser in 1998 at the Frankfurt Book Fair expressing Germany's weariness of the Holocaust enterprise, as well as other reactions by intellectuals to the un-

abating attention to the fate of the Jews and the neglect of other ethnic and political victims of National Socialism, have unfortunately even led some to yield to the temptation of attributing this emphasis to a predominance of Jews contributing to Holocaust scholarship, even verging on implying the behind-the-scenes operation of a "Jewish conspiracy." Their suspicions and criticisms, nevertheless, are countered by the Nigun Society and other sincere gestures of striving to rediscover Germany's lost Jewish community, a movement that has been compared to the American fascination with Native American culture.

Why does the Holocaust still manage to capture the imagination of new generations of Germans, despite the weariness expressed by middle-aged veterans of the 1960s youth movement? Perhaps the Holocaust will always engage successive generations because the revelation of the destruction of European Jewry by Germany and its allies can be said to have shaken two pillars of the very foundations of Western civilization: Christianity and German culture. It revealed, first, the unimaginable extremes to which ancient anti-Semitic teachings of the church could be taken. It also showed that a nation so long respected for its lofty accomplishments in science, literature, philosophy, and music—the nation of "poets and thinkers"—could paradoxically commit barbarous acts. Additionally, though, the destruction of German Jewry by fellow Germans can be considered a form of fratricide. Like Poe's character, Germans resented those who resembled and complemented them the most—musically, intellectually, even ideologically—and they committed the unthinkable act of murdering their *Doppelgänger*. The increasing focus among postwar generations of Germans on Jewish victims of the Holocaust and their lost culture is a way for both Germans and Jews to confront this family tragedy, to come to terms with the loss, and to try to write the missing chapters of their shared cultural history.

One of those missing chapters will clearly have to be devoted to Jewish music. German musicologists have thus far avoided the topic for a variety of reasons. In the early years of the discipline, Jewish music failed to attract the attention of musicologists despite intensive research activity among Russian scholars on Jewish folk music and German-Austrian cantors on synagogue music, as well as a corpus of nineteenth-century German-language works on liturgy, history, and the music of ancient Israel (see the appendix). German Jewish musicologists, themselves firmly rooted in the established confines of German musicological research, for the most part saw no need or felt no desire to initiate scholarly inquiry into Jewish music. Their reasons may simply have been a legacy of assimilation and a need to "blend in," but they may also have been motivated by the discipline's overall desire to promote its scholarly pedigree and distance itself from the work of music practitioners, because the bulk of research on Jewish music to that point, at least in the German-language realm, had been the work of cantors. Once German Jewish scholars started to receive messages that they were no longer regarded as Germans, that their work on Protestant and other German music was no longer welcome, and that they should devote themselves to Jewish

music, the more fortunate among them perceived the dangers that lay ahead and quickly fled. Their responses to this ostracism were varied: some held fast to their Germanness and love of high culture and resisted the unfamiliar musical language foisted upon them as "Jewish music," while others discovered the vast world of Jewish music and devoted the rest of their careers to studying it.

Simultaneously, however, a new legacy for German musicology was in the making, but one which could hardly be pursued beyond World War II. A literature on Jewish music came into being for the purpose of demonstrating the shortcomings and even destructiveness of Jews. Taking on the mantle of scholarship and attempting to build a science of Jewish music on the foundations of anti-Semitic polemics of the previous century, this literature remained for a long time thereafter as the only examples of German musicological inquiry into Jewish music. It served by default as the scholarly foundation for the study of Jewish music, as is implied in the bibliography of the most recent *MGG* entry, but it could hardly offer a point of departure for postwar German scholars to investigate Jewish music. The distasteful legacy of anti-Semitic music scholarship had the effect of making any engagements with Jewish music virtually taboo and diverted German musicology's attention from the otherwise flourishing research activity in Israel, the United States, and elsewhere. Still, Jewish music is a component of German and European music history and warrants a place in German musicological inquiry. Hans Joachim Moser made a clumsy and ill-timed attempt to suggest this in 1957, although scholars such as Walter Salmen had more success in acknowledging the phenomenon and initiating the process. All the same, it will take some time for German musicology to get beyond the stigma left by the brief but effective racist-motivated forays into Jewish music research that began with Wagner and culminated in the Holocaust.

❧

::: **APPENDIX** :::

German-Language Writings on Jewish Music, 1825 to ca. 1900

1825   Saalschütz, Jos. L. (Joseph Levin). *Von der Form der Hebräischen Poesie: Nebst einer Abhandlung über die Musik der Hebräer.* Königsberg: A. W. Unzer.

1829   Saalschütz, Jos. L. (Joseph Levin). *Geschichte und Würdigung der Musik bei den Hebräern, im Verhältniss zur sonstigen Ausbildung dieser Kunst in alter und neuer Zeit, nebst e. Anhange über d. hebräische Orgel.* Berlin: G. Fincke.

1834   Schneider, Peter Joseph. *Biblisch-geschichtliche Darstellung der hebräischen Musik deren Ursprung, Zunahme, Glanzpunkt, Abnahme und gänzlicher Verfall, mit Bezugnahme auf die den Israeliten Sprachlich verwandten Völker.* Bonn: Dunst.

1867   Arends, Leopold Alexander Friedrich. *Über den Sprachgesang der Vorzeit und die Herstellbarkeit der althebräischen Vocalmusik: Mit entsprechenden Musikbeilagen.* Berlin: Friedr. Schulze's Buchhandlung.

1879   Goldschmidt, Israel. *Der jüdische Cantor in der jüdischen Geschichte: oder, Die Musik im Judenthum des Mittelalters.* Briesen: S. Blaustein.

1884   Rabe, Martin. *Die "musica sacra" der alten Hebräer, im Lichte der Ästhetik und der Geschichte.* Berlin: Neuenhahn.

1886   Singer, Josef. *Die Tonarten des traditionellen Synagogengesanges (Steiger): Ihr Verhältnis zu den Kirchentonarten und den Tonarten der vorchristlichen Musikperiode.* Vienna: E. M. Wetzler.

1893   Birnbaum, Eduard. *Jüdische Musiker am Hofe von Mantua von 1542–1628.* Vienna: M. Waizner.

1897   Nobel, Josef. *Die Orgelfrage.* Mainz: Joh. Wirth.

1898   Breslauer, Emil. *Sind originale Synagogen- und Volksmelodien bei den Juden geschichtlich nachweisbar? Vortrag gehalten im Verein für jüdische Geschichte und Litteratur in Berlin.* Leipzig: Breitkopf und Härtel.

1899   Köberle, Justus. *Die Tempelsänger im Alten Testament, ein Versuch zur israelitischen und jüdischen Cultusgeschichte.* Erlangen: Fr. Junge.

1903   Gressmann, Hugo. *Musik und Musikinstrumente im Alten Testament eine religionsgeschichtliche Studie.* Gieszen: J. Ricker.

1906   Leitner, Franz. *Der gottesdienstliche Volksgesang im jüdischen und christlichen Altertum: Ein Beitrag zur jüdischen und christlichen Kultgeschichte.* Freiburg im Breisgau: Herder.

::: **WORKS CITED** :::

Applegate, Celia, and Pamela Potter, eds. 2002. *Music and German National Identity.* Chicago: University of Chicago Press.

Avenary, Hanoch, Bathja Bayer, and Yohanan Boehm. 1971. "Jewish Music." In *Encyclopedia Judaica,* vol. 12, cols. 554–678. Jerusalem: Macmillan, 1971.

Blessinger, Karl. 1938. *Mendelssohn, Meyerbeer, Mahler: Drei Kapitel Judentum in der Musik als Schlüssel zur Musikgeschichte des 19. Jahrhunderts*. Berlin: Hahnefeld.

———. 1941. "Der Weg zur Einheit der deutschen Musik." *Deutschlands Erneuerung* 25: 75–84.

Braun, Joachim, Judith Cohen, Edith Gerson-Kiwi, and Hanoch Avenary. 1996–. "Jüdische Musik." In Ludwig Finscher, ed., *Die Musik in Geschichte und Gegenwart*, Sachteil, vol. 4, cols. 1511–69. 2nd ed. Kassel: Bärenreiter, 1996.

Brinkmann, Reinhold, and Christoph Wolff, eds. 1999. *Driven into Paradise: The Musical Migration from Nazi Germany to the United States*. Berkeley: University of California Press.

Cahan, Judah Loeb. 1952. *Shtudyes vegn yiddisher folksschafung*. New York: YIVO: Yiddish Scientific Institute.

Chamberlain, Houston Stewart. 1911. *The Foundations of the Nineteenth Century*. Trans. by John Lees. London and New York: J. Lane.

Craig, Gordon A. 1982. *The Germans*. New York: New American Library.

Eichenauer, Richard. 1932. *Musik und Rasse*. Munich: Lehmann.

———. 1941. "Händel und das alte Testament." *Musik in Jugend und Volk* 4 (10): 227–31.

Fritsch, Theodor. 1933. *Handbuch der Judenfrage: Die wichtigsten Tatsachen zur Beurteilung des jüdischen Volkes*. Leipzig: Hammer-Verlag.

Gerigk, Herbert, and Theophil Stengel, eds. 1940. *Lexikon der Juden in der Musik*. Berlin: Hahnefeld. (Veröffentlichungen des Instituts der NSDAP zur Erforschung der Judenfrage 2.)

Gerson-Kiwi, Edith. 1938. "Jerusalem Archive for Oriental Music." *Musica Hebraica* 1–2: 40–42.

Ginsburg, S. M., and P. S. Marek. 1901. *Evreiskie narodnye pesni v Rossii* [Jewish Folk Songs in Russia]. St. Petersburg: Voskhod.

Goldhagen, Daniel. 1996. *Hitler's Willing Executioners: Ordinary Germans and the Holocaust*. New York: Alfred A. Knopf.

Gradenwitz, Peter. 1949. *The Music of Israel: Its Rise and Growth through 5000 Years*. New York: W. W. Norton.

Grözinger, Karl E. 1982. *Musik und Gesang in der Theologie der frühen jüdischen Literatur: Talmud, Midrasch, Mystik*. Tübingen: J. C. B. Mohr [Paul Siebeck].

Idelsohn, A. Z. 1917. *Phonographierte Gesänge und Aussprachsproben des Hebräischen der jemenitischen, persischen und syrischen Juden*. Vienna: Alfred Hölder. (Mitteilung der Phonogramm-Archivs-Kommission der Kaiserlichen Akademie der Wissenschaften in Wien, 35.)

John, Eckhard. 1991. "Musik und Konzentrationslager: Eine Annäherung." *Archiv für Musikwissenschaft* 48: 1–36.

———, and Heidy Zimmermann, eds. 2004. *Jüdische Musik? Fremdbilder—Eigenbilder*. Cologne: Böhlau.

Kater, Michael H. 1997. *The Twisted Muse: Musicians and Their Music in the Third Reich*. New York: Oxford University Press.

———. 2000. *Composers of the Nazi Era: Eight Portraits*. New York: Oxford University Press.

Katz, Jacob. 1980. *From Prejudice to Destruction: Anti-Semitism, 1700–1933*. Cambridge, Mass.: Harvard University Press.

———. 1984. "German Culture and the Jews." *Commentary* 77 (2): 54–59.

Katz, Ruth. 2003. *"The Lachmann Problem": An Unsung Chapter in Comparative Musicology*. Jerusalem: Magnes Press of the Hebrew University.

Lach, Robert. 1923. "Das Rassenproblem in der vergleichenden Musikwissenschaft." *Berichte des Forschungsinstituts für Osten und Orient* 3: 107–22.

Lachmann, Robert. 1940. *Jewish Cantillation and Song in the Isle of Djerba*. Jerusalem: Archives of Oriental Music of the Hebrew University. Publication of the full original German text: *Gesänge der Juden auf der Insel Djerba*. Ed. by Edith Gerson-Kiwi. Jerusalem: Magnes Press of the Hebrew University, 1976. (Yuval Monograph Series, 7.)

Lechleitner, Gerda, ed. 2005. *The Collection of Abraham Zvi Idelsohn (1911–1913)*. 3 CDs and CD-ROM, plus booklet. Vienna: Verlag der Österreichischen Akademie der Wissenschaften. (Tondokumente aus dem Phonogrammarchiv der Österreichischen Akademie der Wissenschaften, Gesamtausgabe der Historischen Bestände 1899–1950, Series 9.)

Lorenz, Alfred. 1938. "Musikwissenschaft und Judenfrage." *Die Musik* 31: 177–79.

Mendelsohn, Ezra. 1993. "On the Jewish Presence in Nineteenth-Century European Musical Life." In Ezra Mendelsohn, ed., *Modern Jews and Their Musical Agendas*, 3–16. New York: Oxford University Press. (Studies in Contemporary Jewry, 9.)

Moser, Hans Joachim. 1924. *Geschichte der deutschen Musik: Vom Auftreten Beethovens bis zur Gegenwart.* 3rd ed. Vol. 2, pt. 2. Stuttgart and Berlin: Cotta.

———. 1938. *Kleine deutsche Musikgeschichte.* Stuttgart: Cotta.

———. 1941. *Georg Friedrich Händel.* Cassel: Bärenreiter.

———. 1957. *Die Musik der deutschen Stämme.* Vienna: Wancura Verlag.

Mosse, George. 1964. *The Crisis of German Ideology: Intellectual Origins of the Third Reich.* New York: Grosset & Dunlap.

Nigun Verein zur Förderung und Erforschung jüdischer Musik. 1995–. http://sti1.uni-duisburg.de/netzwerke/gastseiten/nigun/index.xml (accessed 1 October 2007).

Potter, Pamela M. 1998. *Most German of the Arts: Musicology and Society from the Weimar Republic to the End of Hitler's Reich.* New Haven, Conn.: Yale University Press.

———. 1999. "From Jewish Exile in Germany to German Scholar in America: Alfred Einstein's Emigration." In Brinkmann and Wolff, *Driven into Paradise,* 298–321.

———. 2001. "The Politicization of Handel's Oratorios in the Weimar Republic, the Third Reich, and the Early Years of the German Democratic Republic." *Musical Quarterly* 85: 311–41.

Pulzer, Peter. 1992. *Jews and the German State: The Political History of a Minority, 1848–1933.* Oxford: Blackwell.

Rubin, Joel. 1993–94. Review of "*. . . denn die Fiedel macht das Fest*": *Jüdische Musikanten und Tänzer vom 13. bis 20. Jahrhundert,* by Walter Salmen. *Music Judaica* 13: 98–108.

Salmen, Walter. 1991. "*. . . denn die Fiedel macht das Fest*": *Jüdische Musikanten und Tänzer vom 13. bis 20. Jahrhundert.* Innsbruck: Edition Helbling.

Sponheuer, Bernd. 1994. "Musik auf einer 'kulturellen und physischen Insel': Musik als Überlebensmittel im Jüdischen Kulturbund 1933–1941." In Horst Weber, ed. *Musik in der Emigration 1933–1945: Verfolgung—Vertreibung—Rückwirkung,* 108–35. Stuttgart: Verlag J. B. Metzler.

Vetter, Walther. 1939–40. "Zur Erforschung des Deutschen in der Musik." *Deutsche Musikkultur* 4: 101–7.

"Von Klezmorim und Anderen." 1998. Special issue of *Neue Zeitschrift für Musik* 3 (May–June).

Wagner, Richard. 1995 [1869]. "Judaism in Music." In Wagner, *Judaism in Music and Other Essays.* Trans. by William Ashton Ellis, 75–122. Lincoln: University of Nebraska Press.

Walbe, Joel. 1975. *Der Gesang Israels und seine Quellen: Ein Beitrag zur hebräischen Musikologie.* Hamburg: Christians Verlag.

Young, James E. 1993. *The Textures of Meaning: Holocaust Memorials and Meaning.* New Haven, Conn.: Yale University Press.

4

Echoes from beyond Europe

Music and the Beta Israel Transformation

::: KAY KAUFMAN SHELEMAY

Among the more obscure convergences of European and Jewish history is one that occurred mainly outside Europe, in Ethiopia: that of Europeans with the Ethiopian people historically called Beta Israel or Falasha, today known as the Ethiopian Jews in Israel.[1] In this essay I will trace the historical process that culminated in 1991 with what might be termed the end of Falasha/Beta Israel history in Ethiopia and the final transplantation of the Ethiopian Jewish community in Israel. Central to this process was the transformation of Beta Israel ritual life and practice to fit European Jewish models, one that can be traced through its musical content.

How to tell this tale, in fact, presents a central challenge, as we are soberly reminded by the encounters of the Europeans with peoples of the New World. These encounters are recalled by Europeans within narratives of discovery and by New World peoples as tales of conquest (Robertson 1992: 9). I have chosen here to use the metaphor of *midrash* (literally, interpretation of scriptural meaning) because it provides a flexible, multivocal framework for an explanatory process. The choice of *midrash*, too, locates this discussion of encounter within an explicitly Judaic framework, resonant with present-day Beta Israel and Jewish history.

According to Jacob Neusner, there are three types of *midrash*. The first entails taking a series of individual verses and linking the sequence in which they appear as the organizing principle of a "sustained discourse." The second employs the reading of individual verses to test and validate a larger-scale proposition. The third type of *midrash* directs attention not to the concrete statements, but to the larger narrative of which they are part, recasting a story "in such a way as to make new and urgent points through the retelling" (Neusner 1993: 54).

My *midrash* partakes of all three types of interpretation, although scriptural text plays only a small role in the interaction of belief, music, and history traced here. I construct my narrative by linking a series of events over large spans of time and space. Each link gives rise to new liturgical and musical discourses. I hope that the telling of this story will highlight the relation of the Beta Israel with modern Europe, a little-discussed aspect of Beta Israel history that had a transformative impact on a people, their religious traditions, their history, and, of course, their music.

This case study intersects with but does not duplicate other narratives of Jewish modernity. It is a much longer story, commencing well before the emergence of European modernism and continuing long after the cataclysm of the Holocaust stilled the voices of so many European Jews. It moves beyond the local, traveling back and forth across geographical space, encompassing both first contact and continued interaction, which were born not of serendipity or happenstance, but of purposeful union. Finally, in contrast to many other local modernities, played out in increasingly secular contexts, the story of the Beta Israel remains throughout firmly anchored in the realm of the sacred.

The essay is divided into four sections. I first move backward in time to situate the broader historical setting and the Beta Israel past in Ethiopia

that led to the encounters with Europe, beginning in the mid-nineteenth century. The second section, commencing about 1855 or 1860, will explore how Europe came to Ethiopia, and the Beta Israel to Europe. The third part picks up the narrative post-1950, observing the indirect yet substantial impact of the Holocaust on the Beta Israel. The final section, starting in 1991, will arrive at the end of Beta Israel history and the birth of the Ethiopian Jews. Throughout the essay, musical fragments anchor and exemplify each historical moment.

The Beta Israel within Ethiopian History

It is difficult to separate the telling of Beta Israel history from the battles that have been fought over its interpretation in scholarship and the broader world of religious politics.[2] I begin with the centrality of the Five Books of Moses in its Ethiopic translation, the *Orit*, because most perceptions of Beta Israel history from both within and without are grounded in it.

At the center of Beta Israel notions of their own past is a myth or "myth-legend" (Abbink 1990) with biblical roots: the story of the visit of the Queen of Sheba to King Solomon, sketched in 1 Kings 10:1–13 and 2 Chronicles 9:1–12. In brief, the biblical story tells of the Queen of Sheba, who having heard of the fame of Solomon, comes to test him with riddles, bearing gifts of spices, gold, and precious stones. The encounter ends with the king giving to the queen "everything she wanted and asked for, in addition to what King Solomon gave her out of his royal bounty. Then she and her attendants left and returned to her own land" (*JPS Hebrew–English Tanakh* 1999: 737).

This tale of encounter is a deep aspect of the Ethiopian worldview and was recorded and elaborated in the thirteenth century (although it may have had earlier roots) in a document known as the *Kebra Nagast* (The Glory of the Kings). The *Kebra Nagast* recounts the visit of the queen of Ethiopia (Makeda) to King Solomon; the birth of their son, Menelik, after the queen's return to Ethiopia; Menelik's visit years later to his father; and Menelik's return with the ark of the covenant to Ethiopia. This tale became the Ethiopian national epic and legitimized the overthrow of one Christian dynasty by another in 1270, which subsequently became known as the "Solomonic" dynasty (Levine 1973). The *Kebra Negast* has also served to legitimize the "Israelite lineage" of Christian Ethiopian kings, providing "a founding myth" for the royal house and its people (Abbink 1990: 405–6). Understood both as "real history and eternal truth" (ibid.: 407), this tale provides an origin myth for both Christian Ethiopians and for the Beta Israel (ibid.: 411). The Beta Israel also recount this narrative, elaborating the story to describe Menelik's return to Ethiopia, accompanied by learned men and priests who are said to have joined with the Beta Israel (Asres Yayeh 1995: 120–21).

We will return to discussion of the *Kebra Negast* below, but it is important here to emphasize that this narrative at once links the Beta Israel with Christian Ethiopia and with Jewish sources.

In this same manner, the *Orit* has provided a central source for Beta Israel and Christian Ethiopian religious practice and identity throughout their shared history. Modernism is perceived as a secularizing force, yet this tale plays out almost exclusively within a religious domain (Crummey 2000). Thus, the *Orit* both lent legitimacy to the Solomonic dynasty through its claims of Judaic ancestry and provided a core of observances for Ethiopian Christians and Jews alike (including such traditions as the Saturday Sabbath, animal sacrifice, and circumcision). The legend also became the basis for the Beta Israel's twentieth-century claim to Jewish identity. Because Beta Israel religious practice and liturgy lack so many important Jewish elements and because the Beta Israel had no knowledge of post-biblical Jewish writings and practices, their adherence to biblical customs and perpetuation of a history with biblical ties became a central element in discussions of their identity by outsiders as well.

The importance of the *Orit* to Beta Israel worship has since the late nineteenth century been emphasized in writings ranging from the scholarly to the popular. Some emphasize the "fanatical" adherence of the Beta Israel to the teachings of the Torah to counterbalance the absence of Talmudic sources among them ("Jews of Ethiopia" 1972). Beta Israel biblical practices were also frequently credited with defining Beta Israel consciousness as a community and with having buttressed the Beta Israel's will to survive over the centuries despite their marginality as a minority religious community and low-status metalworkers and potters within Ethiopia (Messing 1982: 24). The importance of the *Orit* in Beta Israel practice, especially when wedded to widely circulated medieval legends in Europe connecting them with the lost tribe of Dan (Kaplan 1992: 24–26), further provided a basis for their recognition, after long debate, as Jews. In 1975 they were acknowledged as a "lost tribe" and granted automatic citizenship in Israel under the 1950 Law of Return (Rapoport and Siegel 1975).

Musical Interlude I: Monastic Voices

In striking contrast to the emphasis on the *Orit* within Beta Israel belief and legend, as well as its frequent mention by outsiders as the hallmark of Beta Israel religious practice, there is no regular, cyclical reading of biblical portions within the Beta Israel liturgy. Here we find a major difference between Beta Israel liturgical and musical practice and that of other Jews, who from an early date chanted portions from the Five Books of Moses as part of their weekly observances.

Before the encounter with Europeans, the prayers of the Beta Israel liturgy drew on quotations from the book of Psalms and other biblical texts, along with segments from Beta Israel literature. Although most of the Beta Israel liturgy is in the Ge'ez language (classical Ethiopic), some texts were set in an Ethiopian vernacular (Agawiñña) that the Beta Israel once spoke. The structural core of the Beta Israel liturgy is also strikingly different from that of other Jewish traditions: it is a monastic office, said to been conveyed to the Beta Israel by Ethiopian Christian monks who joined their community beginning in the fifteenth century (Shelemay 1989).

These same monks are also credited with bringing the *Orit* to the Beta Israel, introducing laws of monastic purity, building the Falasha prayer house, and organizing their liturgical cycle. In short, Ethiopian Christian monks were said to have introduced virtually all surviving Beta Israel religious practices. Although I cannot delve here into the complex history of Beta Israel monasticism and its heavily Judaized Ethiopian Christian sources during the fifteenth century, it is important to note that religious authority, as well as transmission of ritual orders among the Beta Israel, was held until the twentieth century by the Beta Israel's own revered monks, who trained priests and liturgical musicians within the Beta Israel religious community. To explore one of the monastic prayers that constituted the Beta Israel liturgy until the departure from Ethiopia opens a window on a musical and liturgical tradition that pre-dated Beta Israel contact with Europe.

We can take as an example the monastic prayer Kalhu Kwellu Mala'ekt, chanted during the Beta Israel morning liturgy before dawn (see fig. 4.1). This text, possibly of Syriac origin, is shared with the Ethiopian Christian liturgy (Shelemay 1989: 115). The division of the topography of heaven into seven layers is thought to draw on the Ascension of Isaiah (ibid.: 133 n. 54). The gong (*qachel*) ostinato accompanying the prayer and the alternation between soloist and chorus are typical of performance practice in much of the traditional Beta Israel liturgy.

Figure 4.1 "Kalhu kwellu mala'ekt" (All the Angels Proclaimed). Transcription and translation from Shelemay 1989: 268–69.

kalḥu kwellu malā'ekt wayeblu qeddus eg"ṣābā'ot
All the angels proclaimed and said, holy Lord of hosts.

kalḥu kwellu malā'ekt bakāle' samāy qeddus eg"ṣābā'ot
All the angels in the second heaven proclaimed, holy Lord of hosts.

kalḥu kwellu malā'ekt bakāle' samāy ekkut eg"ekkut ba'akkwatētu
All the angels in the second heaven proclaimed, the Lord is praised, praised, in his praise.

kalḥu kwellu malā'ekt baśāles samāy gerum eg"bagermā sebḥatihu
All the angels in the third heaven proclaimed, awesome is the Lord, in the splendor of his glory.

kalḥu kwellu malā'ekt barābe' samāy masta'agges eg"zabeka ḥāyl
All the angels in the fourth heaven proclaimed, the Lord is patient, you in whom there is power.

kalḥu kwellu malā'ekt baḫāmes samāy qeddus qeddus eg"waḥeyāw adonāy
All the angels in the fifth heaven proclaimed, holy, holy is the Lord, and Adonay is alive.

kalḥu kwellu malā'ekt basādes samāy manbareka esāt kellul hāllēluyā
All the angels in the sixth heaven proclaimed, your throne is compassed by fire, hallelujah.

kalḥu kwellu malā'ekta aryām basābe' samāy ba'aḥadu qāl nesēbbeḥakka wana'akkwetakka
All the angels of the highest in the seventh heaven proclaimed in one voice, we glorify you and we praise you.

anta tāḥayyu kwellu zanafs amān laka yesaggedu kwellu malā'ekta samāyāt
You make everything that has life live, truly all the angels of heaven worship you.

Both Beta Israel oral traditions and Ethiopian written sources trace the arrival of monasticism— along with monastic prayers—to the Beta Israel during the fifteenth century. Before that time, we find only scattered written references to rebels and Judaized monastic groups (both called *ayhud*, literally "Jew") who left the church, moved to outlying areas, and founded monasteries among peoples not under church control (Kaplan 1992). Musical and textual evidence from the Falasha liturgy (see Shelemay 1989), historical research by Kaplan (1992) and James Quirin (1992), and anthropological inquiry by Jon Abbink (1984, 1990) all point to the fifteenth and sixteenth centuries as the critical period for the religious and political genesis of the Ethiopian community that came to be known as the Beta Israel or Falasha. Following their loss of land during the rule of Emperor Yeshaq (1413–30), we can trace from the sixteenth century forward the first references in the Ethiopian chronicles to the Falasha. Lacking land rights, they soon began working as smiths and potters (Quirin 1992: 62–65), occupations that sustained them until their departure from Ethiopia.

Europe comes to the Beta Israel—and the Beta Israel to Europe

Only in the mid-nineteenth century did Europe come to the Beta Israel. The Jesuits were present in Ethiopia from 1555 to 1633, but they did not directly affect the Beta Israel; it was the arrival of the Christian missionaries in northern Ethiopia in the nineteenth century that opened a new chapter in Ethiopian and Beta Israel history. These Christian missionaries first sought to transform Beta Israel tradition according to Western Christian models. The first, in 1830, was the Church Missionary Society agent Samuel Gobat, a graduate of the Basel Mission training school who was ordained in London (Crummey 1972: 29–31). Several missionaries followed, including Martin Flad, who entered Ethiopia in 1855 and founded a mission in Gondar, the provincial capital, located near a large concentration of Beta Israel (ibid.: 117–18). Closely associated with Flad was Henry Aaron Stern, a German Jew who had converted and been ordained as an Anglican. Representing the London Society for Promoting Christianity amongst the Jews, Stern arrived in Ethiopia in early 1860 (ibid.: 128–29). The rule of the Ethiopian Emperor Tewodros (1855–1868), which saw the weakening of central Ethiopian political power as well as economic hardships, permitted the proliferation of these missions in Ethiopia.

Although the presence of European missions in Ethiopia grew in part out the same colonial sentiments that catalyzed European involvement in much of the rest of Africa during the second half of the nineteenth century, a special situation pertained in Ethiopia. Because Ethiopia already had an ancient and indigenous Ethiopian Orthodox Christian church (founded in the fourth century), the missionaries were allowed to proselytize only among non-Christians in Ethiopia, with any converts to be directed into the Ethiopian church (Kaplan 1992: 118). Thus, many of the missionaries' efforts were directed toward the Beta Israel and other Ethiopian minorities. Research has shown that the impact of the European missions on the Beta Israel was slight (Crummey 1972: 146). Indeed, the proselytizing sparked a religious revival among the Beta Israel, and one religious dispute with the missionaries was even mediated by Emperor Tewodros himself in 1862. In the end, the missionaries offended the emperor and had to be liberated by a British military expedition in 1868 (Kaplan 1992: 119). From then up to the first decades of the twentieth century, the European Protestant missions in Ethiopia were managed by native agents, with only occasional visits from foreign missionaries.

If the Christian missions did not serve to convert a great number of Falasha, it is clear that many Beta Israel joined the Ethiopian Orthodox Church on their own for economic and social reasons. But perhaps the greatest impact of the missions was their success in undermining the authority of the Falasha monks, who had for centuries been the religious leaders of their community:

> Stern and his colleagues not only attacked the priesthood and monasticism as institutions, but also exploited every opportunity to engage individual clerics in disputations in order to demonstrate their opponents' ignorance. Their task was not a difficult one. The Beta Israel monks were honored in their community because of their piety and the communal and ritual roles they filled, not for their skill as debaters. . . . Inevitably, they came out second best in the confrontations engineered by the missionaries. (Kaplan 1992: 124)

News of Christian missionary activity among the Falasha was widely reported among European Jews, and the Alliance Israélite Universelle responded by sending an emissary, Joseph Halévy, to Ethiopia in 1868 to investigate the situation. Yet from the beginning, Halévy's journey was also motivated by a mission to transform the Falashas. His goal, as Halévy wrote in his memoir of these travels, was "to purify the religious ideas of this sect" (Halévy 1877: 61). Halévy was the first to tell the Falashas they shared beliefs with people called Jews, a pivotal encounter that served to define the Beta Israel in relation to Jews abroad. It also began a process of transformation that culminated more than a century later.

During several months in their villages, Halévy encouraged the Beta Israel he met to modify their traditions, and spent a great deal of his time telling them about "the customs and rites of European Jews" (Halévy 1877: 46–47). Halévy was followed by his student, Jacques Faitlovitch, who first visited the Beta Israel during 1904–5. Here what may have been a passing encounter with Jewish modernity was lent great impact by events outside the realm of religion or politics. When Faitlovitch arrived in Ethiopia, he found a people dramatically different from those of Halévy's period, a difference owing in large part to the terrible famine that had devastated Ethiopia between 1888 and 1892 (Kaplan 1992: 143). It is estimated that mortality rates in the northwest regions where Beta Israel lived could have approached as high as 75 percent and that perhaps one-half to two-thirds of all Beta Israel died during this period (ibid.: 147). Beyond its devastating impact on life and community, the famine had encouraged the movement of many of the remaining Beta Israel into the Ethiopian Church. To Beta Israel monks, an elderly and economically dependent segment of the population who were already demoralized and suffering reduced authority in the wake of the missionary challenge, the famine dealt a final blow (ibid.: 151). Although there was evidently a faction that rejected Faitlovitch and actively resisted his efforts (Summerfield 2003: 88), others struggling to sustain a Beta Israel identity drew on memories of Halévy's earlier visit and welcomed Faitlovitch's arrival.

The arrival of other Europeans no doubt paved the way for the Beta Israel embrace of Halévy and his successors. Along with European Christian missionaries and Jewish counter-missionaries who entered the Ethiopian highlands and began to transform Beta Israel tradition, by 1869 the first Italians had arrived on the Ethiopian coast, taking over the port of Assab in 1882. By 1889, following several battles, including one in which the Ethiopian Emperor Johannes was mortally wounded, the Italians and Ethiopians signed a treaty ceding to the Italians a new territory along the Red Sea coast to be named Eritrea.

In addition to Faitlovitch's activities in Ethiopia and introduction of Western Jewish traditions to Beta Israel villages, Faitlovitch set into motion a campaign to bring the Falasha to international awareness and to incorporate the Beta Israel into European Jewish consciousness. Following his first trip to Ethiopia, Faitlovitch went on a lecture tour of Europe and organized a network of Pro-Falasha committees (Quirin 1992: 196). By 1907

the first Falasha Committee had been established in Florence. Within a couple of years there was another in Germany, and others soon followed around the world, including in the United States. The main goal of these committees was the "education" of the community by establishing schools in Ethiopia and supporting the study of young Falashas in Europe.

It is at this point in Beta Israel history, then, that reciprocal travel enters into the narrative, with young Beta Israel replicating the Solomonic origin myth, traveling abroad and returning home with new religious knowledge. In 1905 Faitlovitch took two Beta Israel boys, Gette Jeremias and Taamrat Emmanuel, back to Europe with him; ironically, Faitlovitch had met Taamrat at the Swedish Protestant Mission at Asmara, Eritrea, where Taamrat had converted to Protestantism (ibid.: 194).[3] These two young men, who began their studies in Paris, were the first of more than twenty young Beta Israel boys sponsored for study abroad. Gette accompanied Faitlovitch on a trip back to Ethiopia in 1908–9, but left again, along with his cousin, Solomon Isaac, for a German school in Jerusalem, where Taamrat was being educated. In 1913 Gette again returned with Faitlovitch to Ethiopia and became the first Beta Israel to teach his people at a special school established in Asmara (ibid.: 197). Through the agency of these young travelers, modern Jewish religious practices and music began to enter Beta Israel life.

Following a hiatus imposed by World War I, Faitlovitch again returned to Ethiopia in 1920, bringing Taamrat Emmanuel and Solomon Isaac back to their country and taking four more youths abroad with him. Taamrat was appointed the director of a school founded in 1924 by Faitlovitch for the Beta Israel in Addis Ababa, supported by European and American resources. At its peak in the late 1920s and early 1930s, this school enrolled around eighty Beta Israel students (ibid.: 197).

Among the young Beta Israel men brought by Faitlovitch to Europe and Israel, the most influential for the next half century in Ethiopia would be Yona Bogale. Born in 1911 in Gondar, Yona had grown up with stories about a white Jew who had brought books to his village and taken away Gette Jeremias and Solomon Isaac. Yona was one of the boys Faitlovitch took abroad with him after returning to Gondar with Gette Jeremias in 1920 (Yona Bogale 1986: 37). Yona studied at a school in Jerusalem for two years, after which he spent four years in Germany, one in Switzerland, and a final year in France. Upon his return to Addis Ababa around 1930, Yona taught in the Faitlovitch school in Addis Ababa.

During the Italian occupation, Yona Bogale left the capital and worked as a farmer in the north. After the war, he joined the Ethiopian Ministry of Education for twelve years, one of a group of Falasha men who became prominent in the Ethiopian government. Yona later left his government post to work with the Jewish Agency and other international Jewish organizations on behalf of his community. Fluent in Hebrew, English, and German in addition to his native Amharic, Yona was a scholar whose activities included compilation of an Amharic–Hebrew dictionary. One vital aspect of Yona's role was to serve as a conduit and translator between the Beta Israel and foreign Jewish visitors, and many, including myself in 1973, had their entries into the rural villages eased by Yona. A description of one such visit by an American Jewish rabbi during the Passover holiday in spring 1969 graphically records the transformation well under way in Beta Israel religious life and the trope of exoticism that characterized foreign Jewish interest in this process:

> The service was conducted by . . . their priests, led by the High Priest . . . who is elected by the group. . . . It was a chant in Gheez, the sacred language, to the gentle accompaniment of a drum and a cymbal. This lasted a little over a half hour. I then greeted the Congregation in Hebrew which was translated into Amharic, the Ethiopian dialect, and the High Priest responded. The translations back and forth were rendered by Mr. Bogala.
>
> After the service, the Congregation gathered outside the Synagogue. The group of children recited the Four Questions in Hebrew from Haggadoth which had been brought from Israel. They also read other portions of the Haggadah. Then the High Priest explained in Amharic the general significance of the Festival. The full moon which had risen from behind the hill overlooking the village illuminated this exotic scene. . . .
>
> We were then taken to their Hebrew schools, one of three supported by the Education Department of the Jewish Agency, where the children greeted us with a resounding "bruchim ha'baim" [welcome] in the form of spirited Hebrew songs. (Goldstein 1969: 5, 7)

By the 1950s one outcome of a century of contact—first Europeans in Ethiopia, and later Ethiopians in Europe and Israel—was the formation of a hybrid Falasha religious and musical tradition in Ethiopia.

Musical Interlude II: Juxtapositions

The rabbi describing the scene above sketches a religious tradition in transition, partitioned into a traditional Ge'ez liturgy juxtaposed against newly introduced Hebrew liturgical practices. Throughout the period of foreign contact until the foreigners' departure from Ethiopia, performance of the Beta Israel liturgy remained largely intact, with the traditional liturgy chanted by the priests followed by a Jewish liturgy in Hebrew performed by young Beta Israel trained abroad. The traditional and new ritual complexes were maintained separately. During my extended stay in Beta Israel villages during the fall of 1973, on the eve of the Ethiopian revolution, I had ample opportunities to observe and record such juxtapositions.

Only once did I observe an attempt to combine the traditions, an occasion on which a portion of the Hebrew liturgy was interpolated into a Ge'ez ritual. This singular event took place late on the afternoon of *astasreyo*, the annual Beta Israel fast day, equivalent to the pan-Jewish Yom Kippur. *Astasreyo* consisted of a vigil, beginning around 10:00 P.M. on the eve of the fast and extending throughout the night. Except for an hour between 2:30 and 3:30 A.M., when everyone in the prayer house napped, the singing was contin-

uous until 9:00 A.M.[4] As noted above, there was no cantillation of portions from the Five Books of Moses within Beta Israel rituals, although on the morning of *astasreyo*, several biblical portions were read in Ge'ez, including the Decalogue (Ten Commandments) from Exodus 20. At 9:00 A.M. the Ge'ez ritual adjourned, and while the priests napped, two young Beta Israel men trained in Israel led a standard Hebrew holiday morning ritual.

The Ge'ez ritual resumed at midday. Late in the afternoon, as part of several hours of ongoing chanting, the priests chanted a Ge'ez prayer that began with a text referring to the Orit: "orit zaza'at wahegga zabotu hegomu ladaqiqa esra'el" (the Book of Exodus and the Law that he decreed for the children of Israel). The recording of most of the rest of this chanted prayer text is unintelligible because of background noise and long sections set in the Agawiñña dialect. However, as it concluded, the young men rose to perform the Hebrew prayer "Ashrei yoshvei betecha" (Praiseworthy are those who dwell within your house).

In the Hebrew liturgy performed on the Sabbath, the "Ashrei yoshvei betecha" is sung following the reading of the Five Books of Moses, shortly before the scrolls are placed back in the ark in which they are kept. That this Hebrew prayer was interpolated into the Beta Israel liturgy following a reference to the Ge'ez Orit reflects the considerable knowledge of Jewish liturgy on the part of the young men who stood and sang the prayer and attempted to reconcile the two traditions. They inserted the "Ashrei yoshve betecha" in a manner specifically consistent with European

(Ashkenazic) Jewish tradition, where this prayer is used on the afternoon of the Day of Atonement only during the concluding service (Posner 1972: 736).[5]

Thus, the period between approximately 1850 and 1930 brought Europe to the Beta Israel—and the first Beta Israel to Europe. This contact, expanded in the years following World War II, was reflected in the introduction of Western Jewish Hebrew texts and music into Beta Israel liturgical practice. The period post-1930 and the destruction of Jewish communities in Europe also abruptly severed the relations between European Jews and the Falasha.

The Shadow of the Holocaust: Events and Metaphors

Although the Holocaust did not consume the Beta Israel in the same manner in which it destroyed Jewish communities across Europe, it left its mark on Beta Israel life and thought. In the sections that follow I first explore certain events during World War II that had an impact on the Beta Israel at home and abroad. I then address the long shadow of the Holocaust that reemerged and continued to shape Beta Israel history long after the destruction of European Jewry.

The Events of World War II

The most direct impact of Europeans on the Beta Israel during the period from the late 1930s through the early 1940s came, of course, through the Italian occupation. Following on the heels of the long Italian program, which had begun in the late nineteenth century, to colonize Africa and gain control of the Red Sea, the Italians invaded Ethiopia on 3 October 1935. Despite strong resistance from Ethiopian troops, which included members of the Beta Israel, the Ethiopians were overwhelmed by the Italians and the brutality of their bombings and poison gas attacks. Addis Ababa fell to Italy in the first week of May 1936, evoking considerable sympathy abroad, but no foreign military aid (Boahen 1990: 311–12; Del Boca 1969: 199–206).

Beyond the expected political and economic changes, the Italian occupation had an impact on virtually all aspects of Ethiopian life. The Italians left a permanent mark through a new colonial architecture, which was intended "to demonstrate Italian power over the local audience by designing powerful buildings and cities" (Fuller 1988: 483). In the Ethiopian capital, Addis Ababa, this modernist architectural agenda was superimposed on an existing city, where Italian planners consciously used "the concept [of] acting upon the indigenous mentality, impressing it with the isolated grandeur of power" (ibid.: 476). The fascist building projects separated foreigners from indigenous peoples, ensuring racial segregation. Similar plans were made for northern Ethiopian towns, such as Gondar; however, these never reached fruition as they did in the south. The occupation also left its imprint on Ethiopian traditional culture, through the systematic pursuit and murder of a group of musicians known as *azmari*, who served as a focal point of national patriotism. The Ethiopians resisted the Italians in rural areas

(Shirreff 1994: 858), many of which maintained considerable independence from the occupiers because of the impassable mountainous terrain (Gebre-Egziabeher 1969: 193), but only the entry of British-sponsored forces from the Sudan and Kenya enabled the Ethiopians to defeat the Italians in 1941. Although the official Italian policy during the occupation assured "absolute respect for all religions in so far as these did not conflict with the public order and general principles of civilization" (Larebo 1988: 1), the Italians in fact repressed any group or religious organization that was a source of nationalism and resistance. Their actions extended to the Ethiopian church, most notably following an attempt on the life of the Italian viceroy, Rodolfo Graziani, when the Italians executed all the monks and deacons of the revered Debre Libanos Monastery and murdered an Ethiopian bishop. The Italian policy toward the church has been described as one of "conciliation . . . side by side with terroristic measures" (ibid.: 2).

Although "a superficial examination of Mussolini's oppressive policies has . . . led many researchers to conclude that the Beta Israel were persecuted severely during the Italian occupation of Ethiopia for being not only Ethiopians but Jewish as well," recent research presents a different picture (Summerfield 1999: 5; Summerfield 2003: 97). Some Beta Israel were active in the resistance against the Italians, and some dozens died in a 1937 massacre by the Italians, along with other Ethiopians who had given shelter to a prominent rebel (Summerfield 2003: 54). Yet,

even though it is commonly reported in popular sources that the Faitlovitch school in Addis Ababa closed as a result of the occupation, Faitlovitch's correspondence disputes this widely held view (ibid.: 53). Indeed, Faitlovitch had informed American Pro-Falasha committees well before the invasion that the school was on the verge of collapse for financial reasons. Other documents recently uncovered indicate that the school's director, Taamrat Emmanuel, in fact received a subsidy from a high-ranking Italian official (ibid.: 51).

Many of the educated, urban Beta Israel, such as Taamrat Emmanuel and Yona Bogale, eventually left Addis Ababa to avoid the Italians' persecution of educated Ethiopians. Indeed, the main village in which I carried out my fieldwork in 1973, Ambober, was founded when Beta Israel from other areas were uprooted during the Italian occupation (Shelemay 1989: 5).

Some Beta Israel did lose their lives as a direct result of the Italian occupation.[6] However, Summerfield suggests somewhat ironically that

the legacy of the Italian occupation of Ethiopia for the Beta Israel appears to be an eventual increase in their official recognition as Jews by World Jewry. It would seem that various pro-Falasha organizations attempted to place the Falashas in the arena of world Jewry by exaggerating the impact that the occupation had on the Beta Israel in order to portray them as "suffering Jews" at the same time that European Jewry was being savagely persecuted. (Summerfield 1999: 58)

For a brief moment between 1936 and 1943, it appeared that Ethiopia might become a haven for the Jews, dramatically shifting the field of play. Proposals were made for the mass resettlement of European Jews in Italian-occupied Ethiopia. The initiative evidently began just days after the Italian occupation of Addis Ababa in 1936 (Pankhurst 1973: 235). This odd chapter in the relations among Europe, Ethiopia, and the Jews quickly became a subject of controversy among European Jews, some of whom saw the plan as a possible escape from growing persecution while others perceived it as a threat to the ongoing efforts to found a Jewish state in Palestine. The Ethiopian Jewish-state initiative, which was given considerable publicity in the international press and was a subject of discussion in diplomatic circles, was effectively ended with the beginning of World War II in Europe and the subsequent defeat of the Italians in Ethiopia in 1941. The inception, discussion, and eventual dissolution of the plan did create "a significant amount of interest in the Falashas" (ibid.), as demonstrated by a visit in August 1936 by an Italian Jewish representative to Ethiopia, Carlo Alberto Viterbo.

A final, direct impact of World War II and the Holocaust was the suspension of aid to the Beta Israel from European and American Jews (Winston 1980: 4). This hiatus extended from the inception of the Italian invasion in 1936 until the state of Israel initiated its own aid efforts in 1954. Post–World War II, American Jews assumed the mantle of European activism in Ethiopia. However, there is another dimension of this tragic period of Jewish history in Europe that shaped subsequent events, including the immigration of the Falasha to Israel. It is to that subject that I now turn.

Holocaust Analogies

Perhaps the most startling impact of the Holocaust and the legacy of European Jews on the Beta Israel is one that emerged more than thirty years after the end of World War II. Here I refer to what the American historian Peter Novick has termed "Holocaust analogies" (Novick 1999: 243). Novick questions why the Holocaust has "come to loom so large in our [modern American] culture" (ibid.: 1). Since the 1970s, the Holocaust has been used to signify and draw attention to the Falasha situation, in large part, but not exclusively, by American Jews. By the late 1970s, one finds a proliferation of Holocaust analogies emanating from many quarters: In all these cases, the analogy was invoked as a potent symbol, one that directed the attention of the world to the difficult Beta Israel situation in Ethiopia in order to advance the acceptance of the Falasha as Jews and to ensure the community's immigration to Israel.

The complicated use of Holocaust analogies is the subject of an entire book by Novick, and a number of his statements are germane to the case study in this chapter. There is little doubt that use of Holocaust analogies in publicity mounted on behalf of the immigration of Soviet Jewry during the mid- to late 1970s (as manifest in the slogan "Never Again") was a catalyst for its use in the

Ethiopian context shortly thereafter. The Ethiopian revolution, which began in early 1974, was by 1977–78 marked by domestic disruptions and violence. The Beta Israel's situation during the revolution was not dissimilar to that during the Italian occupation, discussed briefly above: many Beta Israel suffered, as did most of their countrymen and women, although the dimensions of the Beta Israel situation were sometimes overstated by those seeking to galvanize support for Beta Israel immigration to Israel. By the late 1970s fading hopes for Beta Israel immigration as well as concern about their safety in revolutionary Ethiopia provided fertile ground for Holocaust analogies.

The propriety of the use of Holocaust analogies has often been the subject of controversy. It is clear, though, that such comparisons have been widely invoked in respect to the Falasha because of their emotional power. The use of this heavily symbolic "language of crisis" served to bring the Beta Israel yet more firmly into the European orbit, at once incorporating them within a European Jewish framework while reframing them within emotional terms that were beyond debate. The use of Holocaust analogies provided the final rationale for the incorporation of the Beta Israel as Jews within a modern Jewish context.

Wherever we look in the massive literature on the Falasha during the 1970s and 1980s, we encounter Holocaust analogies. The historian Steven Kaplan has noted that "the literature containing these themes is so vast as to defy any bibliography. It includes leaflets, pamphlets, films,

slide shows, newspaper articles, etc." (Kaplan 1993: 651 n. 16). Analogies are invoked in the popular press, in scholarly literature, and by the Ethiopian Jews themselves.

The most graphic examples are, not surprisingly, from the popular press and the world of popular culture. For instance, advertisements for the 1984 film *Falasha: Exile of the Black Jews* noted that "forty years after the Holocaust, the oldest Diaspora Jewish community, the black Jews of Ethiopia, is facing certain and imminent death." Thus the cataclysmic end of European Jewry provides a framework for interpreting the next half century of Beta Israel life.

The journalist Louis Rapoport summarized the use of Holocaust analogies in relation to the Falasha:

> Perhaps it is misleading to draw comparisons between Africa and Europe, Germany or Russia and Ethiopia; yet there are some striking parallels between the pogroms directed against Jews by Europeans, Arabs and Africans alike. The pogroms of today are being directed against a once mighty Jewish tribe, whose history is no less important than the history of German Jews. (Rapoport 1981: 14)

Holocaust analogies were pervasive not only among European and American writers from the late 1970s through the final transfer of the Ethiopian Jewish community to Israel in 1991; the Holocaust was also invoked by Ethiopian Jews in Israel. For instance, a leaflet handed out on 30 October 1979 by Ethiopian Jews who demonstrated in front of the Israeli parliament, the Knesset, for Israeli government support for migration proclaimed that "many opportunities to save and bring out our brothers are passed over as the 'final solution' is carried out on the question of Ethiopian Jews. . . . Our hearts believe, and we are sure that the people of Israel and its delegates in the Knesset will identify with our struggle" (Winston 1980: 10).

Holocaust analogies, thus, have provided a powerful language of crisis that embedded multiple emotional triggers, calling on Diaspora Jewish memory and guilt over American Jewish inaction during the cataclysm in Europe and alluding to important Jewish religious injunctions about saving human life.

Musical Interlude III: The Voices of Children

Beginning in the late 1970s, small groups of Ethiopian Jews made their way to Israel, and the community's connections with Jews of the outside world increased. During this period, the juxtaposition of old Ethiopian Ge'ez liturgy and new pan-Jewish Hebrew traditions described above began to shift. With the priests no longer training anyone in their traditional religion, Beta Israel children in Ethiopia learned only new Jewish traditions brought from the outside. During these years many changes took place in Beta Israel villages as well.

The Euro-American Jewish traditions introduced into Beta Israel villages by the early 1950s included Yona Bogale's Hebrew-Jewish calendar. Yona helped to recruit a second wave of young people to study Jewish ritual and Hebrew in Israel. In the final quarter century of Yona's life and career—he left Ethiopia in 1979 and died in Israel in 1987—we can view the template for the final transformation of Beta Israel religious life on a local level.

Of particular importance in introducing Jewish liturgy and music to the villages was the opening in 1954 of a seminary in Asmara, Eritrea, by the Jewish Agency Department for Torah Education and Culture in the Diaspora. The initial group of thirty-three students brought from the Gondar area included seven Beta Israel priests who were instructed by an Israeli rabbi. The same year twelve students went to Israel to pursue studies. Thirty-three village schools eventually opened in central Falasha villages, and additional Beta Israel students were sent to Israel. Thus, by the mid-1950s, Jewish schools were established in Beta Israel villages in the Gondar area in which hundreds of children were taught Hebrew and Jewish history (Abbink 1984: 93). By 1970 the Joint Distribution Committee (in cooperation with London Falasha Welfare Association) began to provide medical aid to Beta Israel villages, and in 1977 ORT (the Organization for Rehabilitation and Training, an international Jewish relief agency) mounted vocational efforts funded by Swedish, Canadian, West German, and British sources (Bogale n.d.).

Nowhere are these changes more clearly evident than in the generational divide regarding musical transmission. With the old Ge'ez liturgy

Figure 4.2 "Adon 'olam" (Master of the Universe). Unattributed melody, transcribed by K. K. Shelemay.

A - don 'o - lam____ a - sher ma - lakh be - te - rem kal____ ye - tsir - niv - ra . . .

sustained only by Beta Israel priests, the children became heirs to another musical and liturgical tradition, that of Western Jews. No better example exists than the prayer "Adon alom" (Master of the Universe), sung by the Falasha children of Ambober, Ethiopia, to greet the many Jewish visitors from abroad who arrived in their villages.

Beta Israel children learned this prayer not in the prayer house, but in the schoolhouse, taught by teachers who had studied in Israel, where, during the early decades of the Jewish State, "Adon 'olam" (see fig. 4.2) was sung in schools at the end of morning prayers (Herzog 1972: 298). Through song, Beta Israel children could communicate in a language and musical system that was understood by their European and American Jewish visitors. Music thereby affirmed the connection and demonstrated that modern Beta Israel sang in "harmony" with their compatriots from abroad. Part of the heritage of the long European engagement with the Beta Israel was the transplantation of a European-derived Ashkenazic liturgy in Falasha villages and the absorption of a European musical vocabulary during the formative years of Beta Israel children.

The End of Falasha History and the Birth of the Ethiopian Jews

The closing chapter of Beta Israel life in Ethiopia took place between 1980 and 1992. These traumatic years saw a mass exodus of many Ethiopians, including Beta Israel, because of intense drought and famine. By 1983 more than four thousand Beta Israel had crossed the border into the Sudan and were subsequently transported to Israel. Later groups encountered more difficulties, both in reaching the Sudan and in overcoming deteriorating conditions in the refugee camps. Between November 1984 and January 1985 another six thousand Ethiopian Jews were airlifted to Israel in an effort that came to be known as Operation Moses. A subsequent evacuation removed more Beta Israel from the Sudan in March 1985, and another two thousand arrived in Israel from Ethiopia by the end of 1989. By 1990 nearly twenty thousand Ethiopian Jews had converged in Addis Ababa, hoping to travel to Israel. With the fall of the revolutionary Ethiopian government in May 1991, a sum of $35 million was paid to the Ethiopian government, and on 24–25 May 1991 more than fourteen thousand Beta Israel were airlifted to Israel in Operation Solomon. This evacuation, ironically commemorating the community's Solomonic origins, marked the end of the Falasha community in Ethiopia (Westheimer and Kaplan 1992: 3).

The Ethiopian Jews in Israel have largely discarded their traditional liturgy and its music; most Ethiopian Jews have chosen to worship in existing Israeli synagogues. Because of their long-time exposure to European and American Jewish liturgy and music, many affiliate with synagogues that celebrate a European Jewish rite. By the late 1980s Ethiopian Jews in Israel were showing evidence of a strong European influence in many aspects of their daily life and ritual. These changes have been the subject of occasional comment in the press, such as the following observation from a cookbook author who sought to record different ethnic recipes for Jewish holidays: "I ran into lots of problems. . . . When I interviewed the wife of an immigrant rabbi from Ethiopia, she started to spout Ashkenazic customs" (Nathan 1987).

The end of Beta Israel history in Ethiopia and what has been termed "the invention of the Ethiopian Jews" (Kaplan 1993) also spelled the end to claims of the community's descent based on the *Kebra Nagast*. If their Solomonic origins tied the Beta Israel to an Ethiopian elite, this Ethiopian heritage threatened to separate them from their fellow Jews in Israel. By the early 1990s Ethiopian Jews in Israel "almost unanimously" rejected any connection to the tradition of Solomon and Sheba. Rather, they presented themselves either as descendants of Jews who followed the biblical Prophet Jeremiah to Egypt, or, in keeping with

rabbinic opinion, as descendants of the lost tribe of Dan (Abbink 1990: 415–16; Kaplan 1993: 652). Another narrative here begins.

Musical Interlude IV: The Invention of Ethiopian Jewish Music

Another "Adon 'olam" sung by Beta Israel children has been widely distributed on a commercial recording issued in Israel in 1993 (Gronich 1993) and brings Beta Israel music history forward into a framework fully reshaped by European musical styles and sensibilities. This is one of several recordings issued by the Israeli musician Shlomo Gronich, who founded the Sheba Choir, an ensemble consisting of children who had immigrated to Israel from Ethiopia. Gronich's "Adon 'olam" begins with an organ introduction quoting J. S. Bach's Toccata and Fugue in D Minor. Next, the Sheba Choir enters, performing "Adon 'olam" to a melody composed by the Israeli singer/songwriter Uzi Chitman in 1975 (see fig. 4.3) that is widely sung in Israel and the United States.[7] Above the choral refrain, Gronich sings a wordless countermelody. Following a neo-oriental transition played by Middle Eastern drum, violin, and synthesizer and punctuated by vocal cries, yet another "Adon 'olam" begins, this one composed by the Russian cantor Eliezar Gerovitch (see fig. 4.4).[8] In this single recording, the Sheba Choir incorporates several European and European-derived musical styles, just as they have absorbed other European influences over the course of their history.

Figure 4.3 "Adon 'olam" (Master of the Universe). Melody by Uzi Chitman, transcribed by K. K. Shelemay.

"Master of the universe, Who reigned before any form was created
At the time when His will brought all into being—then as 'King' was His Name proclaimed."
(Translation from Scherman and Zlotowitz 1999: 353)

Figure 4.4 "Adon 'olam" (Master of the Universe). Melody by Eliezar M. Gerovitch, transcribed by K. K. Shelemay.

Conclusions

This *midrash* has been about echoes, about the manner in which history reverberates in musical sound, each fading into the distance as another comes into earshot. We have encountered echoes of Europe among Beta Israel in Ethiopia, which after more than a century of intensity, have fallen silent. The echoes of Ethiopia in Europe and America are now resounding, with Ethiopian Jews living and singing not just in Israel, often to tunes of European and American provenance, but throughout Europe and the United States. If the Beta Israel have been transformed into Ethiopian Jews through their long encounter with Europe, their impact on Europeans and Americans remains ongoing. They are for the first time raising their voices in these new contexts, setting off new echoes.

An echo is a reverberation that embeds continuous transformation. It moves between locales, changing as it reverberates through time and space. Similarly, the process of constant transformation that permeated the Beta Israel past remains a powerful force in the Ethiopian Jewish present. A recent ethnography of Ethiopian Jews in Israel suggested that the notion of transformation itself was "a unifying concept" in Beta Israel consciousness, past and present (Salamon 1999: 8). Drawing on old Ethiopian Christian beliefs that Beta Israel men and women possessed the power both to transform objects and to assume different shapes, some have suggested that Beta Israel have absorbed and applied this expectation to enable them to negotiate and survive constant

change. The deep-seated belief in the transformation of people, materials, and objects certainly characterized Beta Israel work as smiths and potters, and it may well be that the transformation of liturgical and musical expression can be posited within this same framework, described as a thoroughgoing and ubiquitous process of the Beta Israel consciousness (ibid.: 117–19).

This *midrash*, with its disputed beginnings, has no single ending. If we take as its metaphorical source the Ge'ez *Orit* and its resonance in Ethiopian culture, we must also acknowledge the irony of the late twentieth-century rejection by the Ethiopian Jews of the myth of their descent from Solomon and Sheba. This *midrash* also leaves many unanswered questions. Told from the point of view of Ethiopian history, the Ethiopian Jews are now an Ethiopian people in diaspora. Told from the perspective of Israel and Jewish Europe, the Beta Israel were too long Jews of the Diaspora and have only now, within the last decade, "come home" to Israel. So in the end, we cannot even be certain where exactly the Beta Israel can be found. Perhaps the answer lies on both sides of this divide: If the Ethiopian Jews were in diaspora in Ethiopia, the Beta Israel are perhaps equally so in Israel.

Europe, long before the modern age, assumed the power of defining the other. For more than 150 years, Europe has sought to remake the Ethiopian Jews in its image. Throughout this period the Ethiopian Jews have increasingly reshaped themselves and redefined the bonds of kinship thought to unite them with Jews around the globe. They have done so through both sounds and silences, by the traditions they maintained, such as the *Kebra Nagast*, and their Geʻez liturgy, and by the traditions they have not observed, such as biblical cantillation. They introduced new elements to our understanding of religious hybridity. The Ethiopian Jews also recast the most powerful image of modern European Jewish history, the Holocaust, charging it with new and contested meanings as it echoed more than half a century after that catastrophe. And throughout, they sang, providing the echoes through which we have been able to trace the end of Falasha history and the transformation of the Ethiopian Jews.

❧⚶☙

::: **NOTES** :::

I thank Philip V. Bohlman for inviting me to participate in the Honigberg Lectures and for his helpful comments on aspects of content and style. I also thank Steven Kaplan for insightful suggestions that strengthened this essay.

1. The Ethiopian people discussed in this essay are known by several names. Their traditional tribal name, Beta Israel, translates as "House of Israel." The name "Falasha," by which they were commonly known for centuries, derives either from a fifteenth-century Ethiopian imperial decree forbidding land ownership to non-Christians or from the word *falasyan*, which means "monk." Since the late 1970s, the name "Falasha" has been considered pejorative, and by the 1980s most in the Beta Israel community had begun to call themselves "Ethiopian Jews." Here I will use "Beta Israel" when referring to aspects of traditional Ethiopian identity, cultural expression, and religion; "Falasha" when discussing Ethiopian historical or ethnographic sources that use that name; and "Ethiopian Jews" when touching on aspects of late twentieth-century identity, especially in Israel.

2. Conflicting interpretations of Beta Israel history both within and outside the community are too complex to revisit here. For commentary about relevant issues relating to the symbolic construction of identity, see the discussions in Cohen 2000. Discussions relating specifically to Beta Israel identity and constructions of Beta Israel history are explored at length in Shelemay 1989 and Kaplan 1992.

3. It is traditional to refer to Ethiopians by their first names.

4. It should be emphasized that the entire Beta Israel liturgy is sung, with no spoken portions except a brief homily in Amharic at the end of rituals.

5. In Sephardic tradition, this prayer occurs twice, once earlier during the morning service and then during the concluding afternoon service.

6. Two teachers from the Falasha School in Addis Ababa—Makonen Levy, who had spent six years in England, and Yonathan Wizkims, who had studied in Germany and France—were evidently imprisoned along with several of their students, and they died in captivity (Abbink 1984: 89; Kessler 1982: 146). Several of the young Beta Israel students taken by Faitlovitch to Europe perished there, although all died during the early 1930s and as a result of illness, not persecution (Trevisan Semi 1999; Weil 1999).

7. I thank Violet Gilboa of the Harvard University Judaica Collection for confirming this date. A recording of Chitman's "Adon ʻolam" performed by the composer can be heard on Chitman 1994.

8. Eliezar M. Gerovitch (1844–1914), born in Rostov, Russia was an important nineteenth-century cantor who published two collections of synagogue song (Weisser

1983: 124). His "Adon 'olam" melody has been widely circulated throughout the twentieth century, including in Europe and the United States (see, e.g., *Union Songster* 1960: 8).

::: WORKS CITED :::

Abbink, G. J. 1984. *The Falashas in Ethiopia and Israel: The Problem of Ethnic Assimilation*. Nijmegen: Institute for Cultural and Social Anthropology.

Abbink, Jon. 1990. "The Enigma of Beta Esra'el Ethnogenesis: An Anthro-Historical Study." *Cahiers d'études africaines*, 120 (XXX-4): 397–449.

Avner, Yossi, Natalia Berger, Kay Kaufman Shelemay, and Uri Ram, eds. 1986. *The Jews of Ethiopia: A People in Transition*. Tel Aviv and New York: Beth Hatefutsoth, Nahum Goldmann Museum of the Jewish Diaspora, and Jewish Museum; New York: Jewish Theological Seminary of America.

Boahen, A. Adu, ed. 1990. *Africa under Colonial Domination, 1880–1935: General History of Africa*. Vol. 7. Berkeley: University of California Press.

Bogale, Yona. 1986. "Memories of an Ethiopian (Falasha) Pupil in the Land of Israel." In Avner et al., *The Jews of Ethiopia*, 36–30.

Bogale, Yona. N.d. "The Beta Israel (Falasha) Schools." Typescript.

Chitman, Uzi. 1994. *Uzi Shar Hitman*. Tel Aviv: Phonokol.

Cohen, Anthony P., ed. 2000. *Signifying Identities: Anthropological Perspectives on Boundaries and Contested Values*. London and New York: Routledge.

Crummey, Donald. 1972. *Priests and Politicians: Protestant and Catholic Missions in Orthodox Ethiopia, 1830–1868*. Oxford: Clarendon Press.

———. 1998. "The Politics of Modernization: Protestant and Catholic Missionaries in Modern Ethiopia." In Getatchew Haile, Aasuly Lande, and Samuel Rubenson, eds., *The Missionary Factor in Ethiopia: Papers from a Symposium on the Impact of European Missions on Ethiopian Society* (Lund University, August 1996), 85–99. Frankfurt am Main and New York: Peter Lang.

———. 2000. "Ethiopia, Europe and Modernity: A Preliminary Sketch." *Aethiopica* 3: 7–23.

Del Boca, Angelo. 1969. *The Ethiopian War, 1935–1941*. Trans. by P. D. Cummins. Chicago: University of Chicago Press.

"Falasha: Exile of the Black Jews." 1984. Publicity for the documentary film, produced by Simcha Jacobovici, Susan Price, and Jamie Boyd of Matara Film Productions.

Fuller, Mia. 1988. "Building Power: Italy's Colonial Architecture and Urbanism, 1923–1940." *Cultural Anthropology* 3 (4): 455–87.

Gebre-Egziabeher, Salome. 1969. "The Patriotic Works of Dejazmatch Aberra Kassa and Ras Abebe Aragaye." *Proceedings of the Third International Conference of Ethiopian Studies* (Addis Ababa, 1966), 293–314. Addis Ababa: Institute of Ethiopian Studies.

Goldstein, Israel. 1969. "The Falashas: Romance, Problem and Challenge (Based on a Passover Visit to the Falashas)." Typescript.

Gronich, Shlomo. 1993. *Shlomo Gronich and the Sheba Choir*. Ramat Gan: Hed Arzi.

Halévy, Joseph. 1877. "Travels in Abyssinia." In A. Lowy, ed., *Miscellany of Hebrew Literature*. 2: 175–256. Trans. by James Picciotto. London: Wertheimer, Lea. (Publications of the Society of Hebrew Literature, 2nd ser.)

Herzog, Avigdor. 1972. "Adon Olam." In *Encyclopaedia Judaica*, 16 vols., 2: 296–98. Jerusalem: Keter.

"Jews of Ethiopia." 1972. (Editorial.) Reprinted from *Pointer: The Journal of the Liberal and Progressive Synagogues*. London.

JPS Hebrew–English Tanakh: The Traditional Hebrew Text and the New JPS Translation. 1999. 2nd ed. Philadelphia: Jewish Publication Society.

Kaplan, Steven. 1992. *The Beta Israel (Falasha) in Ethiopia: From Earliest Times to the Twentieth Century*. New York: New York University Press.

———. 1993. "The Invention of Ethiopian Jews: Three Models." *Cahiers d'études africaines* 132 (XXXIII-4): 645–58.

Kessler, David. 1982. *The Falashas: The Forgotten Jews of Ethiopia*. New York: African.

Larebo, Haile Mariam. 1988. "The Ethiopian Orthodox Church and Politics in the Twentieth Century: Part II." *Northeast African Studies* 10 (1): 1–23.

Levine, Donald N. 1973. "Menelik and Oedipus: Further Observations on the Ethiopian National Epic." In Harold Marcus, ed., *Proceedings of the First United States Conference on Ethiopian Studies*, 11–23. East Lansing: African Studies Center, Michigan State University.

Messing, Simon D. 1982. *The Story of the Falashas: "Black Jews" of Ethiopia*. United States: Balshon Printing & Offset.

Nathan, Joan. 1987. "Hanukkah in Israel: Not by Latkes Alone." *New York Times*, 9 December.

Neusner, Jacob. 1993. *The Way of Torah: An Introduction to Judaism*. 5th rev. ed. Belmont, Calif.: Wadsworth.

Novick, Peter. 1999. *The Holocaust in American Life*. Boston: Houghton Mifflin.

Pankhurst, Richard. 1973. "Plans for Mass Jewish Settlement in Ethiopia (1936–1943)." *Ethiopia Observer* 15 (4): 235–45.

Parfitt, Tudor, and Emanuela Trevisan Semi, eds. 1999. *The Beta Israel in Ethiopia and Israel*. Surrey: Curzon Press.

Posner, Raphael. 1972. "Ashrei." In *Encyclopaedia Judaica*, 16 vols., 3: 736. Jerusalem: Keter.

Quirin, James. 1992. *The Evolution of the Ethiopian Jews: A History of the Beta Israel (Falasha) to 1920*. Philadelphia: University of Pennsylvania Press.

Rapoport, Louis. 1981. *The Lost Jews: Last of the Ethiopian Falashas*. Briarcliff Manor, N.Y.: Stein & Day.

Rapoport, Louis, and Judy Siegel. 1975. "Ethiopian Falashas Recognized as Jews under the Law of Return." *The Jerusalem Post*, 11 April.

Robertson, Carol E. 1992. "Introduction: The Dance of Conquest." In Carol E. Robertson, ed., *The Musical Repercussions of 1492: Encounters in Text and Performance*, 9–30. Washington, D.C.: Smithsonian Institution Press.

Salamon, Hagar. 1999. *The Hyena People: Ethiopian Jews in Christian Ethiopia*. Berkeley: University of California Press.

Scherman, N., and M. Zlotowitz, eds. 1999. *The Complete ArtScroll Siddur*. 3rd ed. Brooklyn: Mesorah.

Shelemay, Kay Kaufman. 1989. *Music, Ritual, and Falasha History*. 2nd ed. East Lansing: Michigan State University Press.

Shirreff, A. D. 1994. "The Ethiopian Patriot Contribution to the 1941 Campaign against the Italians in Gojjam." In Bahru Zewde, Richard Pankhurst, and Taddese Bayene, eds., *Proceedings of the Eleventh International Conference of Ethiopian Studies*, 2 vols., 1: 849–59. Addis Ababa: Institute of Ethiopian Studies.

Summerfield, Daniel P. 1999. "The Impact of the Italian Occupation of Ethiopia on the Beta Israel." In Parfitt and Trevisan Semi, *The Beta Israel in Ethiopia and Israel*, 50–60.

———. 2003. *From Falashas to Ethiopian Jews: The External Influences for Change c. 1860–1960*. London and New York: Routledge Curzon.

Trevisan Semi, Emanuela. 1999. "From Wolleqa to Florence: The Tragic Story of Faitlovitch's Pupil Hizkiahu Finkas." In Parfitt and Trevisan Semi, *The Beta Israel in Ethiopia and Israel*, 15–39.

Union Songster: Songs and Prayers for Jewish Youth. 1960. New York: Central Conference of American Rabbis.

Weil, Shalva. 1999. "The Life and Death of Solomon Isaac." In Parfitt and Trevisan Semi, *The Beta Israel in Ethiopia and Israel*, 40–49.

Weisser, Albert. 1983. *The Modern Renaissance of Jewish Music: Events and Figures, Eastern Europe and America*. New York: Da Capo Press.

Westheimer, Ruth, and Steven Kaplan. 1992. *Surviving Salvation: The Ethiopian Jewish Family in Transition*. New York: New York University Press.

Winston, Diane. 1980. "The Falashas: History and Analysis of Policy towards a Beleaguered Community." *Perspectives*, April 1980. New York: National Jewish Resource Center.

Yayeh, Asres. 1995. *Traditions of the Ethiopian Jews*. Canada: Kibur Asres.

5

Charlotte Salomon's Modernism

::: MICHAEL P. STEINBERG

In recent years, visitors to the Jewish Historical Museum in Amsterdam—scholars and non-scholars alike—have been consistently drawn to the modest, rotating display of the work of Charlotte Salomon. Born in Berlin in 1917, the daughter of a prominent surgeon and from her middle childhood the stepdaughter of a celebrated contralto, Salomon grew up in the privileged, intense, and in multiple ways vexed world of Weimar Berlin. In January 1939, two months after the night of state terrorism known as *Kristallnacht* and its inherent announcement of increased violence against Jews, Charlotte was sent to the care of her maternal grandparents in southern and "unoccupied" France. There, between 1940 and 1942, she produced the single, sustained work for which she is known: a body of some 769 notebook-size gouache paintings, with accompanying text and musical references, which the "reader" is supposed to have in his or her head as the "play" unfolds. She called the work a *Singspiel* and entitled it *Leben? Oder Theater?* Salomon consigned the work for safekeeping to a local doctor and member of the Resistance. An apparently apocryphal anecdote claims that she uttered the words "This is my whole life" as she entrusted her work for safekeeping. The question of their factual status notwithstanding, the words carry analytical accuracy as well as poignancy. Shortly thereafter, she was deported via Drancy to Auschwitz, where, five months pregnant, she was murdered at the age of twenty-six, probably upon her arrival on 10 October 1943.

Since the late 1990s Salomon's work has become increasingly well-known. In the fall of 1998 the Royal Academy of Arts in London presented the most comprehensive exhibition to date of *Life? Or Theater?* Visitors rapidly increased in number as public appreciation of a life's work of art, history, and memory deepened. Yet the work remained interpretatively as inscrutable as it had proved to be accessible. Over the following three years, the exhibition traveled to three North American museums: the Art Gallery of Ontario in Toronto, the Museum of Fine Arts in Boston, and the Jewish Museum in New York. In 2002 it was shown at the Jewish Historical Museum (Joods Historisch Museum) in Amsterdam, its permanent home. The museum is currently expanding and highlighting its rotating display of the work to meet the increasing interest and recognition.[1]

Leben? Oder Theater? traces its artist's own life, scarred both by domestic tragedy and external political events, in the context of her assimilated Jewish family and the rich cultural circles within which it moved in 1920s and 1930s Berlin. The images accrue with increasing stylistic as well as narrational intensity, moving from delicacy to deliberate lack of finesse—at times more Giotto than Spiegelman, at times the reverse, with the passion of both and the secular historical commitment of the latter. And they accrue in compositional haste: the work took shape within a space of two years, and probably less.

Salomon's creative momentum was stirred by her insistence on emotional survival following the suicide of her grandmother in 1940. At the time, her grandfather informed her that the family had been cursed by a long sequence of suicides, mostly of women. The list included Charlotte's maternal aunt as well as her own mother, whose death had been reported to the seven-year-old Charlotte as the result of influenza. In 1940 Salomon seems to have faced the existential choice of either committing suicide or transcending it through a radical act of creativity, to which she referred as "something completely different."

Familiarity with Salomon's work has slowly produced interpretative variety and integrity.[2] Yet the evolving secondary work has not diminished Griselda Pollock's comment, at once instinctive and incisive, that *Leben? Oder Theater?* "is one of our century's most challenging art works—but I for one still do not know what I am looking at" (Pollock 2006). The work remains impossible to classify. In a literal sense, it remains equally impossible to see. Salomon's pages combine gouache images with texts and musical references. Much of the textual material—labels, narrative, quotations of characters' utterances—appears on waxpaper overlays, which must in fact be removed for the underlying image to become visible. In this sense, *Leben? Oder Theater?* unfolds as an imaginary book, a gift to everyone and to no one.

In calling the work a *Singspiel*, Salomon paid homage in tone and principle to a mixed genre of which Mozart's late opera *The Magic Flute* is the most abiding example. Like Mozart, Salomon adopts a combination of genres, a simultaneity of high and low culture, and of an embarrassment of creative riches without the onus of totalization. The prologue reads:

The creation of the following paintings is to be imagined as follows: A person is sitting by the sea. He [*sic*] is painting. A tune suddenly enters his mind. As he starts to hum it, he notices that the tune exactly matches what he is trying to commit to paper. A text forms in his head, and he starts to sing the tune, with his own words, over and over again in a loud voice until the painting seems complete. Frequently, several texts take shape, and the result is a duet.

The *Singspiel* now introduces itself as containing three parts: a prologue, a main section, and an epilogue. The prologue narrates, in paintings supported by tunes and accompanied by texts, original and citations, the history of Charlotte's family, with all figures carrying mildly parodic pseudonyms, from November 1913, four years prior to Charlotte's birth, until the mid-1930s, several years into the Nazi regime. Besides Charlotte herself, the principal characters are her parents, now named "Kann," her maternal grandparents, and her stepmother. The story begins with the suicide of Charlotte's aunt Franziska. A second narrative strand involves the upbringing of the woman who was to become a well-known contralto and Charlotte's stepmother, Paula (Levy) Lindberg, now called Paulinka Bimbam. The main section is the story of Charlotte's infatuation and possible love affair with her stepmother's singing teacher, Alfred Wolfsohn, who appears in the story under the name Amadeus Daberlohn. The erotic charge between Charlotte and Daberlohn is shadowed by the possible romance between Daberlohn and Paulinka. Daberlohn claims the amount of space he does partly because of Charlotte's erotic investment in him, but also because he, and the real Alfred Wolfsohn, provide the story with the side of its aesthetic that might be called neo-Wagnerian, which the author both adopts and scorns. Tristan and Isolde share a track with Hansel and Gretel. The third side of this erotic triangle is defined by the relationship between Charlotte and Paulinka. And the erotic aura is destabilized by the initial announcement of the narrator's male self-gendering.

Alfred Wolfsohn was a survivor of the trenches of the Great War, and specifically of a wartime trauma resulting—at least so he said—from being buried alive under the bodies of dead and dying soldiers. He claims to have derived from this experience a theory of the human voice as holding capacities far beyond the human sound range, sounds he remembered from among the dying soldiers. At its extreme registers, according to his theories, which Charlotte represents faithfully and mocks unforgivingly, this extended human voice is tied to the soul. "Voice" becomes the unifier of text and image, specifically the contralto voice of Paula Lindberg, a.k.a. Paulinka Bimbam, who is imagined as singing most of the lyrics that are to go through the mind of the reader of the account, as they went through the mind of the painter at work. The three signature tunes, often repeated, are Bach's aria "Bist du bei mir"; the Habañera and Toreador Song from Bizet's *Carmen*, the ultimate theatrical, erotic, and—according to Nietzsche—anti-Wagnerian work; and Gluck's aria "*J'ai perdu mon Eurydice*" from his opera *Orphée et Eurydice*. Paulinka performs the role of Orpheus in the only operatic role of hers mentioned; Professor Singsong, however, sings it to himself when he is abandoned in favor of Dr. Kann (Salomon); the Toreador Song is, in turn, Daberlohn's seduction tune.[3]

Throughout, the narrator assumes that the reader/viewer will agree, so to speak, to contribute the musical strand of the story for his or her own internal repertory. An image will state "to the tune 'X'" and the reader is asked to comply. The text is almost never silent. *Almost* never, because at times the narrator states tersely, "No tune." The music is thus separated from the representational, indeed theatrical, practices of the narrative. Silence is framed as the absence of music.

There are two musical worlds in Charlotte Salomon's work: the world of its own referential and visual language and the world of its representations at the level of plot, character, and biographical and historical content. This is the first claim I want to make in this essay. The task of my unfolding argument will be the interpretation of the interface of these two worlds. How does a visual and textual language function as a musical language, and how does this language evolve and transform itself in relation to the story being told? My question addresses a core issue of modernism, namely, its self-reflexivity, its formal, epistemological, and ethical self-consciousness

with regard to representational practices. My second claim assumes the depth of the work's musical sensibility, its control of a musical repertory that, in turn, serves to define modernist form and practice. In this respect, *Leben? Oder Theater?*, as *Singspiel*, understands musical form and practice as fundamental to modernism in general. A sophisticated synaesthetics is thus at work, because we have here a visual practice that defines itself musically and offers music as the defining system of its own aesthetic, its own modernism, as well as modernism in general. I pay particular attention to the work's inscriptions of music as the art of the singing voice and hence of the singing body, in other words, the art of embodiment—physical, erotic, and political.

The unique aesthetic language of *Leben? Oder Theater?*, hovering between text, image, and music, comes more and more to defy the world it engages. Its own modernism enacts a critique of its own representative and narrative work. At this point, history blends fantasy, biography, and autobiography into dreamworlds. At this point also, the Mozartean world cedes to the Wagnerian one, the world of *The Magic Flute* to that of *Tristan und Isolde*. The work's middle section takes shape as an outrageously extended visual trance involving the love affair between the characters of Charlotte and Daberlohn. In relation to this gouache riff on the second act of *Tristan*, speculation as to whether this account mirrors any aspect of the relationship between Charlotte Salomon and Alfred Wolfsohn is utterly beside the point. We cannot know what is true and what isn't; but we can evaluate what is represented as history, via a mode of visual as well as textual historiography, and what is represented as fantasy. The *Tristan*-like idiom of this central love story, with its repetition and excess, catapults the story and its style into adulthood, with its attendant values of eroticism and violence. These are the tools that return to the concluding narration of Nazi violence and Charlotte's own exile. The work culminates in a refusal of image, or more precisely, of the elevation of words into image.

In the middle section of the work, a dreamscape takes over the narrative as well as the visual idiom. Here we might make reference to another fin-de-siècle *Singspiel:* Hugo von Hofmannsthal's libretto as served up by Richard Strauss's opera *Ariadne auf Naxos.* The opera (in its revised 1916 version) unfolds across a prologue and a one-act opera. In the prologue, set in the home of a wealthy Viennese patron, competing troupes of performers prepare for an evening of commedia dell'arte and opera seria. The characters in the prologue (the Prima Donna and the Tenor) appear in costume in the opera as Ariadne, Bacchus, and others. The Composer disappears. And this fact doubles on an instruction that Hofmannsthal supplied to the work's future stage directors. At the end of the opera, he wrote, as Bacchus removes Ariadne from her island, the audience should be no more aware of the opera-within-the-opera structure "than a dreamer is aware of his own bed." Thus does the suspension of belief supply a dreamlike temporality of the radical present. This is how I shall understand the radical presentism and fantasy of the quantitatively dominant middle section of *Leben? Oder Theater?*

The modernism that evolves through the course of *Leben? Oder Theater?* moves away from history in the sense that it moves away from historiography. In earlier writing on Salomon and her work, I emphasized the work's responsibility to history. I reinforced this value, and my own tribute to it, in my introduction above. It would follow that my earlier work focuses on parts 1 and 3 of the work, the parts that narrate history. Here I turn to the suspension of narration and reality that dominates what Salomon calls the main section (*Hauptteil*) of her play, the vast quantity of images between the more historically contingent Prelude (*Vorspiel*) and Epilogue (*Nachwort*). In the table of contents or, rather, list of characters, Salomon also calls her work a three-colored play. She lists the characters associated with the prologue in blue letters, those of the main section in red, and those of the epilogue in yellow.

The prologue contains over two hundred images, with accompanying text and, as described above, indications of relevant musical selections. Its chronology covers the years 1913 to 1934. Thus its reach into the early years of the Third Reich brings it into the political present, from the vantage point of the composition years 1940–42. Spanning autobiography, family history, and political history, it begins in 1913 with the suicide of Salomon's maternal aunt, also named Charlotte, and it continues with the marriage of her sister Franziska to the surgeon Albert Kann. Albert Salomon's sobriquet "Kann" accords him an aura of competence. The family history continues with the birth of the eponymous Charlotte and the depression and suicide of her mother, now told according to the corrected historical understanding of the mature Charlotte. The narrative now cuts to a vignette of Paula Levy, here called Paulinka Bimbam, the contralto who in professional life took the name Paula Lindberg and who as the second wife of Albert became Paula Salomon. Paula brings the Weimar-period musical world into the Salomon/Kann household, including the conductor Professor Kling-klang (Siegfried Ochs); the conductor-impresario Doctor Singsong (Kurt Singer), and the young vocal coach and mystic Amadeus Daberlohn (Alfred Wolfsohn).

Hitler's ascension to power in January 1933 receives attention both as an historical event and as a catastrophe for the family and its milieu. Albert Kann is dismissed from his post and relocates to the Jewish Hospital. Paulinka and Dr. Singsong are heckled on the concert state by uniformed Nazis seated among the audience. Singsong successfully founds the Kulturbund Deutscher Juden—the Cultural Union of German Jews—following well-known and ever controversial historical fact.[4]

The visual palette is intricate throughout the prologue. At the same time, certain patterns emerge, though they are often contradicted. The color scheme remains loyal to the initial declaration of a tricolor structure of blue, red, and yellow. (On such a question the supply of materials at wartime France must of course be taken into account.) The basic associations of color are not surprising. Blue tends to dominate in scenes of family and security; red in depictions of passion, violence, and, whether literally or figuratively, blood. The yellows are the shades of disruption: the traumas that come from family and from the political, historical world.

The images' organization of space divides into two basic options. Where the narrative is advanced, a comic-book style emerges, in which a single image is partitioned into its episodic components, as if individual film frames were being offered for review. For example, the Kanns' Berlin apartment is portrayed as a kind of flattened dollhouse, with each room occupying an asymmetrical square, as if the page's geometry had been fashioned after the sets of the film *The Cabinet of Dr. Caligari:*

PLATE 1 (P. 19)

When the narrative halts to intensify or comment on a moment or a character, a single image fills the page. Thus the fallen and broken body of Charlotte's mother appears with uncompromised violence, and the face of Paulinka Bimbam is portrayed as radiant.

PLATE 2   Paulinka (p. 71)

Both options of visual organization can alternate between image and text. The printed notice of Franziska's suicide, to continue with the same example, appears in straightforward transcription as a full page.

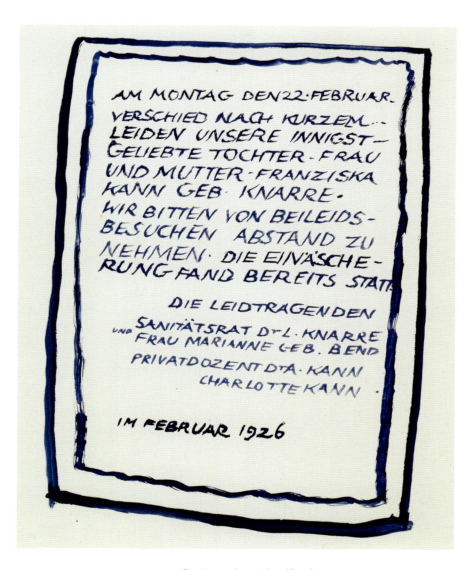

PLATE 3 "Am Montag den 22 Februar" (p. 35)

The narrative's burdensome core precludes neither humor in general nor episodes of light-hearted storytelling and scene painting. The Salomon/Kann family clearly traveled regularly—to the Bavarian Alps, to Greece, to Italy. Several of these trips receive generous coverage. One, the trip to Rome, is particularly interesting, both for the plot and for the work's developing symbolic and visual language, or what may here advisedly be called iconography. A veritable tourist travel log unfolds, accompanied by the imagined tune "Roma aeterna citta divina": St. Peter's, the Palatine, the Sistine Chapel. The same tune accompanies an image of Pius XI, speaking to a group of visitors and saying, "I am Pius XI, God's vicar on earth. *Tiens, tiens, tiens.* What are those little Jews doing here?" The pope wears glasses and a robe that prefigures the ecclesiastical garb created by Matisse, and he holds his arms stretched at his side. A nearby image carries the caption, "And this Pietà, I really loved it."

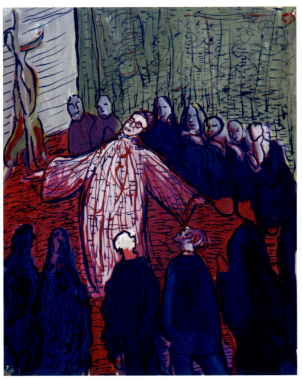

PLATE 4 Pope Pius XI (p. 176)

PLATE 5 Pietà (p. 179)

The scene with the pope involves a fantasy of negative interpellation that is basic to the repertories, private and published, of Jewish anxiety, especially in a climate of heightened anti-Semitism. (The textbook example of such a moment in American popular culture is the scene in Woody Allen's 1977 film *Annie Hall*, in which Allen's character imagines himself in Hasidic garb as he sits at the dinner table of Annie's [Diane Keaton's] midwestern family.)

The episode resonates in the unfolding of *Leben? Oder Theater?* in multiple ways. The pope's bespectacled face and hair resemble those of Amadeus Daberlohn, whose image will dominate the main section of the work with excessive repetition. This proleptic visual joke is a joke on Daberlohn. He will be introduced formally as the prophet of song. Visually, he becomes, by association, the pope of song—ecumenicism at work. Here, in the Rome episode, Pius XI's outstretched arms seem to mimic the posture of crucifixion, as a possible (if perhaps not an unironic) visual commentary on his remark, "I am Pius XI, God's vicar on earth." This posture will also inform the depictions of Daberlohn's bodily postures, especially the more stylized ones. Finally, the image of the character Charlotte gazing at the Pietà has implications for the later depictions of the triangle involving Charlotte, Daberlohn, and Paulinka. Daberlohn will repeatedly refer to Paulinka as his Madonna.

The play's main section opens with an expository scene involving Amadeus Daberlohn's arrival at Dr. Singsong's (Kurt Singer's) office to state his desire to teach voice, despite a lack of formal certification. The text reads "Amadeus Daberlohn,

prophet of song, enters to the tune of the Toreador's Song from *Carmen*." Singsong sends him to audition with "a great singer," which brings Daberlohn into the household of Paulinka and the Kann family. "So we are to work together," says Paulinka, with a sultry intensity in her gaze. Her mouth is pinched shut, but the words surround her profiled mouth and jaw in red block letters. These letters sit at the apex of a mountain-like burst of green and yellow, a kind of mesmeric energy erupting between the two figures.

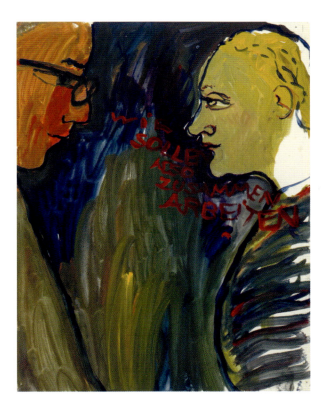

PLATE 6 "So we are to work together" (p. 219)

A professional partnership between Paulinka and Daberlohn develops, but Daberlohn seeks general ratification through eros: "I will make her the greatest of all singers. . . . But for this there's one condition—she must love me!"

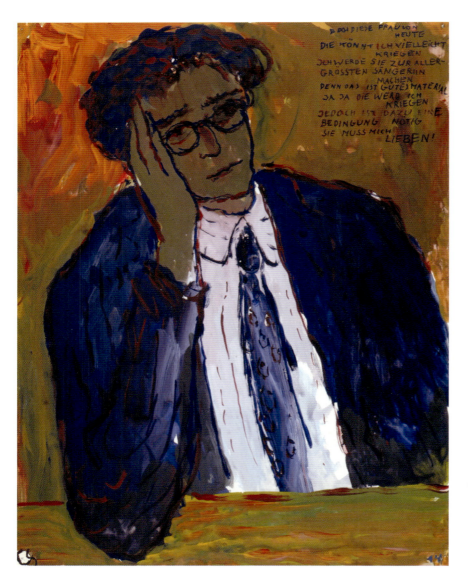

PLATE 7 "But this woman I saw today . . ." (p. 225)

Daberlohn's instruction to Paulinka involves the freeing of her voice. He reminds her of Nietzsche's imperative: "Learn to sing, O my soul." "What does that mean," he insists, "if not the urge to freedom?" Their work together is grounded in J. S. Bach's aria "Bist du bei mir" from the *St. Matthew Passion*. Numerous images depict them working on this aria, which becomes the signature of Paulinka's repertory. (It is part of Paula Lindberg's "recorded legacy.")[5] Daberlohn falls asleep and dreams of Paulinka singing this aria.

PLATE 8 "He falls asleep . . ."(p. 239)

Here we have an initial example of Daberlohn in a suspended position with a hint of the posture of crucifixion, a hint supported by allusion to Bach's sacred music. The confessional reference here is Lutheran, rather than the Roman Catholicism in the potentially precursory image of Pius XI. In the next image, the artist gives the dreaming Daberlohn what she presumes he wants, via a full eroticization of the phrase "Bist du bei mir," which in an emphasis of the subjunctive trans-lates as "Be thou with me": the image and memory of the Pietà are visibly relevant.

The story now gives Daberlohn's own story a chance to unfold, and as it quotes him it repeatedly and increasingly divides his body and head into multiple images, as if by mitosis. Daberlohn's account of war trauma and survival involves a certain identification on the part of the artist who chose creativity over suicide.

PLATE 9 "Bist du bei mir . . ." (p. 240)

PLATE 10 "But I realized that this was not so easy. I realized that no heaven, no sun, no star could help me if I did no contribute by my own will. And then I realized that actually I still had no idea who I was. I was a corpse. And I was expecting life to love me now. I waited and came to the realization: what matters is not whether life loves us, but that we love life" (p. 245)

Daberlohn's interlocutor is Paulinka, and she responds with the consolation of song. She responds visually by occasionally adopting and mirroring the visage of the divided, talking head. Distraught by his transference with regard to Paulinka, Daberlohn claims to leave her house for good. He then falls into a dream, according to the following image:

We seem to have here an intensification of the crucifixion posture, combined with an iconography and cheerfulness of springtime that would suggest resurrection. Upon his return to Paulinka, accompanied by these colors of resurrection, he begins to call her his "Madonna":

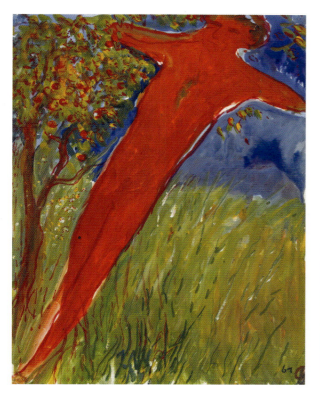

PLATE 11 (P. 271)

PLATE 12 "You are my Madonna and my singer" (p. 283)

"It is no accident, you know," says a later image of Daberlohn *qua* multiple talking head, "that you would rather sing Bach than any other composer and that then you can sometimes look like the true Mater Dolorosa" (p. 335). As this part of the story unfolds, the artist appears to lose the formal reference of the sung play and adopt an implicit referent of the silent film. The split heads can be understood as dissected frames, and there is no indication of accompanying music. (The images proceed silently, which is indeed not an accurate reflection of film: as many theorists have asserted, "silent" film was never silent and was indeed often accompanied by music.)

Paulinka's rejection of Daberlohn's amorous advances causes him to turn to Charlotte. He reviews her drawings and encourages her talent. He pontificates to her on Michelangelo, the character of the ancient Greeks, Rembrandt's *Saul and David*, and the poetry and emotions of Sturm und Drang. He assigns his own new treatise: "Orpheus, or The Way to a Mask." Daberlohn's interest in masks inspires him to have an impression made for his own death mask, without, of course, the presence of death. This story unfolds in a straightforward way, culminating with an un-ironic rendition of the mask itself. Indeed, this episode receives less irony from the artist than most involving Daberlohn. Perhaps he

is thus given credit precisely for his aestheticization of death, for this kitschy but perhaps no less successful self-removal from death via a phony ritual of the casting of the mask.

An episode involving Daberlohn and an unnamed sculptor gives the narrative an opportunity to eroticize Daberlohn's body while at the same time mocking its own eroticizing indulgence. A supine Daberlohn poses for the sculptor, whose product doubles as a giant phallus, accurately placed:

Charlotte depicts herself as the object of Daberlohn's gaze:

PLATE 14 (P. 448)

Daberlohn's seduction of Charlotte is depicted in the presence of an icon now known to the reader as one of death and suicide: the window. The window pervades *Leben? Oder Theater?* as the icon of suicide, its tempter or, where death has occurred, its remnant. A scene of an early childhood memory had placed Charlotte at her mother's bedside while the latter narrated her desire to join the angels; the accompanying image showed repeated figures of the mother passing through a window. Images of the mourning grandmother find her consistently seated in front of the window, the repeated weapon of suicide.

As the boundary between life and death, the window becomes also the boundary of representation. Death disallows representation, as everyone knows but as modernists, for whom representation and its limits form the most consistent aesthetic and ethical principle, know with perhaps more agony. In *The Death of Virgil* (1945) Hermann Broch devoted a novel to this question alone. A virtually real-time narrative traces the poet through his final hours of life, apparently declaring its readiness to follow him into death, which, in keeping with its modernist integrity, it then does not do. In *Leben? Oder Theater?* the window thus becomes the modernist icon, emphasized as the icon of death and the icon of the border between life and death, the border between representability and unrepresentability. In one image, the window appears alone, taking up the page as it fills the empty space of death, marking the absence of the figures whose lives it has helped to take.

PLATE 15 (P. 140)

The image's portrayal of absence, of boundaries, combines with the color palette to form an uncanny precursor to a defining canvas of Mark Rothko's mature style. I refer specifically to *1951 No. 6 (Violet, Green, and Red)* (see Anfam 1998: catalog no. 454).

Rothko of course postdates Salomon and her knowable frame of reference. An iconography of the window that pre-dates her work, and one that was very likely known to her, is Caspar David Friedrich's, specifically his 1811 rendition of his studio window and his 1822 return to the same image, to which he now added the figure of his wife, gazing outward with her back to the viewer.

PLATE 16 Caspar David Friedrich, *Woman at the Window*, 1822

By invoking images from Friedrich and Rothko I am opening the door to all sorts of problems in historical genealogy as well as teleology. Charlotte's three years at the Berlin Academy of Arts provided her with a solid foundation in art history. She did not know Rothko, and Rothko did not know of her. If, alternatively, we think of the history of art according to an externalist model of the history of style, then we slip into the artificial terms of canon building. Whether or not Charlotte Salomon can be engaged by, not to say included in, an art-historical canon is an important question for the politics of the discipline, but this is not my focus here.

Robert Rosenblum has made the link between Friedrich and Rothko (Rosenblum 1975). Rothko's connection is historical and linear, beginning with Friedrich and continuing with discussions of Vincent van Gogh, Edvard Munch, Ferdinand Hodler, Emil Nolde, Franz Marc, Wassily Kandinsky, and Piet Mondrian, on the way to Rothko. For Rosenblum, the central, style-defining metaphor of this canonic trajectory is a depiction of transcendence, in keeping with such aspects of romantic-generation Protestantism as pietism (Schleiermacher) and transcendentalism (Emerson). This stylistic and contextual insight is important. But I would distance myself from Rosenblum's presentation in two ways. First, I find that his analyses of paintings tend to ignore the experiencing subject of/in the images in favor of impersonal assertions of transcendence. This tendency is particularly marked in his discussions of Friedrich's depictions of women: the women themselves are not addressed. Second, I would suggest that an engagement of transcendence may go along with a disavowal of transcendence or of a faith in its possibility, a pessimism and/or reality principle that is key to my reading of Salomon and, indeed, Rothko. On this point my reading jibes with that of Leo Bersani and Ulysse Dutoit (Bersani and Dutoit 1991). The notions of impoverishment, "blocked vision," the "immobilization of perception," and "unreadability" capture Rothko's apparently deliberate convergence of vision and image with blindness and invisibility. The consistent association of seeing with the prohibition on seeing acts as a disavowal of transcendence, while at the same time transcendence is referred to as a forbidden object of desire. Rothko's abstraction precludes the representation of figures, or human bodies.

We can return here to *Leben? Oder Theater?* Now, in the seduction scene between Charlotte and Daberlohn, the window appears as the meeting point of love and death. It appears isolated as if in a modernist stage design by Alfred Roller or Adolphe Appiah. It is the icon of a *Liebestod*. An entirely silent one at that, for text and musical referents are both suppressed.

PLATE 17 Liebestod (p. 511)

The full color palette of *Leben? Oder Theater?* is in play here. In the repetitive iconography of the work's unfolding narrative, the window has long since become a metaphor for the body falling to death. The violence to the body and to life is real; as a boundary between life and death, the window is violently real. Moreover, the narrative of self-destruction and family trauma is consistently linked to the story of cultural and political violence at the level of national history. Thus the real border between life and death stands also as the historical referential history in the work: Europe between 1913 and 1942.

The dreamscape, nonetheless, removes and relieves the narrative from the historical as it removes the bodily. I shall call image no. 511 the *Liebestod.* The lovers are seated at a café table, replete with white coffee or tea cups. They hold hands across the table in a gesture of correct and socially acceptable flirtation, entirely in keeping with their postures and the respectable setting of the coffee table (private or public). According to this dimension of the image, the moment is socially and historically embedded. It is a function of history; it "cannot fall out of this world."[6] Yes, the image's remaining iconography is distinctly otherworldly, for the genre scene of the pair and their coffee table is suspended within a wash of color that fills the page—and suspended as well in spatial relation to the window, the icon of death. The reference to *Tristan und Isolde*, to Wagner's rendition specifically, and to the "Love-Death," is extremely close, though its intentionality cannot be determined. *Tristan* notwithstanding, the image carries no text and no music, nor any reference to music. This image is conspicuously silent.

As figures in the Wagnerian canon, Tristan and Isolde claim removal from the social world through love, eros, and, ultimately, death. Indeed, well-known modernist scenic designs of the act 2 love scene effectively remove the lovers from all definable contexts and space. Occasionally, with the help of hydraulic stage machinery, the lovers appear to float, gravityless, around the proscenium.[7] In a crucial if banal way, however, Wagner's Tristan and Isolde are never silent; as singing voices they are never removed from their bodies. Charlotte and Daberlohn, contra-*Tristan*, are in fact disembodied in this image. Their corporeal figures carry the same bourgeois correctness as the café scenery. Desire and death hover around them. There is no desire in their bodies, and they are voiceless.

Disembodiment informs one side of Charlotte Salomon's modernism. The politics of disembodiment coincide with the removal from desire, the removal from the bodily dimensions of subjectivity.

In arguing for the presence and definition of this kind of disembodiment, I am profiting from Michael Fried's study of the Berlin painter Adolph Menzel (Fried 2002). Fried's central trope is embodiment; "the art of embodiment" titles his first chapter. Presumably he controls the pun on "art" to connote both a made object and a mode of living. Both the painter's embodiment and the viewer's are at stake. Fried associates the body with Maurice Merleau-Ponty's phenomenological principle of "lived perspective," efficiently combining the physical with the experiential, a phenomenological principle with a painterly one (ibid.: 19). He cites Heinrich Wölfflin's assertion, from his 1886 "Prolegomena to a Psychology of Architecture," that "physical forms possess a character only because we ourselves possess a body. If we were purely visual beings, we would always be denied an aesthetic judgment of the physical world" (Wölfflin 1994; cited in Fried 2002: 35). He cites also the phenomenologist Max Scheler's distinction between *Körper* and *Leib* (literally, "body" and "body") as that between the physical and the lived body, as well as Robert Vischer's discussion of the body as a function of "the human psychophysical self" (Fried 2002: 37 and 39).[8] Embodiment thus incorporates the recognition of subjectivity, understood as the life of the human and political subject in the world. Embodiment becomes a principle of painterly realism as "it corresponds to and evokes the actual physical movements—the actual inclinations of the head and neck—with which an embodied viewer would have perceived the original scene."

Fried endows embodiment with the claim of subjectivity:

> To broaden my remarks about the treatment of space . . . we might say that Menzel's art continually asserts the primacy of *situatedness as such*. It is as if Menzel's concern with embodiment called for thematizing the fact that the lived body is always some place, in some particular spatial, actional, and orientational relation to the world, which therefore is never present to artist or viewer as pure "spectacle," the way in which the world appears to have been present to Claude Monet, whom Cézanne once famously described as "nothing but an eye." (Fried 2002: 22)[9]

The world beyond spectacle: Life beyond Theater. With dispatch, Fried moves his terms into the core categories of Charlotte Salomon's work. "Situatedness" is key because it implies a sense of place not only within and outward from the body but also from and in place, culture, history. It is thus the beneficent opposite of banishment and of exile. In this sense, the erotic fantasy of the Charlotte-Daberlohn union (and I repeat that *Leben? Oder Theater?* depicts a fantasy in terms autonomous from the biographical facts) carries the desire for embodiment, for a situatedness at once erotic and political.

Not coincidentally, Adolph Menzel as an artist of embodiment is also an artist of Berlin. Born in Breslau in 1815, he moved to Berlin with his family in 1830 and lived there until his death in 1905. He bequeathed most of his work to Berlin's Nationalgalerie, with the result that most of his work remains in the city. It is work that Charlotte Salomon can be assumed to have known. But the identifications run deeper than that.

In arguing for Menzel's greatness, Fried wants to lift him from the condescension of the adjudicators of a nineteenth-century painterly canon. One problem is that this canon remains largely French. A second problem is that Menzel's work was located mostly in what was East Berlin between 1945 and 1989. Most interestingly, Menzel was rebuked by his most distinguished and most successful local successor, Max Liebermann, for sacrificing, in Fried's words, "the values of painting to those of illustration and anecdote" (Fried 2002: 28). In a polemical study of 1906, Julius Meier-Graefe, in keeping with his Francocentric, modernist valorization of the unity of picture plane and of color, suggested that Menzel had failed to become a great modernist painter owing to his submission to the private and public taste for (Fried's words here) "anecdotal realism" (Meier-Graefe 1906: 75, 274). A similar complaint, among many others, keeps Charlotte Salomon out of the canon of the history of art (for fuller treatment of Salomon and the canon, see N. Salomon 2006).

Fried appears to have difficulty interpreting Menzel's best-known so-called private painting, *The Balcony Room* of 1845. The image (which Fried chose for his book's cover) shows a room empty of people, a wooden floor and a slightly disfigured blank wall at its vertical center, two chairs in mirror position on the right, themselves framing a mirrored armoire. Between these two fields is the image's most-discussed aspect: a pair of French doors, open to the wind, a set of white muslin curtains delicately billowing around them. Earlier commentary on this painting stressed a proto-modernism on the basis of its fragmentariness, emptiness, and loneliness. Fried, however, suggests that the curtains supply a metonym of the bodily, even of a feminine body. He understands the mirror as a metaphor of reflective subjectivity in the philosophical tradition of Fichte, Schelling, Hegel, and Kierkegaard. Thus the painting "interpellates the viewer," Fried argues, asking the viewer "to respond projectively [to]

the multiple evocations of a subjectivity that on the one hand seems to hover everywhere we look and on the other to come to rest, to condense and stabilize, nowhere in particular" (Fried 2002: 87 and 89).[10]

I am not convinced. I do not feel invited into this private space, which, in its austerity of composition and economy of representation, I do in fact find, on its own terms, inviting. Because, according to Fried's rules of embodiment, my own spectator's embodiment is the only embodiment invoked in (his reading of) this picture, I take issue with the application of the main trope to this painting. I see this painting and its display of private space as, rather, a parable of disembodiment. Culturally, ideologically, I read the image therefore as a symptom of a certain north German austerity that disavows the body and its pleasures. This is one side of Berlin, a side of Berlin less known to the studies and evocations of the city of the period of Christopher Isherwood and Marlene Dietrich. Isherwood and Dietrich's Berlin is also, temporally and culturally, Charlotte Salomon's Berlin. This austere, disembodying side of Berlin is also a side of Charlotte Salomon's world and modernism as well as, I dare say, of Menzel's. It is "life" in opposition to theater, self-display, and spectatorship. In *The Balcony Room*, Menzel may in fact disclose a desire for embodiment, in himself and in his culture, just as Salomon may so do in her Tristanesque depiction of two lovers in front of a suspended window. In both cases, however, the presence or achievement of embodiment, of a subjectivity integrating self and world, seems absent.

PLATE 18 Menzel, *The Balcony Room* (Nationalgalerie Berlin A 1 744)

The cultural language of the northern German dialectics of authenticity, into which Protestants and Jews were both interpellated, involved the disavowal of artifice and theater that easily enabled a culture of almost puritanical rigidity. In Charlotte Salomon's case as in the case of her troubled family, the disavowal of theatricality involved what Darcy Buerkle has called the effacement of women. Effacement I understand as a visual metaphor or indeed a real, visual dimension for an existential and indeed political disembodiment, a disembodiment that becomes literally destructive and self-destructive in the epidemic of suicide. Women were glibly understandable as the carriers of theatricality, of inauthenticity, and subsequently also of that more extreme version of theatricality, namely, hysteria. Buerkle thus understands Charlotte Salomon's work as a drive against the effacement of women (Buerkle 2006). With devastating accuracy, Buerkle understands Charlotte's basic question—Life? Or Theater?—in terms both of a reference and of an at least partial adherence to the admonition "mach doch kein Theater"—don't make a scene; don't make a production out of it. Buerkle points out that "it is the admonition that women hear in some form or another throughout the play." Charlotte, or more accurately the Charlotte who narrates *Life? Or Theater?*, I think it is fair to say, heeds the antitheatrical ethic of authenticity, but at the same time undermines its resulting effacement of women. In doing so, she seems, or the work seems, to grasp a crucial distinction between performance and the performative, between "acting" and acting, between representation and presentation. "Life? Or theater?" appears as the most fundamental historical question about the life and claims of German (including German Jewish) culture. "Life? Or theater?" was the central question that German Jews asked themselves, if seldom with Charlotte Salomon's rigor.

It is a question that Salomon's work never resolves, in style or in plot. The Daberlohn story is broken by the text's return to political events on the date of *Kristallnacht*, 9 November 1938. In the pogrom's wake, as the story makes clear, Dr. Kann determines to send his daughter out of Germany. Charlotte respects but resents the decision. The account of her subsequent life in various beautiful spots of the French Riviera abjures the picturesque. Romance is consigned to the past, in its figures (Daberlohn, Paulinka, Singer) and in its visual idioms of dreamscape and repetition. History returns, and with it both political and personal trauma. The end of the story is the survival of the work. Paying homage to it, I would end this essay by endorsing the epigraph Michael Fried chose for his study of Menzel, attaching it as well to Charlotte Salomon's life and work. From Thoreau's *Walden*: "Be it life or death, we crave only reality."

❧❧❧

::: **NOTES** :::

1. For a collection of interdisciplinary analyses of Salomon's work, see Steinberg and Bohm-Duchen 2006.

2. See the fine biography by Mary Felstiner (Felstiner 1997), as well as Kimmelman 2005: 119–30; Steinberg and Bohm-Duchen 2006.

3. Alfred Wolfsohn survived World War II and settled in England, where he taught voice until his death in 1962. He wrote several manuscripts, which were never published, including "Orpheus, oder der Weg zu einer Maske" (Orpheus, or the Way to a Mask), Berlin, 1938; "Die Brücke" (The Bridge), London, 1947; and "The Problems of Limitations," London, 1958. The Alfred Wolfsohn Archives are in the care of Marita Guenther, Malerargues, Ansuze, France. The Jewish Historical Museum in Amsterdam holds copies of "Orpheus" and "Die Brücke." For a portrait of Wolfsohn and his postwar career see Pikes 1999: 29–65, and especially 31 n. See also Newham 1997.

4. This historical narrative receives more detailed analysis in Steinberg 2006.

5. For a discussion of this aria and the place of Bach in the repertory and taste of German Jewish musicians, see Steinberg 2006.

6. As in Freud's citation of Grabbe in chapter 1 of *Civilization and Its Discontents*: "Wir können aus dieser Welt nicht fallen." See Freud 2005.

7. A well-known example of this effect was Günter Schneider-Siemssen's design for the Metropolitan Opera, which premiered in 1971.

8. These citations give credit to the anthology mentioned in the previous citation and to its editors.

9. Fried addresses but deemphasizes the word subjectivity. "Subjectivity is surely to the point but, as I have noted, the effect of lived perspective . . . is as much to emphasize the extreme dearness of some things as to imply the distance of others." This is fair enough. He seems to identify subjectivity with a restricted notion of subject position, related to actual physical and optical position.

In my ongoing work I deploy the term subjectivity as the fully lived, that is, psychological and political, life of the subject (see Steinberg 2004).

10. Fried also compares *The Balcony Room* to Caspar David Friedrich's 1822 painting of his wife at the studio window, which I have discussed with reference to Salomon's depictions of windows (see Fried 2002: 88).

::: **WORKS CITED** :::

Anfam, David. 1998. *Mark Rothko: The Works on Canvas.* New Haven, Conn.: Yale University Press.

Bersani, Leo, and Ulysse Dutoit. 1991. *Arts of Impoverishment: Beckett, Rothko, Resnais.* Cambridge, Mass.: Harvard University Press.

Buerkle, Darcy. 2006. "Historical Effacements: Facing Charlotte Salomon." In Steinberg and Bohm-Duchen, *Reading Charlotte Salomon*, 73–87.

Felstiner, Mary Lowenthal. 1997. *To Paint Her Life: Charlotte Salomon in the Nazi Era.* Berkeley: University of California Press. Orig. publ. 1994.

Freud, Sigmund. 2005. *Civilization and Its Discontents.* Trans. and ed. by James Strachey. New York: W. W. Norton. Modern ed. of German original: Freud, Sigmund. 2000. *Das Unbehagen in der Kultur und andere kulturtheoretische Schriften.* Frankfurt am Main: Büchergilde Gutenberg.

Fried, Michael. 2002. *Menzel's Realism: Art and Embodiment in Nineteenth-Century Berlin.* New Haven, Conn.: Yale University Press.

Kimmelman, Michael. 2005. *The Anecdotal Masterpiece: On the Art of Life and Vice Versa.* New York: Penguin.

Meier-Graefe, Julius. 1906. *Der junge Menzel: Ein Problem der Kunst-Ökonomie Deutschlands.* Leipzig: Insel Verlag.

Newham, Paul. 1997. *The Prophet of Song: The Life and Work of Alfred Wolfsohn.* London and Boston: Tiger's Eye Press.

Pikes, Noah. 1999. *Dark Voices: The Genesis of Roy Hart Theatre*. Woodstock, Conn.: Spring Journal Books.

Pollock, Griselda. 2006. "Theater of Memory: Trauma and Cure in Charlotte Salomon's Modernist Fairy Tale *Leben? Oder Theater?*. In Steinberg and Bohm-Duchen, *Reading Charlotte Salomon*, 34–72.

Rosenblum, Robert. 1975. *Modern Painting and the Northern Romantic Tradition: Friedrich to Rothko*. New York: Harper & Row.

Salomon, Nanette. 2006. "On the Impossibility of Charlotte Salomon in the Classroom." In Steinberg and Bohm-Duchen, *Reading Charlotte Salomon*, 212–22.

Steinberg, Michael P. 2004. *Listening to Reason: Culture, Subjectivity, and Nineteenth-Century Music*. Princeton, N.J.: Princeton University Press.

———. 2006. "Reading Charlotte Salomon: History, Memory, Modernism." In Steinberg and Bohm-Duchen, *Reading Charlotte Salomon*, 1–20.

———, and Monica Bohm-Duchen, eds. 2006. *Reading Charlotte Salomon*. Ithaca, N.Y.: Cornell University Press.

Wölfflin, Heinrich. 1994. "Prolegomena to a Psychology of Architecture." In Henry Francis Mallgrave and Eleftherios Ikonomou, eds., *Empathy, Form, and Space: Problems in German Aesthetics, 1873–1893*, 49–62. Santa Monica, Calif.: Getty Center for the History of Art and the Humanities.

Beyond Jewish Modernism

::: PHILIP V. BOHLMAN

And Abraham lifted up his eyes, and looked, and beheld behind him a ram caught in a thicket by his horns: and Abraham went and took the ram, and offered him up for a burnt offering in the stead of his son.

Genesis 22:13

The biblical story known as the "Binding of Isaac" or, in Hebrew, the Akeda, contains one of the most powerfully transcendent moments in all of Jewish history. Just as Abraham was raising a knife to follow God's commandment to sacrifice his son, Isaac, the angel of God halted him and revealed to him a ram ensnared in a thicket by its own horns. By sacrificing the ram instead of his only son, Abraham assured the lineage of Jewish history and symbolically removed human sacrifice from Jewish ritual practice. Through this transcendent moment, moreover, music comes into being, entering Jewish history as an act of God that was then transformed by human hand. Once the ram had been offered as burnt sacrifice, its horns, which had been the cause of its entrapment, were taken and used as the shofar, the horn sounded to announce beginnings and endings in Jewish ritual, and especially to signal the acts of atonement that accompany Yom Kippur. Throughout Jewish history, but especially in the era of Diaspora, the shofar enjoyed a privileged position as the sole musical instrument allowed in Jewish religious practice after the destruction of the Temple. Played at moments of transition in the Jewish sacred calendar, the shofar reminded Jews of the transformation of material born of sacrifice into the sound issuing forth as the moment of transcendence. The musical meaning of the shofar is also one of in-betweenness, for it occupies an ontological domain between the human voice and the artifice of instrumental music. Its narrative functions as music move between the past, in other words the formative moment in Genesis, and the present, when it articulates each new moment of beginning during the time of transition as one year passes into the next. It renews the transcendence at one of the earliest defining moments in Jewish history by affording it a specific place in the present.

The constant renewal of metaphorical meaning in the story of the Akeda has empowered it to serve as one of the most forceful narratives for the representation and interpretation of Jewish history. In the essay that closes this volume, I also draw upon the metonymic potential of the Akeda, particularly upon the ways it opens up the narrative spaces of Jewish modernism. The narrative qualities of the biblical story are, in fact, critical in any attempt to explore the ways Jewish modernism emerges along the borders between myth and history. As a story that offers up its metaphors

through hermeneutical interpretation, the Akeda directs us toward the type of empirical evidence that usefully represents Jewish modernism. The story should remind us that transcendence is not simply an abstract, directionless transition in Jewish history. Quite the contrary, the moment of Jewish modernism is one in which history is being reconfigured. New goals and directions supplant the old. Once the teleology of European history is suspended, there is a deliberate move toward identifying a new telos consistent with Jewish modernism. Just as Abraham substituted the ram for Isaac at the sacrificial altar, Jewish modernism fulfilled its goal of transition by reconfiguring its symbolic contexts, specifically so by enhancing what the modernists understood to be Jewishness.

In the extended section that constitutes the core of this epilogue I examine five distinctive forms of reconfiguring history that emerged from the border between myth and history opened by the transcendence of Jewish modernism. Several of these forms represent clearly temporal metaphors—beginnings and endings—while others are more broadly geographical or spatial—border crossing and utopia. Modernism, the fourth case of reconfiguring history I examine in this section, is neither clearly temporal nor spatial, but rather embodies metaphorical qualities of both. Each of the five cases introduces different historical processes and, even more significantly, different sets of historical actors, whose individual contributions to the shaping of Jewish modernism were distinctive and, at times, catalytic. The cases below were not always related to each other, even if they reflect responses to roughly the same historical period.

To add a further level of interpretation to the convergence of the different historical processes represented by the cases, I turn to another narrative framework in Jewish history, the *Torah*, or Five Books of Moses. As a compilation of biblical texts meant to convey the laws for Jewish life through exemplary laws and historical narratives, the Torah relies on a texture woven from both mythological and historical strands that even when viewed from the perspective of contemporary thought, yield new, sometimes radically new, processes in Jewish history. The Torah is equally rich with musical metaphor, and as a text with a performative basis in cantillation and song, it reveals the ways in which music was often present at specific moments, charging them with the especially powerful meanings that accompanied transcendence.[1]

Genesis/Beginnings

Beginnings and endings overlapped and blurred as Jewish history entered modernity. To some extent, they overlapped because of a tension that resulted from the fact that Jewish history is not primarily imagined as teleological (see Funkenstein 1993: 22–49). Jewish history became teleological precisely when it confronted modernity, moving toward moments of crisis, among them the crises of Jewish modernism that enable the authors in the present volume to locate Jewish music in twentieth-century history.[2] As we begin to examine the transcendence of the teleological anxieties of modernity, it becomes necessary to reflect on the nature of Jewish history and historiography, especially to understand how the moments of beginning are identified and constructed.

Whereas there is no single, unassailably authoritative model of Jewish historiography, there are several that recur with some frequency yet nonetheless parse the *longue durée* in quite different ways. The first truly overarching model is that of cycles. The cyclical view of Jewish history makes a case for events that occur in repeated fashion, gathering momentum at a point of beginning and then progressing through a series of stages, which in turn are followed by a return to the point of beginning before starting all over again. The most common framework for cyclical history is the cyclicity that accompanies life itself. Patterns of cyclicity are often invoked to represent musical practices as Jewish, both sacred and secular. The most widespread textual and melodic cycle for Jewish sacred music is that of the Torah cycle, in other words the cantillation of all five Books of Moses during the course of a year. The cyclical nature of reciting the Torah is musically emphasized in several Jewish communities, notably the Eastern communities, whose use of distinctive *maqāmāt* at certain points in the cycle has been canonized as the dominant liturgical tradition in modern Israel, the so-called Jerusalem-Sephardi tradition (see Seroussi in this volume). Published anthologies of liturgical or cantorial repertory (*ḥazzanut*) also employ the framework of liturgical and holiday cycles, thus musically inscribing the repetitive overlapping of beginnings and endings. Anthologies of Jewish folk song, too, have been represented as a constellation of repertories, each of which has meaning according to functions associated with the life cycle (e.g., marriage songs, lullabies, and children's songs).[3]

The second model of Jewish history is myth. There are many different ways of defining myth, but I use it here as in one of the most basic models, in which myth contrasts with history because it incorporates sequences of events that largely belie the human life cycle; hence, they lie outside of history. In myth, people may live in ways that are not always human, as in the case of Moses, the eponymous figure of the Torah, whose lifetime spans some 140 years. Much that cannot be explained through history is situated in myth. Accordingly, many folklorists and structural anthropologists have treated myth as if it were ahistorical, or even as if it were the non-teleological counterpart to history, where nothing really changes. The meaning of myth for Jewish historiography is all the greater because the great mythical cycle is the Torah. Torah cantillation, emphasizing the stichic (line-by-line) structure common to mythological texts, incorporates myth into the performative properties of cantillation. By extension, it is possible to interpret Torah cantillation as performatively constitutive of the epic, the musical genre most often associated with the performance of myth.

Diaspora has provided Jewish historiography with one of its most complex and durable models. Within the model of diaspora, beginning and ending are specified and geographically located in *eretz yisrael*, the land of Israel. Diaspora is itself teleological, nonetheless, because it is temporary as well as temporal, at least in an idealized sense. It also manifests the conditions of history, as opposed to the conditions of myth, in such a way that the movement between Israel and the Diaspora are equivalent to crossing the border between history (diaspora) and myth (Israel before and after diaspora). Diaspora demonstrates the properties of cyclicity, especially if one takes into consideration the possibility of multiple diasporas.[4]

Not to be forgotten as a model for Jewish history is messianism, which is characterized by two periods of relative historical stasis, one prior to the arrival of the Messiah, the other beginning with the arrival of the Messiah. Messianism reflects a very particular metaphysics of beginning and ending, for the epoch of expectation gives way completely to the epoch of fulfillment; beginning, in essence, brings about ending. Messianism, moreover, specifies place in historically significant ways, again emphasizing the juxtaposition of geographical and temporal points of beginning and ending.

Historical consciousness grew in European Jewish society in many of the same ways that Jewish self-consciousness intensified and reached a moment of crisis at the beginning of the twentieth century (Funkenstein 1993: 220–56). These different models of Jewish history, therefore, become extraordinarily relevant because they signify the convergence the essays in this volume broadly attribute to Jewish modernism. If historical beginnings and endings are manifest in each of the models, they undergo a process of competing for the spaces immanent in Jewish society (Bohlman 1997). I use the designation "space" here quite deliberately, for it is another condition of modern Jewish history that space became available to Jews—that they gained the power, for example, to own the land on which they might build their homes or locate their businesses—more or less across the globe.

Making space Jewish became a crucial problem for modern Jewish society. We witness this in the history of Zionism, for example, and its struggle to determine just how sacred or secular the historical geography of Israel needed to be. Jewish modernism provided a context for the ways in which the competition for historical spaces was played out, and it laid the groundwork for surveying what Homi Bhabha has called a "third space" (Bhabha 1994), a "location of culture" that could be transformed in such a way that it provided radically new possibilities for realizing Jewish identity. Throughout the present volume, we have examined how the alternative spaces of modern Jewish history were opened through Jewish thought, through scientific and artistic expression that is identifiably Jewish. Within these spaces of Jewish thought and expressive culture, music occupies a distinctive place, both because of its historical and narrative qualities and because of its capacity to represent myth and give it historical meaning.

Only at the end of the nineteenth century did it become common to speak unequivocally of an historiography of Jewish music. In other words, only as Jewish modernism began to coalesce was it possible to discuss specific histories of Jewish music that unfolded from identifiable beginnings. One of the most sweeping cases of a Jewish music discussed in the emerging historical discourse was folk music. I have already remarked upon the fact that, prior to the 1880s, there was no phenomenon, repertory, or set of expressive practices that bore the name "Jewish folk music." European folklorists had so completely read Jewish music out of folk music that when examples appeared in canonic repertories, they were given regional or national classifications.[5] The absence of a specific name to use for Jewish folk music around 1880 notwithstanding, by 1900 the search for Jewish folk music was preoccupying a broad range of Jewish musicians and intellectuals, whose common endeavor displayed the characteristics of a discourse history. Within a generation an anxiety had arisen that Jewish folk music had already been lost, even sacrificed to modernity, and as a response to that anxiety the collection and canonization of Jewish folk music and the accompanying search for its origins spread across the Diaspora.

Almost from the first passionate calls for retrieving disappearing repertories and practices, Jewish folk music possessed the rhetoric of a discourse history, which required that one first identify and name a music "Jewish" and then create a space in modern Jewish history for that music. With that space given musical resonance, the beginnings of a modern Jewish music history were in place, and it became possible, for the first time, to explode the categories that ascribed Jewishness to the musical practices of modern Jews.

The beginnings of Jewish modernism were firmly established.

Exodus/Diaspora

History and myth overlap and intersect to form the cultural geography of diaspora. The historical meaning of diaspora—the separation from a homeland and the teleology of a return—enhances and is enhanced by the constellation of metaphors that accompany diaspora. Worldly and sacred dimensions, for example, interact, as the metaphors of sacred journey and escape from persecution intersect. Diaspora ascribes meaning in especially powerful ways precisely at the moments when the intersection of history and myth is the greatest, when the distinctions between them blur in the most unexpected ways. In the Torah the narrative of diaspora is set in motion by the Second Book of Moses, Exodus. In modern Jewish history diaspora reaches its greatest crisis during the half century that led to and culminated in the Holocaust.

Each author in the present volume has addressed the dilemma of diaspora in different ways. There is, nonetheless, a common set of questions that connect all the essays to the moment of Jewish modernism. Do the conditions of diaspora enhance or weaken the ways in which music reflects Jewish identity? Is the culture of diaspora a bulwark against acculturation, or does it hasten the processes that lead to the disintegration of Jewish society? Does diaspora hasten the fragmentation of Jewish history, or does it forge a new teleology predicated upon the possibilities of return? The individuals we encountered in the previous chapters responded to the explicit crises laid bare by such questions in remarkably different ways, but again we can also perceive a set of common responses. It is not by chance that music, indeed, Jewish music, has provided one of the central languages for giving voice to those common responses.

Music occupies a very special place in diaspora. Not only is it possible to speak of the ways in which music accrues to expressive practices that are diasporic, but music may extensively undergird the capacity of certain practices to be diasporic. In some diasporas music may even provide a sort of historical receptacle for those cultural practices and traces that directly embody and transmit diaspora. Perhaps most important, music frequently serves as a performative text for the inscription of diaspora, representing and even narrating the journey embedded in the history of diaspora. The presence of music in diaspora raises a question about the representation of history that has been critical to the essays in this book. Music, so many scholars in music or completely outside it would argue, represents history and the past in very distinctive ways (see Bohlman 2005). Language or dialect, for example, survives in song after disappearing elsewhere in a diasporic culture. Certain genres of music possess the function to narrate the history of diaspora itself, telling the stories of journey, encounter, and homeland. The *romancero* and *romance* of Sephardic Jews, narrative practice and genre, accrue as a corpus of historical texts, not only for the centuries of residence in Iberia, but also for the confrontations resulting from centuries of searching for a new land in which to settle. Music also weaves the various historical narratives of diaspora into a common fabric, which in turn allows music to symbolize diaspora itself, even though that fabric is constitutive of the contradictions and crises that accompany diasporic cultures as they confront modernity.[6]

Crucial to the way diaspora served as a precondition for the transcendence of Jewish modernism is that one of the characteristics distinguishing diaspora from other types of migration or displacement is religion. Diaspora takes shape as a communal journey with sacred dimensions. The original homeland—*eretz yisrael*—is symbolically sacred, and return to the homeland is therefore possible only upon completing a sacred journey, which invests diaspora with a religious teleology. This means that embarking on and continuing along the journey is not entirely a matter of personal volition. The culture of diaspora responds to the sacred nature of diaspora, which, by extension, is a primary condition in the separation of the diasporic community from the culture around it. The sacred history that musical repertories shaped in diaspora convey has the potential to inscribe the sacred landscape of the diaspora itself. The musical and ritual practices accompanying the three pilgrimage festivals of Judaism—Passover, Shavuot, and Succot—serve as performative texts for the sacred geography of Jewish history, in the cases of Passover and Succot of the exodus from Egypt itself. It is because of diaspora's sacred dimensions that its mythological character becomes important. In diaspora, mythological time

forms along the temporal border with history, but there is no prehistorical or posthistorical dualism. Quite the contrary: the mythological world is that of the homeland, the place from which Jews in diaspora came and to which its sacred teleology pulls them. By stressing the sacred quality of music in diaspora, however, I do not want to bracket off musical practices that are not directly sacred in function. The point I wish to make, instead, is that all musics in diaspora do not have to be directly connected to or dependent on diaspora. Accordingly, at moments of crisis, music is invested with the power to transcend diaspora.

Without pushing the matter of paradigms and precedence too far, I should like to suggest that diaspora has such a uniquely powerful presence in Jewish music history that ontologies of Jewish music depend on it to a remarkable degree.[7] Concepts of what Jewish music is, therefore, have historically been argued from the standpoint of their location in the Diaspora, temporally and spatially. If one can justify or even prove the connections to prediasporic traditions, especially musical practices supported by biblical evidence, the identity of Jewish music is presumably secure.[8]

Above all, the music of the Jewish Diaspora is paradigmatic because the relation between the music of a homeland and that of the Diaspora has sustained a remarkably consistent historical tradition over the course of several millennia. There are several distinctive ontological conditions that we might schematically represent as follows. First, in the historical imagination Jewish music survives in a temporal stasis, and through its putative lack of changeability Jewish music is imagined to embody the homeland in diaspora. Second—and paradoxically—music thought to be truly Jewish reflects an historical dynamic, insofar as it possesses an ideal toward which the communities in diaspora should aspire. Third, the musics of the homeland and the musics of the Diaspora coexist in an historical counterpoint, constantly juxtaposing diaspora and homeland.

Even though the ontologies of Jewish music are inseparable from the historical frameworks of diaspora, they are nonetheless both constructions and emblems of larger myths about the dynamics of Jewish historical identities. In the commonsense arguments about Jewish music, it is the claim that a given musical repertory, musical practice, or musical sound has remained stable and unchanging in diaspora that is most broadly held. By and large, empirical evidence, even from outside the Diaspora, is mustered to back up such claims. Clearly, they rely on an historical tautology, whereby different diasporic communities maintain that their centuries of isolation—in Yemen, Iraq, or South Germany—mean they have preserved the *true* music of the period before the destruction of the Temple in Jerusalem in 70 CE.[9]

A history of Jewish music in the Jewish Diaspora raises complex issues about the nature of authenticity and its possibility in displaced cultures (see Shelemay in this volume). As a condition of diaspora, Jewish music's authenticity displays a particularly heightened meaning, for the really crucial issue is whether or not authenticity (1) can be sustained or retained and (2) can serve as a metaphorical telos or goal toward which

the diasporic community strives. The authentic becomes, therefore, idealized. The authentic enters an historical space in which the present is distinguished from both the past and the future. A specifically diasporic historical dynamic accrues to authenticity, transforming it into one of the most highly charged emblems for Jewish modernism, even when—or especially when, as Michael Steinberg illustrates with his chapter on Charlotte Salomon—perils accompany that authenticity. Once appropriated during the moment of Jewish modernism, diaspora was therefore more than a persistent condition of Jewish history: It became the symbol of that which most desperately called out for transcendence.

Music that was imagined as Jewish provided the Diaspora with a multitude of options for slipping from the historical present into a mythological elsewhere. Jewish music at the turn of the century acquired important temporal qualities that could invert the usual relation between myth and history. Whereas theories of myth, among them those of structuralists such as Claude Lévi-Strauss (e.g., Lévi-Strauss 1969), held that history followed from myth, diaspora creates the possibility of returning to a mythical world, in which physical mortality and time itself would take on different meaning. An implicit authenticity in that mythical world would invest it with the power of transcendence. As the many displaced Jewish cultures at the beginning of the twentieth century endeavored to respond to the changing conditions of diaspora (e.g., emigration from Europe to the Americas or the growing multiculturalism of European communities), music came increasingly to provide an important domain for the imagination of authenticity and for the historical inscription of myth. During the moment of Jewish modernism diaspora ultimately came to result from the counterpoint formed by two temporal worlds, one displaced from the other, but neither fully realized through a cultural geography of modernity. Music, precisely because it could represent both worlds, succeeded in differentiating the contrapuntal temporalities of myth and history, thereby, if paradoxically, sustaining the counterpoint itself as an historical framework for Jewish modernism.

Leviticus/Utopia

It was in the city that the counterhistories of Jewish modernism converged and then coalesced as transcendence. The heightened musical ontology of Jewish modernism depended at once on the traditional polity of the Jewish community as an urban institution and the emergence of the modern European city, which had become cosmopolitan in part by permitting Jews to enter the culture of its public sphere. Jewish music was a city music, and the history of Jewish music is one of cosmopolitanism. In the modern European city, Jewish music underwent a radical transformation in the process of crossing the boundaries between Jewish and non-Jewish sectors. Paradoxically, music became in many ways more Jewish, surely self-consciously more Jewish, precisely because it aspired to the conditions of transcendence that the modern city afforded. In the course of the half century prior to the Holocaust it was because the

music of Jewish modernism was so fundamentally a product of the city that it could yield the transcendence of utopia.

The utopian potential of the city is first evident in the Third Book of Moses, Leviticus, for it is in that book of laws that conditions for giving Jewish society cosmopolitan dimensions are most clearly evident. The historical narrative of the Torah comes to a standstill in Leviticus, while Moses and the people of Israel turn inward toward themselves to create their own world, a society of humans on earth, who take time to carry out ritual and obey laws in order that they might fulfill a covenant with God. The detailed description of laws and their concomitant fulfillment through a priesthood should serve as the foundation for an ideal world, a utopia. I use the concept of utopia here in two ways. First, I use it as it is most commonly understood and applied, namely as a society that is in some way perfect and unique to a particular culture, which is to say, cut off from the rest of the world. Second, I use the concept as it was originally used by Thomas More in his book of the same name, for which he coined the word "utopia" from the Greek *oitopia* (a good place) and *outopia* (a place that does not exist). Such images of utopia help us understand Leviticus as a moment outside history, in which the future was envisioned as a society in which every action could be accounted for by law, and every transgression against other human beings could be resolved through sacrifice.

Utopia is one of the most common metaphors in the imagination and construction of Jewish polities. As European Jewish communities confronted the expanding conditions of modernity in European society, utopian responses proliferated, both as alternatives to modernity and as communities that may demonstrate a polity of hypermodernity. The genealogies and courts of Hasidic Jews that emerged in Eastern Europe as a response to the Enlightenment were, in this sense, no less utopian than the Jewish state that early Zionists envisioned. Utopian responses to modernity were practical and philosophical,[10] and they appeared as religious tracts and belles lettres.[11] So pervasive is the imagination of utopia during the moment of Jewish modernism that we need to look even beyond such obvious works dedicated specifically to utopia (Buber 1985). The typologies of diaspora community, for example, the shtetl and the ghetto, function historiographically as utopias. In very similar ways, the kibbutz has become the most recent modern community structure to reflect Jewish visions of utopia.

The emergence of Jewish city culture during the moment of Jewish modernism was the product of utopian responses. In Eastern Europe, Jewish modernism contributed to the metropolises to which I refer as Jewish "fantasy cities," cities such as Czernowitz, Lvov, and Sarajevo, all of which fell victim to the end of modernism in the late twentieth century. Jewish utopian movements, moreover, are inseparable from the dystopian tendency that brought modernism to its end.[12] Dystopia forms the counterpart to utopia, describing a place where all laws break down and society undergoes thorough destruction. Unquestionably, the Holocaust became the ultimate dys-

topia at the end of Jewish modernism. There was, moreover, recourse during the early twentieth century to heterotopia, a place between utopia and dystopia, representing a lived-in world, a reality of sorts, where utopian visions became realized in human lives. Their distinctive realizations of modern city culture notwithstanding, utopia, dystopia, and heterotopia all formed responses to modernism (cf. Bettauer 1996; Bohlman 2002; Corbea-Hoisie 1998; Corbea-Hoisie 2003).

Throughout the transformation to early modern and then to modern Europe, Jewish music increasingly became a phenomenon of the city and of urban spaces. The transformation was not so much a process of urbanization in and of itself as it was an unfolding of historical processes that shaped Jewish music as a response of the Jewish community to modernity. Across the musical landscape of the Jewish community virtually every kind of music began to acquire cultural markers of Jewishness that bore witness to the processes of urbanization. Even in the early modern Jewish community there were traditional concepts of local or city character in traditional Jewish music, particularly that of the synagogue, with its genealogy of cantors responsible for transmitting the music of a particular Jewish ethnic community (*kehilla*) within the city. These laws and customs, written and unwritten, fall generally into the traditional set of practices belonging to *minhag* (Hebrew: custom, practice). *Minhag* reflects the folkloristic or ethnographic sense of customs forming systems that provide identity for a community in a particular place. As a term *minhag* also describes a canon of written works that include descriptions of the practices that distinguish the Jews of a particular city, extending even to bodies of literature (*minhagim*) that chronicle the community and its traditions. Within the larger *minhag* of a community music takes its place, again embracing oral traditions (e.g., repertories of *pizmonim*, songs crafted to celebrate a specific holiday or rite of passage) and written traditions, above all the cantorial repertories of a given community, especially those preserved in manuscripts passed from cantor to cantor (see, e.g., Bloemendal 1990).

Musical style also generates a discourse about place, generating markers of a city music. Most important is the concept—a fairly modern concept—of *nusach*, a hard-to-define term that refers not only to the sound that characterizes the music of a particular Jewish community, but also to the performance practices and the processes of acquiring local tradition (see Summit 2000). *Nusach* provides structural guidelines for the cantor in his or her choice of repertories and in the musical decisions he or she makes about the performance of given liturgies, but it also informs the congregation *qua* community that the repertories they hear belong to them. *Nusach* is not simply passed from generation to generation; rather, one acquires it or even learns it when entering fully into a Jewish community.

The urban qualities of traditional—in this sense, premodern—Jewish music also depend extensively on genealogy. Cantorial practices, or *ḥazzanut*, encompass not only the *ḥazzanim* (Hebrew: cantors) of a given community, but also the repertories the *ḥazzanim* embody as their own history. The cantor both maintained a community's *ḥazzanut* and personalized it, which often meant introducing new styles and variants to the repertory. The *ḥazzanut* was not, therefore, simply a repository of unchanging tradition. It was a set of performance practices that successive cantors used to inscribe history itself through the catalytic acts of cantors who consolidated different traditions in order to create a cosmopolitan music history (cf. Bloemendal 1990, 1: xxi; Bohlman 2000; Idelsohn 1932; also see Seroussi in this volume).

Jewish music symbolized the heterotopian dimensions of modern city culture in quite different ways, and perhaps no other European metropolis displayed those dimensions as extensively as Sarajevo. Sarajevo fulfilled all the conditions of a border city in the Habsburg monarchy, particularly as a cosmopolitan culture that blurred East and West. It is because of its functions as a border city, indeed, that Sarajevo so powerfully marked the beginning and end of the twentieth century—the onset of World War I and the contested city in the Balkan Wars—thus symbolizing the historical borders of modernism and postmodernism. From the beginning of early modern Europe into and almost to the end of the twentieth century, the Jewish community of Sarajevo was largely Sephardic, settled initially in the sixteenth century by Jews expelled from the Iberian Peninsula but gradually occupying a pivotal position in the cosmopolitan culture of the Balkans (Levy 1996). Sarajevo's Jews, as Mediterranean, had enjoyed a long history of interaction with Muslims, especially in the urban cultures of the North Africa,

Turkey, and the Levant.

The city music of Jews in Muslim society was fundamentally different from that of the Jews of northern Europe, and it accordingly reflected Jewish self-consciousness in ways that both resonated and conflicted with Jewish modernism in the early twentieth century; above all, Jewish music in Sarajevo was fundamentally not bound by a European teleology of modernism. Jewish musicians had thriven in Muslim courts, where there was exchange between Jews and Muslims. Jewish city music in Sarajevo forces us to rethink the presence of Jewishness within a much more expansive music culture beyond that of Europe (Gauß 2001: 7–50).

The question that arises is just how the distinctive music culture of Jews in Sarajevo represents the historical narrative of twentieth-century modernism. Clearly, at the beginning of the twenty-first century, when there is no longer a significant Jewish presence in Sarajevo, it would be hard to make a case for utopia. What was once heterotopian—a city-music culture constituted of Jewish, Muslim, and Christian traditions—has proved to be dystopian in the successive waves of civil war in the former Yugoslavia. What remains, however, is the model of an alternative Jewish city music, where even the borders between utopia, dystopia, and heterotopia are fragile, but where the histories of Jewish modernism proliferate, insisting that Jewish music respond in highly distinctive ways to the cosmopolitanism of the modern city.

Numbers/Modernism

Accounts and theories of modernism frequently treat it as if it were an aesthetic or condition of art or science in which identity is minimized and camouflaged, or in which identity collapses altogether through modernism's implicit self-referentiality. The idealism that humanized modernity in the nineteenth century, so such theories hold, gave way to the two-dimensionality of a twentieth-century modernism that depended almost entirely on words and the structure of language (Bell 1999: 16–20). If modernism is the result of a system of self-referential symbols or if it results from the emancipation from history—the history of musical style, as in Schoenberg's emancipation of dissonance—then it might seem paradoxical to examine Jewish modernism as the condition of an historical moment and a specific set of historical conditions in which self-identity is actually strengthened (see Ash in this volume). Paradox, however, runs through the moment of Jewish modernism that the authors in the present book chronicle.

We might state the paradox of modernism accordingly: However nebulous and multivalent Jewishness in music is in the general sense, it became more easily identifiable in the musical practices of European Jews during the early decades of the twentieth century and then in the Weimar and Nazi periods than it was prior to the codification of European anti-Semitism at the end of the nineteenth century. In the modernist moment, then, music could become at once more modern and more Jewish. Certain social and political conditions that obtained initially after World War I but that impinged particularly on Jewish society after 1933 forced Jews to reckon with self-identity. The aesthetic of Jewish modernism resulted from deliberate decisions to make music more Jewish. Composers who never would have written "Jewish music" prior to 1933 did so afterward. Even the aesthetic experimentation that could lead to a greater presence of Jewishness multiplied, for example, with the expansion of systems of Jewish harmony by Joseph Yasser and others (Yasser 1938).

In contrast, new historical contexts for creating a self-consciously Jewish music developed. By the 1920s European Jewish communities had become generally aware that there was some kind of nascent music culture in the Yishuv (Hebrew, literally "settlement," in other words the Jewish settlements in mandated Palestine), and that this new music culture, whatever its musical contents, was very Jewish (Hirshberg 1995). Publications of folk songs during the 1920s, for example, expanded their sections devoted to Hebrew songs by including songs sent from the Yishuv, especially those collected on kibbutzim, which therefore possessed the extra patina of authenticity. By the 1930s communities in the Diaspora could sing from anthologies entirely filled with Hebrew songs from the Yishuv, such as Jakob Schönberg's *Schireh eretz jisrael* (Songs of Eretz Yisrael; see Schönberg 1938).[13] The Jewish music of the Yishuv was modern and secular, hence it came to be recontextualized as a form of aesthetic expression in the twentieth century. The songs of the Yishuv were in modern Hebrew, and their imagery contrasted the traditional culture of the Levant with the modern images of growing cities, such as Tel Aviv and Haifa.

Typical of the paradox of Jewish modernism is that many of the emerging Jewish musical practices had deliberately antimodernist dimensions. Of those genres that seemed to resist modernism, none was a clearer or more public genre than Jewish cabaret. The central ethos of cabaret is the use of parody to poke fun and to voice social criticism, and it is for these reasons that it served as a calculus for the complex interaction of modernism and antimodernism.[14] By the end of the nineteenth century, the Jewish popular stage and Jewish cabaret had come to provide two of the most public sites in for signifying and representing Jewish self-identity as modern. Jewish cabaret (e.g., on the CD by the New Budapest Orpheum Society that accompanies this book) grew from the convergence of two different paths of Jewish cultural history: Yiddish theater in Eastern Europe and the tradition of *Couplets* (literally, couplets, or popular songs that made frequent use of dialogue) and urban dialect songs and other stage genres of Central Europe (Bohlman 1994).[15] In the mid-nineteenth century Yiddish theater had broken ranks with the tradition of nonrepresentation, employing instead the representation of everything from biblical allegories to rags-to-riches stories of Jews journeying out into the public sphere of a modern world (Dalinger 1998). In essence, Yiddish theater was a venue for staging Jewish lives for Jewish audiences.

The Jewish cabaret took this tradition of representation one step farther, albeit a step that was implicit in the cabaret tradition itself: Self-irony intensified self-identity. The cabaret depended on a cultural climate that tolerated stereotyped images of selfness. Stereotyping transformed the self into the other, while relying on the familiarity of self that Jewish audiences shared. The ne'er-do-wells that increasingly appeared in the skits and longer plays of the Yiddish theater provided a stock of characters who appeared again and again in Jewish cabaret songs. Many of these stock characters make appearances on the CD accompanying this book (e.g., the East European immigrant to Vienna who does not want to join the Jewish regiment in the Austro-Hungarian army, portrayed in "Der jüdische Landsturm").

Jewish cabaret historically unfolded across a very specific cultural geography, which in turn serves as one map for the landscape of Jewish modernism. The first regions of the map to come into focus are in Eastern Europe, and from there the journey across the landscape moves with Jewish theatrical and musical troupes into the cities transformed by Jewish cosmopolitanism in the nineteenth century—Czernowitz, Lvov/L'viv/Lemberg, Großwardein/Oradea—before accelerating toward the metropolises of Central Europe. By the end of the nineteenth century, Jewish cabaret had become a firmly established institution of popular culture in the rapidly expanding new Jewish neighborhoods of Berlin and Vienna, such as the Scheunenviertel and Leopoldstadt, respectively. The cultural geography of songs from the Jewish cabaret continued to chart the course of European Jewish history into the Holocaust, especially in the Kulturbund and then later in the ghettos of Eastern Europe, where, because and in spite of their inherent paradox, they continued to flourish (cf. Freund, Ruttner, and Safrian 1992; Wacks 2002).

The paradox of Jewish modernism also depended on the historicist pull that formed a counterpoint with the intensification of Jewish self-consciousness. Cultural historians identify the period between the world wars as an historical moment in which Jewish culture underwent a resurgence, indeed, an explosion unleashed by modernism. That resurgence is not infrequently referred to as a Jewish renaissance (see especially Weisser 1954; Brenner 1996). Jewish composers in Eastern Europe, especially in the Soviet Union, began to compose works that had specifically Jewish themes and that used melodies from Jewish folk music and Jewish harmonic systems. The institutions that supported the Jewish musical renaissance proliferated and prospered financially. Lists for the publication of Jewish music appeared in the catalogs of the larger music publishers (e.g., Jibneh-Juwal at Universal Edition), and, no less important, there were other Jewish presses that began to publish music with self-determined Jewish content, notably Jüdischer Verlag and Benjamin Harz in Berlin, and M. W. Kaufmann and Friedrich Hofmeister in Leipzig (see Belke 1983). Within the Jewish community itself there were burgeoning programs dedicated to the study of Jewish culture and Judaism, such as the *Lehrhaus* movement established by Franz Rosenzweig in Frankfurt.

The Jewish renaissance between the world wars was extraordinarily complex, but two factors stand out as emblems of the deepening paradox in Jewish self-consciousness. First, there was an intensified interested in secular and humanistic Jewishness. Second, as much as the designation "renaissance" reflects an historicist engagement with the past, the growing Jewish self-consciousness received additional impetus from the ways it interacted with and became a vehicle for modernism in the arts. The aesthetic modernism of the Jewish renaissance was stylistically very eclectic. Above all, the hybridity that stimulated aesthetic experiments also permitted an intensification of an identifiably Jewish modernist aesthetic, but insisted that there was nothing specifically Jewish about it. Instead, it was the eclecticism itself—the mixture of western and eastern elements, the juxtaposition of the sacred and the secular, the blurring of myth and history—that was fundamentally Jewish.

Throughout the Fourth Book of Moses, Numbers, the historical narrative of the Torah demonstrates an accelerating teleology, in which the utopia of Leviticus gives way to a more complex heterotopia, in which the Jewish people, journeying across the wilderness, are "numbered," in other words, their identities are specified in more distinctive ways. The historical narrative itself shifts in tone during Numbers, returning from the mythological to the historical; the journey of the exodus, in short, moves forward much more dramatically, reaching its final stage on the plains of Moab in what is today Jordan. The transformation from utopia to heterotopia loomed as a specter in the early 1930s, paradoxically, because the multiple modernisms of the 1920s and the

diverse aesthetic language left Jewish modernism exposed and fragile. Both the parody and the celebration of Jewishness in the cabaret and in Yiddish popular song would cease to broaden the public for Jewish music, with its utopian implications for the breakdown of difference, and would be forced instead into the heterotopia of the Jüdischer Kulturbund and the ghetto, and eventually into the dystopia of the concentration camp and the Holocaust.

Deuteronomy/Endings

The Final "Song of Moses"

1. Give ear, O heavens, and I will speak:
    and hear, O earth, the words of my mouth.
2. My doctrine [law] shall drop like rain,
    my speech shall distill as the dew,
as the small rain upon the tender herb,
    and as the showers upon the grass:
3. Because I will publish the name of the Lord:
    ascribe ye greatness unto our God.
4. He is the Rock, his work is perfect:
    for all his ways are judgment:
a God of truth and without iniquity,
    just and right is he. . . .

40. For I lift up my hand to heaven, and say,
    I live forever.
41. If I whet my glittering sword,
    and my hand take hold on judgment;
I will render vengeance to my enemies,
    and will reward them that hate me.
42. I will make my arrows drunk with blood,
    and my sword will devour flesh;

and that with the blood of the slain and of the captives,
  from the beginning of revenges upon the enemy.

43. Rejoice, O ye nations, with his people:
  for he will avenge the blood of his servants,
and will render vengeance unto his land, and to his
  people.

[The "Song of Moses" ends]

44. And Moses came and spoke all the words of this
  song in the ears of the people, he, and Hoshea, the
  son of Nun.

45. And Moses made an end of speaking all these
  words to all Israel.

> Deuteronomy 32:1–4, 40–43

The Torah approaches its end with Moses's final song, one of several passages given the appellation "Song of Moses," in which Moses breaks from the line-by-line structure of epic, the standard form of cantillation, and marks his words instead as ballad—also a narrative genre, but one that transcends the heightened speech of epic, indeed, a genre that crosses the boundary from myth to history. It is not just the Torah that ends with Moses's final song; it is Moses's life itself, for he raises his voice in song as he looks from the mountains of Moab across the Jordan and views the land of Israel. Moses will die before reaching that land, the goal of the exodus, the telos of the Five Books of Moses. Music marks this moment of ending by calling attention to the absence of ending in ending itself. The "Song of Moses" looks into the future, albeit a future that the singer, Moses, the chronicler and agent of exodus, will not inhabit. In the performance of the song, however, we witness a transcendence that the writers of Deuteronomy entrusted especially to song: in the moment of ending, as the death and finality of the journey across the wilderness are nigh, song announces the life beyond the borders of the present and chronicles history as it unfolds in the future.

In the 1930s and 1940s metaphors of death and the end of history well up within Jewish music, and music powerfully comes to mark the tragedy that was overwhelming the Jewish communities of Central and Eastern Europe (Bohlman 1999). As in Deuteronomy, music was present at a moment of ending, even as death was knowingly confronted. The remarkable presence of music at the most profound of all crises of Jewish modernism is surely one of the greatest paradoxes of modern Jewish historiography. Of all the moments that have revived the attributes of endism in modern history, the Holocaust serves as the ground metaphor, a locus classicus of the convergence of historical conditions that permit no transcendence.[16] The essays in this book, however, draw attention to the end of modern Jewish history in a different way, raising the possibility that transcendence was realized through music. Jewish music became all the more concentrated and unexpected as the moment of Jewish modernism appeared to be drawing to a final conclusion. The transcendence we witness as the destruction of the Holocaust unfolded poses many of the most difficult, unanswerable questions of Jewish history. We do not pretend to answer those questions in this book; rather, we pose new questions about why music was so powerfully present at the end.

We turn to the music of the concentration camps to raise again the troubling questions about the transcendence that responded to the crisis of the Holocaust, and I take as a case in point one of the several composers whose life as a Jewish composer ended in the camp at Theresienstadt/Terezín:[17] Viktor Ullmann (1898–1944). My choice to examine the end of Jewish modernism through a brief examination of Ullmann is not the result of the generally held assertion that he was the most successful of the Theresienstadt composers, but rather that his compositions in the concentration camp and during the Holocaust concentrated the conditions of transcendence through Jewish music in particularly trenchant ways. The more one looks at Ullmann's compositions and writings (e.g., Schultz 1993; Klein 1995) from the years of incarceration, the more clearly one sees a common set of themes unifying his thought and creative activity. It is as if a new metaphorical relation between his thinking as a composer and his life in the concentration camp had coalesced. The special forms and functions of this unity were palpable in *Der Kaiser von Atlantis* (The Emperor of Atlantis), making the opera far more than a collection of fragments that document an imploding world through their lack of finality, far more than merely a sign of dystopia.[18] Quite the contrary: the opera was a musical work whose component parts connect to each other, to the life of Theresienstadt, and beyond to a Europe unthinkable without Jews, in other words to all the conditions of heterotopia. These connections form the calculus that ultimately supports the processes of transcendence that project *Der Kaiser von Atlantis*

beyond the Holocaust to the past and the present, beyond the beginnings and endings of the historical moment of Jewish modernism.

One of the most strikingly transcendent techniques Ullmann employed was his metaphorical connection of music to language through the formal processes of polyphony and fugue. For modernist composers of the Austro-German tradition, fugue represented the ultimate compositional form, an ironic inversion of modernism. I refer to fugue in its modernist forms as ironic both because it represented the highest craft for the composer and because it often came at the end of a larger compositional project, thereby symbolizing the culmination of a composition, the closing gesture of time.[19] The counterpoint that Ullmann weaves between language and music also has historical dimensions, which themselves have specific implications for his aesthetic practices. By powerfully drawing the listener into the most complex temporal dimensions of music, Ullmann uses music and poetry to create alternative temporal worlds. In *Der Kaiser von Atlantis* time and history serve as measures of human society and human mortality, but the opera itself allows these to be suspended while musically participating in and making possible their suspension. The suspension of war and death serves as one of the voices in Ullmann's dramatic texture as it might in the musical texture of a fugue.

Ullmann also employs the aesthetic device of irony in *Der Kaiser von Atlantis*, especially in its extreme form, parody. Parody results specifically from the ways in which music masks meaning, and here, too, the functions of counterpoint and alternative temporal and historical narratives are at play. Parody is evident during every scene in *Der Kaiser von Atlantis*, and it penetrated the very cultural life of Theresienstadt. The immanence of parody is also important for a deeper understanding of the world from which many of the concentration camp's residents came, the cosmopolitan Jewish culture of Central and East Central Europe, where Jews contributed so crucially to cabaret and the aesthetics of high modernism (cf. the CD accompanying this volume). Parody accentuated the end of history itself, drawing attention to it, as if to negate it in a final act of self-consciousness.

In the final decade of the twentieth century scholars of Jewish history undertook a radical rethinking of their methods and paradigms, particularly of the insistence on interpreting the present as the outcome of critical moments in the past. The new Jewish historiography calls for a rethinking of several crucial moments in Jewish history, especially the ways in which these signify beginnings and endings. Accordingly, certain events, movements, and historical agents that have been seen as providing essentializing explanations for Jewish history are called into question.[20] Rather simplistically stated, the new Jewish historiography admits to the possibility of multiple modernities and multiple historical narratives (see, e.g., Funkenstein 1993; Cheyette and Marcus 1998).

The essays in the present book open up new possibilities for an intensified rethinking of the relation of music to modern Jewish history, and in so doing they offer additional perspectives on the debates in the new Jewish historiography. Many often, if not usually, contradictory narratives converge when music becomes self-consciously Jewish, and the music itself gives voice and meaning to these narratives in multiple ways. In this epilogue I have traveled dangerously close to essentialism myself, arguing that music—music rendered Jewish by its historical contexts—provides the crucial voice for reckoning with the crisis of modernism and the paradox of meaninglessness that surround the end of history. The more complex question posed by music's power to give meaning at moments of ending surely also results from the incapacity of words, sacred or even theodical, to represent the inexpressible.

It is not a question of music's ability to express the inexpressible when words cannot; rather, it is one of music's allowing us to confront the very dilemma of expressing the historical narratives that cluster around the end of history. Music does not necessarily resolve the dilemma or even provide clues for solving the mystery of ending, but it does sharpen our ability to fathom the dimensions of the dilemma and the mystery. This is surely one reason that the language of the Torah is heightened through its historical dimensions. It is surely why sound is used in so many different ways—with multiple modalities that arise from the multiple subjectivities of different Jewish ethnic communities and languages—to aspire to Jewish music, at the same time complicating the problem of its ontology, which ineffably resists unity. At the beginning of the twenty-first century we continue to seek an ontological unity that seems to explain all Jewish musics, in other words some metaphysics of Jewish music as a whole, but perhaps it is the inexpressibility of such an ontology that determines what its musical and extramusical dimensions really are.

In the final "Song of Moses" the end emerges through music, in Moses's musical voice, but the historical narrative of the Torah fails to realize that end. The dilemma of the ending that brings Deuteronomy to its close returned again as a specter in the moment of Jewish modernism, which, too, came to an end without a sense of closure. Ironically, it is in a work of high modernism, of high Jewish modernism—Arnold Schoenberg's unfinished opera, *Moses und Aron*—that the inexpressibility of ending is most disturbingly made manifest.[21] In the fifth scene of act 2, Moses seeks the word that he himself does not possess, the word of God, because it is to that word that history ultimately returns. With Moses's song in the wilderness, which concludes act 2 and is thus the last music Schoenberg composed for the opera, a modernist song of Moses draws this epilogue and this book toward a close, in counterpoint with his final utterances—highly musical utterances—which epigrammatically opened the chapter.

Inconceivable God! Unspeakable idea, with so many
    meanings!
Will you permit such a conclusion? May Aaron, my
    mouth, fashion this image?
Thus, I made myself an image, a false image, as only
    an image can be!
Thus, I am totally defeated! Thus, everything was
    insanity that I had thought,
And it cannot and may not be spoken!
Oh word, you word, that I cannot find![22]

In Lieu of Ending

On 8 July 2005 a Jewish film swept the honors at the annual Deutscher Filmpreis (German Film Awards) ceremony. Dani Levy's 2004 hit comedy *Alles auf Zucker* (translated into English as *Go for Zucker: An Unorthodox Comedy*), received awards for best film, best leading actor (Henry Hübchen), best screenplay, best director (Dani Levy), best costume design, and best musical score (Niki Reiser). Whether or not there really was a genre or style of film identifiable as Jewish deterred few of those who lavished praise on *Alles auf Zucker*. Similarly, in the explosive reception history that followed the ceremony, there was no debate about whether the screenplay, the dialogue, or the musical score was Jewish; there was, however, a proliferation of reviews and ancillary literature that celebrated the very possibility that Jewishness had so successfully reentered the arts and the public sphere in Germany today.[23]

It was lost upon few that *Alles auf Zucker* marked a moment of historical beginning, just as other events in the weeks prior to the Deutscher Filmpreis had marked a moment of historical ending (see, e.g., Bühler 2004). The film prizes, in fact, were awarded at the Berlin Philharmonic, less than a kilometer from the Monument for the Murdered Jews of Europe (Denkmal für die ermordeten Juden Europas), which had been dedicated only two months earlier, together with remembrance of the sixty years since the end of World War II and the liberation of the concentration camps. If there had been debates about specifying the Jewishness of the monument, there was none about celebrating the Jewishness of *Alles auf Zucker* and laying claim to its Jewishness as a new beginning in Germany.

The Jewishness of *Alles auf Zucker* was not, in fact, invented for or by the German public. By no means was it prophetic of a "new Jewish film" genre in Germany, in post-Holocaust Europe, or anywhere else. *Alles auf Zucker* was explicitly Yiddish theater, and its staging of the modern conflict of Jewish culture—East versus West, orthodox versus secular Judaism, ritual bound to the past versus change responding to the present—also owed its heritage to the theatrical and musical traditions of the Berlin of an earlier fin de siècle. That the "East" had become East Germany and the "West" had become West Germany, and that the modern conflict played out through the exploitation of stereotypes, were merely historicized variants of the traditional. Musically, too, Niki Reiser's score successfully evoked the multiple modernisms of the traditional. Rather than succumbing to the din of klezmer that has filled Berlin since the destruction of the Wall, anachronistically evoking a Jewish past that never was, Niki Reiser's score is a potpourri, an abundant mix drawn from worship in the synagogue to the ambient sounds of the clubs and entertainment venues that are not so different from the Jewish cabarets of the Berlin Scheunenviertel, where *Alles auf Zucker* was shot.

In the modern history of Jewish music, *Alles auf Zucker* reminds us, in an uncanny way, that we have been here before. There may be debates about its Jewishness, but those debates, too, remind us of the past. So superabundant is the interplay of identities and the surfeit of musical styles that questions of authentic Jewishness in music miss the point. Jewish identity—in the screenplay, in a cast of characters from Yiddish theater, in the historical context of multiple musical styles—is remixed in ways we recognize as totally modern in its recognition of tradition. Jewish music is not subtle in its reflection on the silence of the past, but cacophonous in its proclamation of tradition's modernism. Jewish music has survived the end of history, and accompanying its survival is Jewish modernism itself.

Approaching the end of my epilogue, I return to the non-closure at the end of Schoenberg's *Moses und Aron*, itself a musical representation of the absence of conclusion in the final biblical narrative of the Torah. "Oh word, you word, that I cannot find!" A suggestive epigraph, indeed, but one I ultimately reject. At first glance, Schoenberg's prophetic pronouncement of speechlessness would seem to confirm the eschatological themes that run through this book. In the word that Moses cannot find resides the end of history, the literal impossibility of narrative. How convenient it would be to end the epilogue and this book here, with the enunciation of closure itself. How conclusive it would be to submit to the conclusiveness of Jewish modernism in silence.

The prophecy of silence that haunts the multiple narratives in this book has not, however, been fulfilled. The apocalypse, realized in the Holocaust, tragically drew nearer, but it too passed. In the twenty-first century—after Jewish modernism—we witness the Jewish music of a different prophecy, albeit a prophecy, too, that each chapter in this volume voiced. This was the prophecy of multiplicity and complex counterpoint, the envoicement of more rather than fewer musics, the expansive presence of many Jewish musics in a lived-in world, not the silence at the end of time (see, e.g., the essays in Köster and Schmidt 2005). Jewish music, in the ethnographic and historical moments that close this book, has never before been performed in so many genres, and Jewish musicians have never before drawn from so many repertories that allow them consciously to express Jewish identity. In the post-Holocaust world, Jewish music has survived the eschatology of endism and proved, instead, to possess the resilience of a soteriology unimaginable to the Jewish modernists. Jewish music today—beyond modernism—is anything but unimaginable.

::: NOTES :::

1. Translated probably more often and into more languages than perhaps any other literary corpus, the Torah continues to provide literary theorists and theologians alike with contemporary tools for the analysis of literature and history (see most recently Five Books 2004).

2. Jacob Katz places the crisis that arose from the confrontation between Jewish history, anchored in traditional polity and culture, and teleological history at a somewhat earlier moment of Jewish history, namely at the threshold of early modern Europe or the end of the Middle Ages (Katz 1993).

3. Most anthologies of Yiddish folk song published since the Holocaust have been organized cyclically into distinct sections (see, e.g., Rubin 1950; Goldin and Zemtsovsky 1994).

4. The expulsion of Jews from the Iberian Peninsula at the end of the fifteenth century, for example, brought about the Sephardic diaspora, which became a diaspora within diaspora.

5. The German folk-music canon, the three-volume *Deutscher Liederhort*, contains numerous cases of Jewish songs, some even used to celebrate Jewish holidays (see Erk and Böhme 1893–94). Furthermore, Jewish songs, such as the ballad "Die Jüdin" (The Jewish Woman) in *Des Knaben Wunderhorn*, were stripped of Jewishness upon entering the canon (see Arnim and Brentano 1806 and 1808; Bohlman and Holzapfel 2001).

6. Music often provides scholars theorizing diaspora with a special type of tool for specifying the empirical conditions of diaspora (see, e.g., Chow 1993; Gilroy 1993; Lavie and Swedenburg 1996).

7. I realize the possibility of interpreting such a claim as essentialist. My point is historical rather than subjective: other models drawing upon diasporic metaphors derive from the Jewish Diaspora, which is no doubt one of the reasons that the Diaspora in American usage is capitalized and accompanied by a definite article when referring specifically to Jewish history. Theorists of diaspora generally acknowledge such historical precedents (see, e.g., Gilroy 1993; Clifford 1994).

8. Musical instruments, both ancient and modern, often acquire biblical names—or, rather, names deriving from a biblical etymology—for this reason. The piano, thus, is called a *psanter* in Hebrew, a name derived from the generic term for hammered dulcimer–type instruments (cf. the *santur* in West and South Asia).

9. A. Z. Idelsohn reports such claims about the different community traditions in his ten-volume *Thesaurus*

(1914–32). At times he provides empirical evidence to support some aspects of the claims, but he also generally refutes them, for not all assertions of the absence of musical change can be equally valid.

10. Martin Buber summarized and assessed many of these after immigrating to the Yishuv, which was for him the culmination of a personal utopian journey (see Buber 1985).

11. Theodor Herzl's *Der Judenstaat* (1896) and *Altneuland* (1904) are both utopian works, the former an outline for a modern Jewish state, the latter a novel in which successes of that state are enacted on the fictional stage of the future. Fictional literature also blurred the distinctions between utopia and dystopia. In his 1922 *Stadt ohne Juden* (City without Jews) Hugo Bettauer ironically portrays the collapse of the Viennese economy and the bankruptcy of Austrian culture once the Austrian government rids the country of all Jews (Bettauer 1996).

12. The Jewish fantasy cities were multicultural and multilingual, and they occupied the political and geographical borderlands of empires and nation-states. Lvov/L'viv/Lemberg, for example, lies in Ukrainian Galicia, and even in the twenty-first century Poland lays claim to it.

13. *Schireh eretz jisrael* remains in print and is available in an inexpensive paperback edition published in Israel.

14. In his study of German modernism in music and the arts, Walter Frisch traces the constant present of antimodernism as a condition, at times distinctly dialectic, of modernism. Responses to Richard Wagner, for example, vary wildly between reception of his works and aesthetics as either radical or reactionary. Following Frisch, we might observe that modernism does not eliminate its counterpart, but rather depends to some degree upon it (Frisch 2005).

15. In Vienna, for example, the dialect songs are simply called *Wienerlieder* (Viennese Songs), and they constitute a repertory that remains popular at the beginning of the twenty-first century. The slippage between *Wienerlieder* and cabaret has always characterized the tradition.

16. Critics have described and theorized the end of history in quite different ways (see, e.g., Fukuyama 1992; Sim 1999). For a sweeping historical survey of theories of endism, see Baumgartner 1999.

17. I shall use the German "Theresienstadt" rather than the Czech "Terezín" to refer to the small city in northwestern Bohemia because it was originally built as a garrison city, with military functions in the Austro-Hungarian Empire, and as an outpost for defensive purposes during the reign of Maria Theresa, after whom it was named "Theresa's City." The best comprehensive study of Theresienstadt remains Joža Karas's *Music in Terezín* (1985).

18. Completed in 1943, *Der Kaiser von Atlantis* was not performed during the remaining year that Ullmann spent in Theresienstadt before he was deported to Auschwitz in the autumn of 1944, where he was, in all probability, murdered on the day of his arrival. Because the opera itself contains so many references to the Holocaust, to Nazi persecutions throughout Europe, and, arguably, to Hitler himself as the eponymous figure of the emperor, many critics speculate that Ullmann fully recognized that censors in the concentration camp would never approve its performance. Briefly summarized, Peter Kien's libretto for *Der Kaiser* is the story of a warring nation whose emperor accepts an offer by the figure of Death to suspend all death in war. When, however, death is no longer a factor, human misery and suffering only magnify, and the emperor implores Death to return at the end.

19. These are the qualities, also, that we find in the most famous of all Holocaust poems, Paul Celan's "Todesfuge," or "Death Fugue" (Celan 2003: 40–41). In much of his poetry Celan set themes of music and death in counterpoint (see Celan 1983; Felstiner 1995; cf. also John 1991).

20. Zionism, for example, would be stripped of its centrality as an explanation for the founding of a modern, secular state of Israel. The Holocaust, too, would cease to serve as an inevitable cause for the establishment of a modern Jewish state.

21. Schoenberg completed the first two acts, both the libretto and the musical score. The final act survives in the text for a single scene, at the end of which Schoenberg has placed the directions "Ende der Oper" (end of the opera). In the published score the composer's wife, Gertrud Schoenberg, reproduces excerpts from his letters from 1931 to 1951 that reveal the struggle that obsessed him as he endeavored to resolve the dilemma of composing the final act (see Schoenberg 1958: 542–43).

22. Unvorstellbarer Gott! Unaussprechlicher, vieldeutiger
     Gedanke!

  Läßt du diese Auslegung zu? Darf Aron, sein Mund,
     dieses Bild machen?

  So habe ich mir ein Bild gemacht, falsch, wie ein Bild
     nur sein kann!

  So bin ich geschlagen! So war alles Wahnsinn, was ich
     gedacht habe,

  Und kann und darf nicht gesagt werden!

  O Wort, du Wort, das mir fehlt!

My translation differs slightly from that in the published score (Schoenberg 1958: 538–40).

23. In commentary on the film it has become customary to explain its Jewish content and style, in detail and with caution. The press release for the film, for example, begins with the question, "Jakob Zuckermann ein Jude?," answering the question itself by employing Jaeckie Zucker's "real," hence Jewish, name. The play of stereotyped Jews in the film—the orthodox and secular Jewish families, for example—lend themselves to explanations of the "Jewish joke," with the usual historical trimmings that Freud's writings on the joke provide. Crucial to the Jewish identity of the film is the biography of director Dani Levy (b. 1957, Basel), who was able to carve out a successful theater and film career as a Jew in Germany. The National Center for Political Education has even published a booklet to help interested Germans organize seminars for public discussions about the film and Jewish culture in Germany, complete with glossary, explanation of the thematic tropes (e.g., with sections such as "Between Communists and Christian Democrats: Jews in Postwar Germany" and "'Kosher like a Pork Chop': Secular and Orthodox Jews"), and bibliography; see Bühler 2004).

::: **WORKS CITED** :::

Arnim, L. Achim von, and Clemens Brentano. 1806 and 1808. *Des Knaben Wunderhorn: Alte deutsche Lieder.* Publ. in 2 parts. Heidelberg: Mohr & Zimmer.

Baumgartner, Frederic J. 1999. *Longing for the End: A History of Millennialism in Western Civilization.* New York: St. Martin's.

Belke, Ingrid, ed. 1983. *In den Katakomben: Jüdische Verlage in Deutschland, 1933–1938.* Special edition of *Marbacher Magazin* 25.

Bell, Michael. 1999. "The Metaphysics of Modernism." In Michael Levenson, ed., *The Cambridge Companion to Modernism*, 9–32. Cambridge: Cambridge University Press.

Bettauer, Hugo. 1996. *Die Stadt ohne Juden: Ein Roman von Übermorgen.* Hamburg and Bremen: Achilla Presse Buchhandlung. Orig. publ. 1922.

Bhabha, Homi K. 1994. *The Location of Culture.* New York: Routledge.

Bloemendal, Hans. 1990. *Amsterdams chazzanoet: Synagogale muziek van de Ashkenazische Gemeente.* 2 vols. Buren: Frits Knuf.

Bohlman, Philip V. 1994. "Auf der Bima—Auf der Bühne: Zur Emanzipation der jüdischen Popularmusik um die Jahrhundertwende in Wien." In Elisabeth T. Hilscher and Theophil Antonicek, eds., *Vergleichend-systematische Musikwissenschaft: Beiträge zu Methode und Problematik der systematischen, ethnologischen und historischen Musikwissenschaft: Franz Födermayr zum 60. Geburtstag*, 417–49. Tutzing: Hans Schneider.

———. 1997. "Il passato, il presente e i popoli del Mediterraneo senza storia musicale." *Musica e storia* 5: 181–204.

———. 2000. "Composing the Cantorate: Westernizing Europe's Other Within." In Georgina Born and David Hesmondhalgh, eds., *Western Music and Its Others: Difference, Representation, and Appropriation in Music*, 187–212. Berkeley and Los Angeles: University of

California Press.

———. 2002. "World Music at the 'End of History'." *Ethnomusicology* 46 (1): 1–32.

———. 2005. "Music as Representation." *Journal of Musicological Research* 24 (3–4): 205–26.

———, and Otto Holzapfel. 2001. *The Folk Songs of Ashkenaz*. Middleton, Wisc.: A-R Editions. (Recent Researches in the Oral Traditions of Music, 6)

Brenner, Michael. 1996. *The Renaissance of Jewish Culture in Weimar Germany*. New Haven, Conn.: Yale University Press.

Buber, Martin. 1985. *Pfade in Utopia: Über Gemeinschaft und deren Verwirklichung*. 3rd revised ed. Heidelberg: Lambert Schneider.

Bühler, Philipp. 2004. *Alles auf Zucker! Dani Levy, Deutschland 2004*. Bonn: Bundeszentrale für politische Bildung.

Celan, Paul. 1983. *Gesammelte Werk*. Ed. by Beda Allemann and Stefan Reichert, with Rolf Bücher. 5 vols. Frankfurt am Main: Suhrkamp.

———. 2003. *Die Gedichte*. Ed. by Barbara Wiedemann. Frankfurt am Main: Suhrkamp.

Cheyette, Bryan, and Laura Marcus, eds. 1998. *Modernity, Culture and "The Jew."* Stanford, Calif.: Stanford University Press.

Chow, Rey. 1993. *Writing Diaspora: Tactics of Intervention in Contemporary Cultural Studies*. Bloomington: Indiana University Press.

Clifford, James. 1994. "Diasporas." *Cultural Anthropology* 9: 302–38.

Corbea-Hoisie, Andrei. 2003. *Czernowitzer Geschichten: Über eine städtische Kultur in Mittel(Ost)-Europa*. Vienna: Böhlau Verlag.

———, ed. 1998. *Jüdisches Städtebild: Czernowitz*. Frankfurt am Main: Jüdischer Verlag.

Dalinger, Brigitte. 1998. *Verloschene Sterne: Geschichte des jüdischen Theaters in Wien*. Vienna: Picus.

Erk, Ludwig, and Franz Magnus Böhme. 1893–94. *Deutscher Liederhort*. 3 vols. Leipzig: Breitkopf & Härtel.

Felstiner, John. 1995. *Paul Celan: Poet, Survivor, Jew*. New Haven, Conn.: Yale University Press.

Five Books. 2004. *The Five Books of Moses: A Translation with Commentary*. Trans. by Robert Alter. New York: W. W. Norton.

Freund, Florian, Franz Ruttner, and Hans Safrian, eds. 1995. *Ess firt kejn weg zurik . . . : Geschichte und Lieder des Ghettos von Wilna, 1941–1943*. Vienna: Picus.

Frisch, Walter. 2005. *German Modernism: Music and the Arts*. Berkeley: University of California Press. (California Studies in Twentieth-Century Music)

Fukuyama, Francis. 1992. *The End of History and the Last Man*. New York: Avon.

Funkenstein, Amos. 1993. *Perceptions of Jewish History*. Berkeley and Los Angeles: University of California Press.

Gauß, Karl-Markus. 2001. *Die sterbenden Europäer: Unterwegs zu den Sepharden von Sarajevo, Gottscheer Deutschen, Arbëresche, Sorben und Aromunen*. Vienna: Paul Zsolnay Verlag.

Gilroy, Paul. 1993. *The Black Atlantic: Modernity and Double Consciousness*. Cambridge, Mass.: Harvard University Press.

Goldin, Max, and Izaly Zemtsovsky, eds. 1994. *Evreiskaia narodnaia pesnia: Antologii* [Jewish Folk Songs: An Anthology]. St. Petersburg: Kompositor.

Herzl, Theodor. 1896. *Der Judenstaat: Versuch einer modernen Lösung der Judenfrage*. Leipzig and Vienna: M. Breitenstein.

———. 1919. *Altneuland*. Berlin and Vienna: Benjamin Harz. Orig. publ. 1904.

Hirshberg, Jehoash. 1995. *Music in the Jewish Community of Palestine, 1880–1948: A Social History*. Oxford: Oxford University Press.

Idelsohn, A. Z. 1914–32. *Hebräisch-orientalischer Melodienschatz*. 10 vols. Berlin etc.: Benjamin Harz etc.

———. 1932. *Die traditionellen Gesänge der süddeutschen Juden*. Leipzig: Friedrich Hofmeister. (Hebräisch-orientalischer Melodienschatz, 7)

John, Eckhard. 1991. "Musik und Konzentrationslager: Eine Annäherung." *Archiv für Musikwissenschaft* 48 (1): 1–36.

Karas, Joža. 1985. *Music in Terezín, 1941–1945*. New York:

Beaufort Books.

Köster, Maren, and Dörte Schmidt, eds. 2005. *"Man kehrt nie zurück, man geht immer nur fort": Remigration und Musikkultur.* Munich: edition text + kritik.

Katz, Jacob. 1993. *Tradition and Crisis: Jewish Society at the End of the Middle Ages.* Trans. by Bernard Dov Cooperman. New York: New York University Press.

Klein, Hans-Günther, ed. 1995. *Viktor Ullmann Materialien.* 2nd ed., rev. and expanded. Hamburg: Von Bockel Verlag.

Lavie, Smadar, and Ted Swedenburg, eds. 1996. *Displacement, Diaspora, and Geographies of Identity.* Durham, N.C.: Duke University Press.

Lévi-Strauss, Claude. 1969. *The Raw and the Cooked: Introduction to a Science of Mythology.* Trans. by John and Doreen Weightman. New York: Harper & Row. Orig. publ. 1964.

Levy, Moritz. 1996. *Die Sephardim in Bosnien: Ein Beitrag zur Geschichte der Juden auf der Balkanhalbinsel.* Klagenfurt: Wieser. (Bosnisch-österreichische Beziehungen, 1) Orig. publ. 1911.

Rubin, Ruth. 1950. *A Treasury of Jewish Folksong.* New York: Schocken.

Schoenberg, Arnold. 1958. *Moses und Aron: Oper in drei Akten.* Partitur. Mainz: B. Schott's Söhne.

Schönberg, Jakob. 1938. *Schireh eretz jisrael.* Berlin: Schocken Verlag.

Schultz, Ingo, ed. 1993. *Viktor Ullmann: 26 Kritiken über musikalische Veranstaltungen in Theresienstadt.* Hamburg: Von Bockel Verlag. (Verdrängte Musik, 3)

Sim, Stuart. 1999. *Derrida and the End of History.* New York: Totem Books. (Postmodern Encounters)

Summit, Jeffrey A. 2000. *The Lord's Song in a Strange Land: Music and Identity in Contemporary Jewish Worship.* New York: Oxford University Press. (American Musicspheres)

Wacks, Georg. 2002. *Die Budapester Orpheumgesellschaft: Eine Varieté in Wien, 1889–1919.* Vienna: Verlag Holzhausen.

Weisser, Albert. 1954. *The Modern Renaissance of Jewish Music: Events and Figures in Eastern Europe and America.* New York: Bloch.

Yasser, Joseph. 1938. "Foundations of Jewish Harmony." *Musica Hebraica* 1–2: 8–12.

Moments Musicaux et Modernes

Jewish Modernism in Popular and Political Music

Accompanying CD by the New Budapest Orpheum Society

::: PHILIP V. BOHLMAN, artistic director
ILYA LEVINSON, music director
DEBORAH BARD, soprano (track 4)
JULIA BENTLEY, mezzo-soprano (tracks 1, 2, 3, and 7–19)
STEWART FIGA, baritone (tracks 5 and 6)
PETER BLAGOEV, violin
STEWART MILLER, bass violin
HANK TAUSEND, percussion

Jewish music mapped both the geography and the history of Jewish modernism. As the landscapes of tradition shifted and exposed the fissures of modernism, Jewish music was there, articulating the borders between the Jewish and the non-Jewish, the private and the public, and, above all, the selfness and the otherness that dissolved as modernism transformed the old into the new. Even as they opened the possibility of transcendence, the musical repertories and multiple identities that accompanied Jewish modernism insistently revealed paradox. The *moments musicaux* that accompany this book similarly reflect the multiple modernisms of the historical moments in which they were conceived and performed. As musical works, they wantonly mix metaphors and genres. Folk, popular, and art music intersect; languages and dialects commingle; the sacred presents itself only to be rendered secular; social boundaries rigidly etch traditional identities while yielding to the dismantling potential of new identities. To the mixing of metaphors, nonetheless, accrues the force of modernism, for the songs on the accompanying CD have also become trenchantly self-referential. They map individual moments of Jewish modernism, and from them emerges the landscape charted by Jewish history during its modernist moment.

Drawn from the repertory of the New Budapest Orpheum Society, an ensemble dedicated to the performance of Jewish cabaret, popular, and political songs from the first half of the twentieth century, the *moments musicaux* on the accompanying CD form the polyphonic voices of modernist counterhistories (see New Budapest Orpheum Society 2002). With homage to the original Budapester Orpheumgesellschaft (1889–1919), the most famous Jewish cabaret troupe from fin-de-siècle Vienna, which set the standards for modern Jewish cabaret for two generations after its dissolution at the end of World War I, the New Budapesters cast their nets wide, historically, geographically, and linguistically, at once expanding the very identity of modern Jewish cabaret and recontextualizing popular and political song as Jewish and modern. The teleology of modern European history is challenged through these repertories by music's ability to recalibrate the relation of past to present precisely because of the mixing of metaphors. The many themes and identities made possible by this mixing announce the multiple modernisms of a music whose context is that of modern Jewish history, in its multiple, one might even say countless, narratives. The songs sample and remix the themes in this book. Diaspora and exile are never absent; the paradox of East and West, multiple identities within Jewish modernity itself, is discomfiting through its insistence on stereotype; the power of modern science envoices those silenced by war; and humor and hopelessness entwine in the counterpoint of fleeting contemporaneity.

The multiple modernisms of this book are hardly foreign to the New Budapest Orpheum Society, whose performances, never the same, bear witness to multiple interpretations of Jewish modernism. Whether performing in synagogues or the cabarets of the metropolis, whether accompanying an academic conference or educating the broader public in the auditorium of a Holocaust museum, the New Budapest Orpheum Society ceaselessly seeks to provide new and alternative readings of Jewish modernism. The ensemble's repertory grows constantly, on one hand through the excavation of the past, on the other through the performativity with which each of the members, individually and collectively, respond to the musical moment at hand. The instrumentalists improvise, and the singers experiment with alternative verses and translations. The artistic director, Philip V. Bohlman, locates long-lost variants in the archives of Central and Eastern Europe, and the musical director, Ilya Levinson, realizes them through arrangements. The musical moments of modernism in the songs proliferate, revealing the fragile ways in which they narrate the many experiences of modern Jewish history itself.

In the first group of songs, "*Altneuland*: Modern Landscapes of Diaspora," folk and art song form a complex counterpoint, with melodies from oral tradition inscribed through literate forms of mediation: the postcards exchanged between the Keren Kayemeth in Palestine and Jewish composers throughout the world. The Hebrew language would seemingly signal the past, were it not modern rather than biblical Hebrew. Its power, nonetheless, rests in an ability to give modern form to biblical imagery, hence even to contradict history.

In the second group of songs, "Crossing Borders between Old and New," we witness the soft underbelly exposed through the play of oral and written traditions. Based on Jewish broadside ballads and sheet music that circulated and then recirculated folk and popular songs on the streets of European Jewish metropoles at the turn of the twentieth century, these songs self-consciously express an awareness of the social, religious, and racial divisions that marked and encumbered modernism. Not by chance, each song contains its own map of the boundaries between Jewish and non-Jewish worlds, and by extension between tradition and modernity.

In the third section, "Multiplying Jewish Modernism," the breakthrough into modernism has fully asserted itself. The question the songs pose is whether the breakthrough is Jewish or modernist, or whether it could even couple Jewishness and modernism. The key to interpreting the map of modernism lies in cabaret and its multiple stagings of a world turned inside out—indeed, in these songs, a modern world inverted and subtly subverted. In these songs we encounter Arnold Schoenberg not as the nestor of musical modernism but as the cabaret musician. Friedrich Holländer, too, imagines the alternative worlds of modernity here for the Berlin stage, not for the world of exile in Hollywood.

The fourth group of songs represent "Exile from Modernity" through their failure to effect historical closure. Composed for the most part in exile, these songs by Hanns Eisler, with texts by Bertolt Brecht and Kurt Tucholsky, realize historical moments stripped of teleology. Their language of hope is poignantly hopeless, even as the machines of modernism are all that give voice to the possibility of survival in exile. The song texts do not shy from the despair of modernism, the victims of war who never return in Tucholsky's antiwar anthem, or the specter of Jewish otherness in Brecht's modernization of a broadside narrative.

The final section comprises six songs from the single collection known as the *Hollywooder Lieder-*

buch (Hollywood Songbook). With texts by Bertolt Brecht and music by Hanns Eisler, the *Hollywood Songbook* narrates a path toward the everyday worlds of exile, the modern reality of displacement and the destruction of war. Brecht's texts are stark narratives of the place of exile, and Eisler's settings, at once beautiful and haunting, afford the narratives a numinous transparency, reminding us of an aesthetics we find at many moments in this book, not least in the Charlotte Salomon paintings that fill Michael Steinberg's chapter. The *Hollywood Songbook* nonetheless reaches a moment of closure in a final song of *Heimkehr* (homecoming) to the site of modernism, the metropoles of Jewish Europe, destroyed by modernity itself.

As an historical landscape of modernity, the CD ends at the same moment it began, at the moment of most profound crisis. In the music, however, that moment both is and is not the same. Clearly, the songs on the CD do not bring us to a point of arrival, but rather call into being a course of transit. The Jewish modernism that the songs chart might seem to have reached its final stage, but there is a total absence of finality. The *moments musicaux* on the CD thus provide no exit from history. Instead, they draw us into the moment of Jewish modernism, whose limitless dimensions are given shape by music.

THE SONGS

I. *Altneuland*: Modern Landscapes of Diaspora

1. "Banu" (We've Come): music by Aaron Copland (1900–1990) based on a melody by Joel Walbe; text by Nathan Alterman

Folk song and folk dance converge in the *shireh chalutzim* (pioneer songs), plumbing the past to retrieve symbols for the present. The convergence of different musical forms and genres symbolizes the ingathering of Jews from throughout Europe, the Mediterranean, and the Middle East. In "Banu," Nathan Alterman, one of the first modern poets to turn deliberately to modern Hebrew, has contributed a poem to the emerging culture of communal living on the kibbutzim of the Yishuv, replete with images of dance in the Diaspora, specifically the *hora*, which would quickly become the national folk dance of Israel. In Aaron Copland's setting, folk dance thus fully expresses explicit modern, and nationalist, meanings (see Nathan 1994).

2. "Gam Hayom" (Day after Day): music by Darius Milhaud (1892–1974), based on a melody by Shalom Postolsky; text by Levi Ben-Amitai

As Edwin Seroussi reveals in his contribution to this volume, the Sephardic voice often entered twentieth-century Jewish music history from the periphery, passing from the timeless world of the Mediterranean into the timeboundedness of modernity. Darius Milhaud's contributions to the pioneer songs introduce the Sephardic voice in very distinctive ways—in "Gam Hayom" through the meditative quality of prayer. The music of modern Israel, nonetheless, would actually seize upon these Sephardic qualities, employing them after the Holocaust to displace the dominant presence of Ashkenazic influences and the European history they inscribed.

3. "Ba'a M'nuḥa" (There Comes Peace): music by Kurt Weill (1900–1950) based on a melody by Daniel Sambursky; text by Nathan Alterman

The teleology of history without telos. Of the composers contributing to the pioneer songs, no one managed this modernist contradiction with more craft than Kurt Weill. The composer of stage works that juxtaposed opera and cabaret, classical and popular media, Weill's pioneer songs, not just "Ba'a M'nuḥa" but also "Havu L'venim" (Bring the Bricks), found their way into the modern spaces between folk and popular music in Israel, where Weill's authorship quickly gave way to an imagined authenticity. Unlike the juxtaposition of imagined and real geographies in Weill's operas, the places in "Ba'a M'nuḥa"—Beth-alpha and Nahalal—were real, indeed, modern rather than biblical settlements in the Yishuv.

II. Crossing Borders between Old and New

4. ". . . Nach Großwardein" (. . . To Großwardein): music by Hermann Rosenzweig; text by Anton Groiss

The borders between folk and popular music formed metonyms for the borders between myth and history in the *Altneuland* of Jewish modernism. The Jewish cabaret in fin-de-siècle Central Europe seized upon multiple meanings of these metonyms and appropriated them for performance on the stages of the Jewish quarters of the metropoles (e.g., the Leopoldstadt in Vienna and the Scheunenviertel in Berlin). Cabaret songs, such as ". . . Nach Großwardein," rely on a familiarity with the traditions of the past—the world of orthodox Jews in the Hungarian-Romanian border city Großwardein (today Oradea, Romania)—and the modernist juxtapositions of popular songs from the day. The song succeeds because of its hybridity, which in turn undoes the stereotyped images of authenticity that punctuate the song's potpourri of tunes.

5. "Jüdisches Fiaker Lied" (Jewish Coachman's Song): music by Gustav Pick (1832–1921); text by Carl Lorens (fin-de-siècle broadside)

Fin-de-siècle popular song ceaselessly poked fun at the paradoxical conflicts raised by the interstices between assimilation and modernity. Whereas Gustav Pick's "Wiener Fiakerlied," the rags-to-riches story of a Viennese coachman, was a hit song for decades, from its composition in 1885 until World War I, the Jewish cover versions treated the coachman more ironically. Through the *Kleinkunst* (popular theatrical tradition) of the metropoles, this semiautobiographical song by a Jewish composer—Pick was born in Jewish Burgenland but made his fortune in Vienna as an industrialist—becomes more markedly Jewish when circulated on broadsides, such as the one from which this version was taken.

6. "Liebeslied an ein Proletariermädchen" (Love Song to a Proletarian Girl): music by Gerhard Bronner (1922–2007); text by Peter Hammerschlag (1902–ca. 1942)

A Vienna divided by class and socioeconomic mobility takes to the historical stage with the "Liebeslied an ein Proletariermädchen" by Peter Hammerschlag, one of the most brilliant social critics and cabaret poets of the "Red Vienna" period between the world wars. With echoes of nineteenth-century broadside traditions, not least in the deliberate but brilliant use of dialect, Hammerschlag addresses the impact of modernity on social conditions in the Habsburg metropole, which nonetheless left him the "poor and hapless" Jew. Weaving its way through written and oral traditions from the 1930s until the present—Hammerschlag himself died in Auschwitz in 1942—this version uses the musical arrangement of Gerhard Bronner, perhaps the greatest contemporary Jewish cabaret singer in Vienna.

III. Multiplying Jewish Modernism

7. "Mahnung" (Warning): music by Arnold Schoenberg (1874–1951) from *Brettl-Lieder* (1901); text by Gustav Hochstetter

With his cabaret songs, the *Brettl-Lieder* of 1901, Arnold

Schoenberg paused briefly before making his boldest move toward modernism. Cabaret afforded Schoenberg a different view of modern art, not least when he turned to the circle of poets in Berlin known as the Literarisches Kabarett (Literary Cabaret). Still, Schoenberg entered the Berlin cabaret scene by joining an ensemble known as the Überbrettl as its "Kapellmeister." For more than two years he worked intensively with Ernst von Wolzogen and Oscar Strauss, carving out an aesthetic space between popular music and art music, a space that after 1903 became the field for his own modernist experimentation.

8. "Ich bin von Kopf bis Fuß auf Liebe eingestellt" (From Head to Toe I Am Ready for Love): music and text by Friedrich Holländer (1896–1976)

The popular stage quickly opened to the new media of the twentieth century, particularly to film. With the advent of sound film in the late 1920s, Jewish composers and cabaret musicians were among the first to seize the opportunity to expand the potential of recorded sound. Not least among these was Friedrich Holländer, whose career began in Berlin with troupes such as the Weintraub Syncopaters and ensemble at the Café Größenwahn, as well as his own Jazz-Symphoniker, and included a spate of film collaborations in Germany before he left for Hollywood in 1933, where his film scores pushed against many different aesthetic boundaries. "Ich bin von Kopf bis Fuß auf Liebe eingestellt" remains one of his most memorable songs, not least for its performance by Marlene Dietrich in *Der blaue Engel*.

9. "Eine kleine Sehnsucht" (Do a Little Dreaming): music and text by Friedrich Holländer

One of the persistent themes of modernist aesthetics, the relentless routine of the everyday, provides Friedrich Holländer with the text for "Eine kleine

Sehnsucht." More literally translated as "A Little Longing," the song musically spawns the possibilities for transcending the repetitive world of the office. Slowly dancing to a tango, the song's narrator and his partner view themselves together in a dream in which the drab world suddenly takes on brilliant colors. It is hardly by chance that Holländer juxtaposed a traditional genre, the "song of longing," with one of the most popular dance forms of interwar Central Europe, the tango, which was itself imagined to be Jewish precisely because of its exotic and modern sound.

10. "Gigerlette": music by Arnold Schoenberg from *Brettl-Lieder*; text by Otto Julius Birnbaum

The second Schoenberg *Brettl-Lied*, "Gigerlette," seems at first hearing almost antimodernist because of its apparent lack of self-referentiality. Ironically, the keyboard and vocal styles run strikingly close to those of Richard Strauss, but they are no less reminiscent of moments in Hugo Wolf. As a cabaret song, however, "Gigerlette" raises a different set of questions about modernism, for what is clear is that the song fitted the context for which it was written. It projected a different kind of self-awareness, that of the popular stage performer who must convince her audiences that the song functions as a mirror of their own existence in a modern world. It was hardly lost upon Schoenberg that the song's aesthetic pushed against different boundaries between the composer and his listeners, boundaries he would increasingly cross in the early decades of the twentieth century.

IV. Exile from Modernity

11. "Der Graben" (The Trenches): music by Hanns Eisler (1898–1962); text by Kurt Tucholsky

In the penultimate group of songs, exile and transcendence form counterhistories that struggle against the telos and ahistoricism of modernity. In Hanns Eisler and Kurt Tucholsky's "Der Graben," the historical narrative could not be more explicit in the wake of one world war and on the eve of another. A biting satirist and writer whose texts quickly found their way to the cabaret stage (e.g., Friedrich Holländer also set "Der Graben"), Tucholsky wrote such songs not so much as an historical reminder as a cynical interrogation of the inevitable. The musical vocabulary crafted by Hanns Eisler is one of remarkable honesty, neither hopeful nor hopeless, but transforming the song itself into a moment outside of history.

12. "Ballade von der 'Judenhure' Marie Sanders" (Ballad of the "Jewish Whore" Marie Sanders): music by Hanns Eisler; text by Bertolt Brecht (1898–1956)

Music and poetry themselves provide the framework for the unexpected juxtapositions of genre and form in the "Ballade von der 'Judenhure' Marie Sanders." Formally, the song functions as a broadside ballad about broadside ballads, and a popular song about the quotidian onslaught of the popular. As an historically accurate index of the implementation of the Nuremberg Laws concerning racial purity, the "Ballade" tells several different stories, first about the humiliation of Marie Sanders, and second about the degradation of German society. Eisler's moves between musical forms and textures transform music itself into social and historical critique, empowering it to serve as the vehicle for transcendence through the balladlike narrative of modern political song.

13. "Und es sind die finstren Zeiten" (And the Times Are Dark and Fearful): music by Hanns Eisler; text by Bertolt Brecht

In the *moments musicaux* of displacement during war, exile begins to emerge as a form of transcendence itself. The historical moments of the popular broadside are blurred, which is to say, rendered general, if not universal, rather than specific. Modernity ceases to characterize the everyday and begins to loom as a foreshadowing of what lies ahead. Even the individual characters of the cabaret stage give way to the voice of a singer whom we now encounter on a very different kind of stage. History in the dark times of this slow dance by Eisler and Brecht seems almost to come to a halt; the transcendent moment is almost coeval with the crisis of modernity.

V. Beyond Modernism: Hanns Eisler and Bertolt Brecht, *Hollywooder Liederbuch*

14. "An den kleinen Radioapparat" (To the Little Radio)

In the first song chosen here from the *Hollywooder Liederbuch*, Hanns Eisler and Bertolt Brecht's stunning "An den kleinen Radioapparat," modernism and modernity unite in the single voice of the radio that one forced into exile takes with her on her journey. Even the path of exile is explicitly modern, no longer fully in control of the singer who must flee the conditions of the present. It is not, however, the voice of the radio, the symbol of modernism, that is itself the enemy, for ironically it is in voice itself—in the music that sings in these final *moments musicaux*—that transcendence remains, still resonant as music resisting the teleology of the very history of the present.

15. "Hotelzimmer 1942" (Hotel Room 1942)

The bitter irony of exile occupies the place of displacement, the hotel room given its precise coordinates. The poet and the composer describe the confining landscape of displacement with painful precision. Here is the place of creativity, but at what cost? The radio of the first song in the section remains the only companion, and its messages remain the same. The song's pace projects the ennui of a history sliding to-

ward its end. The narrator still refuses to abandon himself to silence. The masks of modernism—the artistry of poet and composer—are still there, waiting.

16. "Der Kirschdieb" (The Cherry Thief)

The third song from the *Hollywooder Liederbuch* interrupts the everyday of exile. So sudden is the cherry thief's arrival at dawn that it is unclear whether his deeds take place only in a dream. With this song, Eisler and Brecht make an antimodernist intervention. The bare electric lights of the previous song are replaced by the gentle brush of dawn across the garden. The barking radio voices give way to the joyful whistling of a little tune. Eisler transposes the song to a different world, beyond modernity, the briefest of *moments musicaux*.

17. "Über den Selbstmord" (On Suicide)

"In this land and during these times." The modernity of the moment could not be more precise. Danger lurks in time itself, and time itself stretches forever into the past and future. The everyday envelops Everyman, and Everywoman, in suffering, which in turn becomes the calibration of time itself. In this vast expanse of time, sustained by Hanns Eisler through the plodding of measureless chords from which meter has departed, it is life that intervenes and that captures the fleeting moment in which the human comes to know herself or himself. Defining that moment are the brutal juxtaposition and the explosive flash of music, stark premonitions of the last resort, in which life is extinguished.

18. "Vom Sprengen des Gartens" (On Watering the Garden)

We might at first wonder whether this song renders the everyday banal. At the boundaries of modernity, what could be more banal than pausing to water the garden? The clarity of the text and the musical setting, however, might also be deceptive, for, in contrast to the previous song, it is life here for which the garden is a metaphor. The nature we witness is surely an antimodernist symbol, but there is an eerie agency in the humanness of the intimate form of address—*du*—with which the singer celebrates the possibility of life-giving refreshment. Banality, too, joins the multiple musical moments that draw us toward the end of the CD.

19. "Die Heimkehr" (The Homecoming)

It seems only fitting to bring the CD to a close with a song of homecoming. The irony in Eisler's and Brecht's "Homecoming" is, however, anything but welcoming. The song, written in the middle of World War II and in the midst of exile, bears the enormous burden of modernity. Destroying what is familiar are the most modern weapons of war, which alter the landscapes of all that the poet knows. The exile's home is both familiar and unfamiliar in this staging of the uncanny moment in the future when one must confront the place from which one came. The melodic beauty of Eisler's setting belies the horror of the still unknowable present. It is that beauty that transcends past and future, that draws the old and the new together in a final musical moment of Jewish modernism.

Permissions

Tracks 1–13 are used by permission of Cedille Records, Chicago, Illinois, www.cedillerecords.org.

Further Reading and Listening

Ammersfeld, Anita, Gerhard Bronner, and Ethan Freeman. 1997. *Ich hab' kein scharfes Messer: Jüdische Lieder und andere Weisheiten*. AEJ CD E1718.

Bei uns um die Gedächtniskirche rum. . . . Berlin Cabaret: Friedrich Holländer und das Kabarett der zwanziger Jahre. 1996. Edel 0014532TLR.

Bohlman, Philip V. 1989. "Die Verstädterung der jüdischen Volksmusik in Mitteleuropa, 1890–1939." *Jahrbuch für Volksmusikforschung* 34: 25–40.

———. 1994. "Auf der Bima—Auf der Bühne: Zur Emanzipation der jüdischen Popularmusik um die Jahrhundertwende in Wien." In Elisabeth T. Hilscher and Theophil Antonicek, eds., *Vergleichend-systematische Musikwissenschaft: Beiträge zu Methode und Problematik der systematischen, ethnologischen und historischen Musikwissenschaft: Franz Födermayr zum 60. Geburtstag*, 417–49. Tutzing: Hans Schneider.

———, and Otto Holzapfel. 2001. *The Folk Songs of Ashkenaz*. Middleton, Wisc.: A-R Editions. (Recent Researches in the Oral Traditions of Music, 6)

Brusatti, Otto. 1998. *Verklärte Nacht: Einübung in Jahrhundertwenden*. St. Pölten: NP Buchverlag.

Budzinski, Klaus. 1961. *Die Muse mit der scharfen Zunge: Vom Cabaret zum Kabarett*. Munich: Paul List Verlag.

———. 1985. *Das Kabarett: 100 Jahre literarische Zeitkritik—gesprochen—gesungen—gespielt*. Düsseldorf: ECON Taschenbuch Verlag.

Czáky, Moritz. 1996. *Ideologie der Operette und Wiener Moderne: Ein kulturhistorischer Essay zur österreichischen Identität*. Vienna: Böhlau Verlag.

Dalinger, Brigitte. 1998. *Verloschene Sterne: Geschichte des jüdischen Theaters in Wien*. Vienna: Picus Verlag.

Eisler, Hanns. 1988. *Lieder für eine Singstimme und Klavier*. Ed. by Manfred Krebs. Leipzig: VEB Deutscher Verlag für Musik. (Hanns Eisler, *Gesammelte Werke*: Serie I, Band 16)

Ewers, Hanns Heinz. 1904. *Das Cabaret*. Berlin: Schuster & Loeffler.

Fechner, Eberhard. 1988. *Die Comedian Harmonists: Sechs Lebensläufe*. Munich: Wilhelm Heyne Verlag.

Henneberg, Fritz. 1984. *Brecht Liederbuch*. Frankfurt am Main: Suhrkamp Verlag.

Holländer, Friedrich. n.d. *Von Kopf bis Fuß.* . . . Berlin and Munich: Ufaton-Verlag.

Jelavich, Peter. 1993. *Berlin Cabaret.* Cambridge, Mass.: Harvard University Press.

Klösch, Christian, and Regina Thumser. 2002. *"From Vienna": Exilkabarett in New York 1938 bis 1950.* Vienna: Picus Verlag.

Nathan, Hans, ed. 1994. *Israeli Folk Music: Songs of the Early Pioneers.* Madison, Wisc.: A-R Editions. (Recent Researches in the Oral Traditions of Music, 4)

New Budapest Orpheum Society. 2002. *Dancing on the Edge of a Volcano: Jewish Cabaret, Popular, and Political Songs, 1900–1945.* Cedille Records CDR 90000 065.

Pressler, Gertraud. 1995. ". . . 'an echt's Weanakind'? Zur Gustav Pick-Gedenkfeier am Wiener Zentralfriedhof." *Bockkeller: Die Zeitung des Wiener Volksliedwerks* 1 (1): 6–7.

Ringer, Alexander L. 1990. *Arnold Schoenberg: The Composer as Jew.* Oxford: Clarendon Press.

Rösler, Walter, ed. 1991. *Gehn ma halt a bisserl unter: Kabarett in Wien von den Anfängen bis heute.* Berlin: Henschel Verlag.

Scheu, Friedrich. 1977. *Humor als Waffe: Politisches Kabarett in der Ersten Republik.* Vienna: Europaverlag.

Segel, Harold B. 1987. *Turn-of-the-Century Cabaret: Paris, Barcelona, Berlin, Munich, Vienna, Cracow, Moscow, St. Petersburg, Zurich.* New York: Columbia University Press.

Teller, Oscar. 1985. *Davids Witz-Schleuder: Jüdisch-Politisches Cabaret; 50 Jahre Kleinkunstbühnen in Wien.* 2nd ed. Darmstadt: Verlag Darmstädter Blätter.

Veigl, Hans. 1986. *Lachen im Keller: Von den Budapestern zum Wiener Werkel; Kabarett und Kleinkunst in Wien.* Vienna: Kremayr & Scheriau.

———, ed. 1992. *Luftmenschen spielen Theater: Jüdisches Kabarett in Wien, 1890–1938.* Vienna: Kremayr & Scheriau.

Wacks, Georg. 2002. *Die Budapester Orpheumgesellschaft: Eine Varieté in Wien, 1889–1919.* Vienna: Verlag Holzhausen.

CD Texts and Translations

I. *Altneuland*: Modern Landscapes of Diaspora

1. "Banu" (We've Come)

Composed by Aaron Copland
Text by Nathan Alterman; melody by Joel Walbe

1. Banu vli kol vachol,
   Anu aniyei etmol;
   Lanu hagoral masar
   Et milyonei hamaḥar.

   Refrain
   Hora, ali na li,
   Esh hadliki b'leili;
   T'hora rabat ora,
   Hora m'dura.

2. Tze na lam'gal,
   Ten na shir mizmor ladal;
   Hine ne'esfu lirkod
   B'nei haoni v'hashod.

   Refrain

1. Poor and needy came we here,
   Paupers of the yesteryear;
   Yet the future has in store
   Millions for us by the score.

   Refrain
   Dance the hora, brethren; rout
   Shades that girdle us about.
   Dance the hora, do not tire,
   Hearts aflame and breasts afire.

2. Join the circle, dance along,
   Sing aloud the pauper's song.
   Lo, the children of distress
   Dance and shout with mirthfulness.

   Refrain

2. "Gam Hayom" (Day after Day)

Composed by Darius Milhaud,

Text by Levi Ben-Amitai; melody by Shalom Postolsky

Gam hayom kitmol shilshom,	Day after day, in the selfsame way,
Al haḥof omdim baḥurim minyan.	The youths are standing on the shore.
Lo sadeh lahem, lo bayit,	No field have they, no house,
Lo sadeh lahem, lo bayit v'kinyan.	No field have they, no house, no store.
Umi pakad: harpe?	Who bade them pause from work?
Pi mi tziva: ḥadol?	Who bade them to stand by?
Hoy, baḥurim! Od hayom gadol,	Up, up, brave youths! The day is yet high.
Tnu, tnu ḥol! Hava zifzif, zifzif labinyan.	Bring clay, bring sand, to build our land.

3. "Ba'a M'nuḥa" (There Comes Peace)

Composed by Kurt Weill

Text by Nathan Alterman; melody by Daniel Sambursky

1. Ba'a m'nuḥa layagea
   Umargoa leamel.
   Laila ḥiver mistarea,
   Al s'dot emek yizr'el.
   Tal mil'mata ul'vana meal,
   Mibeit-alfa ad nahalal.

   Refrain
   Ma, ma laila mileil?
   D'mama b'yizr'el.
   Numa, emek, eretz tif'eret
   Anu l'ḥa mishmeret.

1. There comes peace unto the weary
   And rest unto the toiler.
   A bright night is spreading
   O'er the fields of Emek Yezreel.
   The dew glistens below and the moon shines above
   From Beth-alpha to Nahalal.

   Refrain
   What of the night? What of the night?
   Silence reigns in Yezreel;
   Slumber, Emek, land of splendor,
   We are thy sentinels.

2. Yam hadagan mitnoe'a,
   Shir haeder m'tzaltzel.
   Zohi artzi us'doteha,
   Zehu emek yizr'el.
   T'voraḥ artzi v'tithalal,
   Mibeit-alfa ad nahalal.

   Refrain

2. The sea of corn is swaying,
   The song of the flock is ringing,
   This is my land and its fields,
   This is Emek Yezreel.
   Blessed and lauded may thou be
   From Beth-Alpha to Nahalal.

   Refrain

3. Ofel b'har hagilboa,
   Sus doher mitzel el tzel.
   Kol z'aka af gavoa,
   Mis'dot emek yizr'el.
   Miyara umi zeh sham nafal
   Bein beit-alfa v'nahalal?

   Refrain

3. Darkness wraps Mount Gilboa,
   A horse is galloping from shade to shade,
   A cry of lamentation is borne aloft
   From the fields of Emek Yezreel.
   Who fired the shot and who fell slain
   Between Beth-Alpha and Nahalal?

   Refrain

II. Crossing Borders between Old and New

4. "...Nach Großwardein!" (...To Großwardein!)

Composed by Hermann Rosenzweig
Text by Anton Groiss

1. Eine Stadt in Ungarland—doi deridi ridi ridi
     roidoi,
   Ist deswegen so bekannt,—doi deridi . . .
   Weil die allerschönsten Madlech dort zu
     finden sein,—doi deridi . . .
   Und e Czárdás können alle tanzen, Gott wie
     fein.
   [Doi deridi . . .]
   Darum reisen voller Freud'—doi deridi . . .
   Männer hin von weit und breit.—doi deridi . . .

     Trio
     Aron Hersch und Itzig Veitel,—doi deridi . . .
     Moische Bär und Natzi Teitel,—doi deridi . . .
     Und die ganze Schnorer-Verein—doi deridi . . .
     Fahren erein nach Großwardein.—doi deridi
       . . .

2. Kobi Gigerl mit sei' Schnas—doi deridi . . .
   Will auch gehen auf der Ras',—doi deridi . . .
   Weil der Zonentarif eingeführt ist auf der
     Bahn,—doi deridi . . .
   Ist das Reisen heutzutag' der allerneuester
     Schau.

1. There's a place in Hungary—doi deridi ridi ridi
     roidoi,
   Why so famous? You will see—doi deridi . . .
   All the raving beauties live there, ev'ry one
     a gem.
   God, how nice to see them dance the *csárdás.*
     Look at them!
   [Doi deridi . . .]
   Joyful men from far and wide—doi deridi . . .
   Off they go, they take the ride—doi deridi . . .

     Trio
     Aharon Hirsch and Itzik Veitel,—doi deridi . . .
     Moishe Baer and Nachum Teitel,—doi deridi . . .
     Not one cent, but dressed up fine—doi deridi . . .
     All take that trip to Großwardein.—doi deridi . . .

2. Kobi Gigerlel wore his suit—doi deridi . . .
   He wants to join us on the route—doi deridi . . .
   He has heard they've put a brand new toll upon
     that stretch.
   So he wears his finest just to show he's not a wretch.

[Doi deridi . . .]
Im Coupé, da sieht man heut'—doi deridi . . .
Drinnen sitzen üns're Leut'.—doi deridi . . .

> *Trio*
> *Hier in Ungarn ist ein Städtchen,—doi deridi . . .*
> *Dorten sein die schönsten Mädchen.—doi deridi . . .*
>
> *Alle Männer jung und fein—doi deridi . . .*
> *Fahren erein nach Großwardein.—doi deridi . . .*

3. Wenn ist Markt in Großwardein,—doi deridi . . .
   Seht man Jüden groß und klein,—doi deridi . . .
   Kaufleut', Schnorrer und Hausirer mit e
      Povel-Waar,—doi deridi . . .
   Ganefjüngel und dann Gigerl eine ganze Schaar.

[Doi deridi . . .]
Alle rechnen schon voraus—doi deridi . . .
Auf der Bahn den Rebach aus.—doi deridi . . .

> *Trio*
> *Kobi Gigerl mit sei' Dalles—doi deridi . . .*
> *Will bekücken sich de Kalles,—doi deridi . . .*
> *Und er mant, er kenn' auf Leim—doi deridi . . .*
> *Fahren erein nach Großwardei.—doi deridi . . .*

[Doi deridi . . .]
See that fancy carriage there?—doi deridi . . .
They're all inside, they'll have to share—doi deridi . . .

> *Trio*
> *Hungary has got an Eden,—doi deridi . . .*
> *Gorgeous girls, but not from Sweden.—doi deridi . . .*
>
> *Young men come to buy them wine—doi deridi . . .*
> *They're on their way to Großwardein.—doi deridi . . .*

3. Market day and ev'ry stall—doi deridi . . .
   Shows you Jews, both short and tall,—doi deridi . . .
   Merchants, beggars, hawkers, ev'ry type the mind
      conceives.
   Rough men, tough men, loud men, crowd men, watch
      for little thieves.

[Doi deridi . . .]
All of them are out for gain—doi deridi . . .
Looking forward to each train.—doi deridi . . .

> *Trio*
> *Kobi Giberlel has no money—doi deridi . . .*
> *He desires a bride. That's funny!—doi deridi . . .*
> *What's he got to bait his line?—doi deridi . . .*
> *He'll take that trip to Großwardein!—doi deridi . . .*

5. "Jüdisches Fiaker Lied" (Jewish Coachman's Song)

Music by Gustav Pick
Text by Carl Lorens

1. Iach hab' zwa faine Rappen,
   Mei Wag'n, der is e soi!
   Denn iach bin e Fiaker
   Von Baden und Vösloi.
   Mein Wagen der ist koscher,
   Er dürft' von Rothschild sein,
   Iach fahr auch lauter fainer Leut,
   Ka Bocher steigt nix ein,

1. My carriage has two horses,
   Both strong and sleek and fine!
   I'm proud to be a coachman.
   At work I really shine.
   Take note: My coach is kosher.
   No riff-raff rides with me.
   I once drove Rothschild through the park.
   Says I, "The ride is free."

E Trapp gehn meine Rappen
E Trapp—soi eins, zwei, drei!
Iach fahr als wie e Dampfmaschin',
In zwa Täg bin iach schon in Wien.
E Tax thu iach nich kennen,
Steigt ein e Passagier,
Laß iach bei zwa Gülden handeln,
Sag: "Geb n Sie halt e Einserl her!"
Statt Geld nehm' iach auch Werthpapier,
Versatzzetteln, ist Aner stier.

> *Refrain*
> *Denn iach bin e Fiaker a koscheres Kind,*
> *Gebor'n auf'n Salzgries und leicht wie der Wind.*
> *Mei Mame, mei Tate hab'n mit mir e Freud'.*
> *Denn ich bin e Fiaker von ünsere Leut'.*

2. Iach war als klanes Jüngel
   Vor'm dreinundsiebziger Jahr
   E Laufbursch an der Börse,
   Bevor der Krach noch war.
   Dann bin iach wor'n e Kutscher
   Beim reichen Silberstein,
   Hab' geführt e Equipasche
   E soi! Nobel, superfein!
   Doch wie der Krach gekümmen ist,
   Püh! haben Sie gesehn!
   Kapores war der Fleckeles,
   Der Silberstein, der Schmeckeles!
   Das war e groiß' Gewurre!
   Iach muß es frei gestehen,
   Man hat uns Alles weg' gepfänd',
   's war nix mehr da am End.
   Sechs Jahr hat kriegt der Silberstein,
   Iach bin gestanden ganz allein.

   > *Refrain*

3. Gebor'n bin iach am Salzgries
   Mei Tate war e Jüd,

Clip-clop, you'll hear me coming,
Clip-clop, all over town.
"Just climb aboard, right up that stair.
Sit tight, I'll get you anywhere."
This guy jumps in my taxi.
He looks so dignified.
"Oh no," he says. "My wallet's gone.
"I can't afford this ride."
He seemed to me an honest Jew.
I gladly took his IOU.

> *Refrain*
> *I drive a Fiaker, a nice Jewish boy.*
> *I fly through Vienna's streets, just like a goy!*
> *My mother and my dad are still proud of me.*
> *I drive a Fiaker for all to see.*

2. Right after my bar-mitzvah,
   Way back before the crash,
   I worked for Moishe Silver.
   Oh boy, did he have cash.
   I started as a gofer,
   Helped keep his carriage clean.
   I soon became his main chauffeur,
   The best you've ever seen.
   But then the market tumbled,
   And Silver lost his wealth.
   It ruined all those millionaires,
   And people mostly said, "Who cares?"
   So, Moishe went to jail,
   And me, I lost my job.
   But the biggest loser of this tale
   Was Silver, that poor slob.
   They took him off to prison, sure,
   But as a coachman, I'd endure.

   > *Refrain*

3. I live in Vienna's ghetto,
   My dad, a kosher Jew.

Der hat gelebt, gehandelt,
Das liegt soi im Geblüt,
Mit alte Hoisen, Stiefeln,
Zerbroch'ne Paraplui.
Mein Mame war ä Ganslerin
Am Salzgries, vis a vis.
Mich hat nix gefreut das Handeln,
Hab' g'sagt zum Tateleb'n:
"Iach möcht emal Fiaker werd'n."
"Zerbrach den Krag'n, iach werd Dich lehr'n!"
Hat er zu mir geschrieen, doch
Iach hab nix aufgepaßt,
Iach bin gleich auf e Bock gestiegen,
Und auch Fiaker blieb'n.
Beim Wettfahr'n bin iach Erster g'wiß,
Weil mei schöne Nas die längste is.

Refrain

He ran our family business,
A small-time merchant, nu!
He sold old pants and shmates,
And old umbrellas too.
My mother's pious family
Were small-time merchants too.
I felt that I was different,
Declared to my old man,
"I want to be a coachman, dad."
"You must be crazy, son," he said.
"I simply won't allow it."
I did not even care.
I climbed up in that driver's seat,
And my new life was there.
When racing, my hack really goes.
I'll come in first place by a nose.

Refrain

6. "Liebeslied an ein Proletariermädchen"
(Love Song to a Proletarian Girl)

Text by Peter Hammerschlag
Music by Gerhard Bronner

Ich bin a armer, kleiner Jud
und hab ka scharfes Messer.
Du bist aus altem Vorstadtblut,
ans nix von meiner Liebesglut,
und wahrlich: dir ist besser.
Ja, mir, dir geht es gut.

Du kennst die Spittelberger Buam
mit Mahagonipratzen.
Die sind sie der Novembersturm,
allweil fidel und hoch in Furm,
und hab'n statt Mädchen "Katzen."
Die Spittelberger Buam.

I'm just a poor and hapless Jew,
No knife, I'm not a cutthroat.
You've always lived on easy street.
I'm used to cold, and you have heat.
It's true, I'm not your dreamboat,
But still I think you're sweet.

You're with the hoity-toity crowd.
Your deep roots help you fit in.
Nice in November, I mean when
Storms keep you right as rain, but then
They call their women kitten,
Those hoity-toity men.

Die treten dir im Maienwind
verliebt ins weiße Bäuchlein,
und machen dir ein Sonntagskind
Flugs hinterm Fliedersträuchlein.

Dazu fehlt mir die innre Kraft,
so heiß kann ich nicht werben.
Jedoch von deiner Jungfernschaft,
die schon vor langer Zeit erschlaft,
da sammle ich die Scherben,
weil ich bin in dich vergabt.

Ich bring dir süße Mehlspeis dar
(Auch die ist nicht verächtlich),
und sind wir auch nicht ganz ein Paar,
ich denk an dich, allnächtlich.

Das Naserl streich ich dir zurecht
und dann die Augenbrauen.
Doch kann ich dir, selbst wenn ich möcht,
und wär' ich auch total bezücht,
die Pappen nicht zerhauen,
drum bin ich dir zu schlecht.

Sei mir auch so ein bisserl gut,
auch wenn ich werd einmal gresser!
Zwar fehlt es mir nicht Liebesglut,
weil ich kan seh'n kein frisches Blut,
ich hab ka scharfes Messer,
und nennt man mich auch Professor,
für dich bin ich a armer klaner Jud.

They come to you like breeze in May
In love with their white bellies,
And romp through glens on Sabbath day,
With Saras and with Nellies.

For that I've got no time at all.
I cannot court in clover.
But for your sweet virginity,
Which went to sleep eternally,
I'll take what they've left over,
And my all you'll get from me.

Each day, I'll bring a chocolate bar,
Though now and then I'll doubt you.
We'll be as normal couples are.
At night I'll dream about you.

I would caress your nose and cheeks,
And then each lovely eyebrow.
If I have flipped, well, I don't know.
I'll kiss you on your lips like so.
Of course, that's all so highbrow,
And I'm no Romeo.

If you'll be good, then I'll be good.
I'll be your fond caresser.
If I don't sing you love refrains,
I cannot change what's in my veins.
No knife, no snappy dresser.
I'm clearly no professor.
To you, I'm just a poor and hapless Jew.

English translations by Philip V. Bohlman in the previous
section adapted for American performances of the New
Budapest Orpheum Society by Jon Steinhagen and Stewart
Figa.

III. Multiplying Jewish Modernism

7. "Mahnung" (Warning)

Composed by Arnold Schoenberg
Text by Gustav Hochstetter

1. Mädel sei kein eitles Ding,
    Fang dir keinen Schmetterling,
    Such dir einen rechten Mann,
    Der dich tüchtig küssen kann
    Und mit seiner Hände Kraft,
    Dir ein warmes Nestchen schafft.

2. Mädel, Mädel, sei nicht dumm,
    Lauf nicht wie im Traum herum,
    Augen auf! ob Einer kommt,
    Der dir recht zum Manne taugt.
    Kommt er, dann nicht lang bedacht!
    Klapp! die Falle zugemacht.

3. Liebes Mädel sei gescheit,
    Nütze deine Rosenzeit!
    Passe auf und denke dran,
    Daß du, wenn du ohne Plan
    Ziellos durch das Leben schwirrst,
    Eine alte Jungfer wirst.

4. Liebes Mädel sei gescheit,
    Nütze deine Rosenzeit,
    Passe auf und denke dran!
    Denk daran. . . .

1. Please, young lady, don't be vain,
    Sunshine soon will change to rain,
    Real men are the men for you,
    Who will kiss you and mean it, too.
    With the strength of his two hands alone,
    One will build you a nest all your own.

2. Darling girl, employ your brain,
    Stay here on this earthly plane,
    Just in case one comes along,
    You are certain is wrong, all wrong.
    Don't you give him a thought or a whim!
    Snap! The trap should not open for him.

3. Use your youth, but please be wise,
    Don't go chasing butterflies!
    Fly through life without a plan—
    That is, if you think you can.
    Dream on, you can be my guest,
    You'll end up an old spinster, at best.

4. Use your youth, but please be wise,
    Don't go chasing butterflies.
    Stop and think and please take care.
    Please take care. . . .

8. "Ich bin von Kopf bis Fuß auf Liebe eingestellt" (From Head to Toe I Am Prepared for Love)

Music and text by Friedrich Holländer

1. Ein rätselhafter Schimmer,
    Ein je ne sai pas quoi,
    Liegt in den Augen immer
    Bei einer schönen Frau.
    Doch wenn sich meine Augen

1. I don't know what is glowing,
    A "je ne sais pas quoi,"
    But women worth the knowing
    Hold in their eyes, "à moi."
    Yet when you look within mine

Bei einem vis a vis
Ganz tief in seine saugen,
Was sprechen dann sie?

Refrain
Ich bin von Kopf bis Fuß auf Liebe eingestellt,
Denn das ist meine Welt und sonst garnichts.
Das ist, was soll ich machen, meine Natur:
Ich kann halt lieben nur und sonst garnichts.
Männer umschwirrn mich wie Motten um das
*   Licht,*
Und wenn sie verbrennen, ja, dafür kann ich
*   nicht.*
Ich bin von Kopf bis Fuß auf Liebe eingestellt,
Denn das ist meine Welt und sonst garnichts.

2. Was bebt in meinen Händen,
   In ihrem heißen Druck,
   Sie möchten sich verschwenden,
   Sie haben nie genug.
   Ihr werdet es verzeihen,
   Ihr müßt es halt versteh'n,
   Es lockt mich stets von neuem,
   Ich find' es so schön.

   Refrain

Before I look away,
Before you chance to win mine,
What, what do they say?

Refrain
I am ready for love, my heart has told me so,
And love is all I know, I can't help it.
I've always cared for love, and that is how I live:
I've nothing else to give, I can't help it.
Men become moths as they flutter to my light.

They burn up so quickly because I burn so bright.

I am ready for love, my heart has told me so,
And love is all I know, I can't help it.

2. They hold me in a fashion,
   They long to call my bluff,
   They give me all their passion,
   They never give enough.
   And when they try to land me,
   They have to pay the price.
   You have to understand me:
   I find it so nice.

   Refrain

9. "Eine kleine Sehnsucht" (Do a Little Dreaming)

Music and text by Friedrich Holländer

1. Mein Tag ist grau, dein Tag ist grau;
   Laß uns zusammen geh'n!
   Wir wollen beide an den Händen uns fassen
   Und uns so recht versteh'n!
   Lang ist der Weg, bang ist der Weg,
   Sicher wird man belohnt;
   Wir soll'n recht fest an etwas Schönes denken
   Und an ein Schloß im Mond!

   Refrain

1. My day is gray, your day is gray;
   How could we stay apart?
   I want to hold your hand, and you want the same, so
   You understand my heart!
   One way is long, one way is wrong,
   We'll be rewarded soon;
   We need to concentrate on beautiful things, like
   Castles upon the moon.

   Refrain

Eine kleine Sehnsucht braucht jeder zum
*   Glücklichsein!*
Eine kleine Sehnsucht, ein Stückchen Sonnen-
*   schein.*
Eine Sehnsucht für den grauen Tag;
Eine Sehnsucht, ganz egal wonach!
Eine kleine Sehnsucht, ein flüchtiges Traum-
*   gebild,*
Eine Sehnsucht, die sich niemals erfüllt!

Do a little dreaming, and happiness may appear!

Do a little dreaming, when skies of gray appear.

Have your pipe dreams, I don't care what for;
Overripe dreams that you can't ignore.
Do a little dreaming, imagine your skies of blue.

Dream away, but know they'll never come true!

2. Lügen wir uns, trügen wir uns
   In eine Welt hinein,
   Und laß uns dann in dieser Welt ganz verzau-
   bert
   Prinz und Prinzessin sein!
   Du bist aus Gold, ich bin aus Gold,
   Und unser Tag ist froh;
   Vergessen der Student im Dachstübchen und
   das
   Mädelchen vom Büro!

   Refrain

2. Sigh to yourself, lie to yourself.
   Enter that dreaming place.
   Turn into royalty, and laugh at the world,

   The one that is hard to face!
   You're made of gold, I'm made of gold,
   What else to do but smile?
   The lonely student and the girl at her desk

   Can smile for a little while!

   Refrain

10. "Gigerlette"

Composed by Arnold Schoenberg
Text by Otto Julius Birnbaum

1. Fräulein Gigerlette lud mich ein zum Tee.
   Ihre Toilette war gestimmt auf Schnee;
   Ganz wie Pierrette war sie angetan.
   Selbst ein Mönch, ich wette,
   Sähe Gigerlette wohlgefällig an.

2. War ein rotes Zimmer, drin sie mich empfing,
   Gelber Kerzenschimmer in dem Raume hing.
   Und sie war wie immer Leben und Esprit.
   Nie vergess ichs, nimmer:
   weinrot war das Zimmer, blütenweiß war sie.

1. Fräulein Gigerlette invited me to tea.
   Dressed up like Pierette, she was a joy to see.
   What a vision in her gown, as white as snow;
   And though I was rather shy,
   I gazed upon her for an hour or so.

2. Gigerlette received me in a room of red,
   Candlelight, a golden halo 'round her head.
   And she was, as always, bubbling with esprit.
   I can see her still, like blossoms on a cherry,
   Snowy white was she.

3. Und im Trab mit Vieren fuhren wir zu zweit
   In das Land spazieren, das heißt Heiterkeit.
   Daß wir nicht verlieren Zügel, Ziel und Lauf,
   Saß bei dem Kutschieren
   Mit den heißen Vieren Amor hinten auf.

3. Then we two went riding in a coach and four,
   Saw the country scenery and so much more.
   But as a precaution, so we would not lose our way,
   Guiding us that evening with our steaming stallions,
   Cupid saved the day!

IV. Exile from Modernity

11. "Der Graben" (The Trenches)

Composed by Hanns Eisler
Text by Kurt Tucholsky

1. Mutter, wozu hast du deinen aufgezogen?
   Hast dich zwanzig Jahr mit ihm gequällt?
   Wozu ist er dir in deinen Arm geflogen,
   Und du hast ihm leise was erzählt?
   Bis sie ihn dir weggenommen haben.
   Für den Graben, für den Graben.

1. Mother, what did you raise your son to live like?
   All that quarreling for twenty years?
   Why does he return to you for what you give, like
   Gentle stories as you dried his tears?
   You have done all this so they may take him
   To the trenches, Mother, to the trenches.

2. Junge, kannst du noch an Vater denken?
   Vater nahm dich oft auf seinen Arm.
   Wollt dir einen Groschen schenken,
   Spielte mit dir Räuber und Gendarm.
   Bis sie ihn dir weggenommen haben.
   Für den Graben, Junge, für den Graben.

2. Sir, may I ask: Do you still recall your father?
   How he held you by the hand and smiled?
   How he gave you coins when no one else would bother?
   He knew what it was to be a child.
   After all the games, they only took him
   To the trenches, young man, to the trenches.

3. Drüben die französischen Genossen
   Lagen dicht bei Englands Arbeitsmann.
   Alle haben sie ihr Blut vergossen,
   Und zerschossen ruht heut Mann bei Mann.
   Alte Leute, Männer, mancher Knabe
   In dem einen großen Massengrabe.

3. Over there, you'll find the French lieutenants
   Side by side with British working men.
   Blood flowed freely from each one, like pennants,
   Scarlet flags that marked the carnage then.
   Men of every age are still together
   Sharing one final grave in the trenches.

4. Seid nicht stolz auf Orden und Geklunker!
   Seid nicht stolz auf Narben und die Zeit!
   In die Gräben schickten euch die Junker,
   Staatswahn und der Fabrikantenneid.
   Ihr wart gut genug zum Fraß für Raben,
   Für das Grab, Kameraden, für den Graben.

4. Don't love medals or the way they rank you!
   Not the scars and not the present day!
   Rich men send you to the grave to thank you,
   Likewise businessmen throw us away.
   We are good enough for crows to dine on,
   For the graveyard, comrades, for the trenches.

5. Denkt an Todesröcheln und Gestöhne.
Drüben stehen Väter, Mütter, Söhne,
Schuften schwer, wie ihr, ums bißchen Leben.
Wollt ihr denen nicht die Hände geben?
Reicht die Bruderhand als schönste aller Gaben
Übern Graben, Leute, übern Graben!

5. Think about the ghosts who gather, groaning.
Over there are families, not one owning,
Anything but debts, yet see them slaving?
Don't you think these souls are worth us saving?
They need a brother's hand, most precious gift!
Reach across the trenches! Across the trenches!

English adapted from Eric Bentley.

12. "Ballade von der 'Judenhure' Marie Sanders"
(Ballad of the "Jewish Whore" Marie Sanders)

Composed by Hanns Eisler
Text by Bertolt Brecht

1. In Nürnberg machten sie ein Gesetz,
Darüber weinte manches Weib,
Das mit dem falschen Mann im Bette lag.
"Das Fleisch schlägt auf in den Vorstädten,
Die Trommeln schlagen mit Macht,
Gott im Himmel, wenn sie etwas vorhätten,
Wär' es heute nacht."

1. In Nürnberg they made a law,
Giving women cause to weep,
Who had been sleeping with the wrong man.
"The meat's going up in the city shops,
The drums beat louder each day,
God above, if there's something you've not done,
Do it right away."

2. Marie Sanders, dein Geliebter hat zu
schwarzes Haar.
Besser, du bist heut zu ihm nicht mehr
Wie du zu ihm gestern warst.
"Das Fleisch schlägt auf in den Vorstädten,
Die Trommeln schlagen mit Macht,
Gott im Himmel, wenn sie etwas vorhätten,
Wär' es heute nacht."

2. Marie Sanders, your sweetheart's hair is far too dark.

Better to reconsider
Love is such a very fleeting thing.
"The meat's going up in the city shops,
The drums beat louder each day,
God above, if there's something you've not done,
Do it right away."

3. Mutter, gib mir den Schlüssel,
Es ist alles halb so schlimm.
Der Mond schaut aus wie immer.
"Das Fleisch schlägt auf in den Vorstädten,
Die Trommeln schlagen mit Macht,
Gott im Himmel, wenn sie etwas vorhätten,
Wär' es heute nacht."

3. Mother, give me the key,
Please, everything will be all right.
The moon looks like it always did.
"The meat's going up in the city shops,
The drums beat louder each day,
God above, if there's something you've not done,
Do it right away."

4. Eines Morgens früh um neun fuhr sie durch die
    Stadt im Hemd,
Um den Hals ein Schild, das Haar geschoren.
Die Gasse johlte. Sie blickte kalt.
Das Fleisch schlägt auf in den Vorstädten,
Der Streicher redet heute nacht.
Großer Gott, wenn sie ein Ohr hätten,
Wüßten sie, was man mit ihnen macht.

4. And at nine one morning, she rode through the city
    in her slip,
With a board round her neck, her head was shaven.
The crowd was jeering. Their eyes cold.
The meat's rising up in the city streets,
Herr Streicher's speaking tonight.
God above, how can they be so blind,
As to dream it will all come out right.

13. "Und es sind die finstren Zeiten" (And the Times Are Dark and Fearful)

Composed by Hanns Eisler
Text by Bertolt Brecht

Und es sind die finstren Zeiten in der fremden
    Stadt,

Doch es bleibt beim leichten Schreiten und die
    Stirn ist glatt.

Harte Menschheit unbeweget, lang erfrornem
    Fischvolk gleich.

Doch das Herz bleibt schnell geregelt und das
    Lächeln weich.

And the times are dark and fearful in the foreign town,

Yet how light is every footstep and untroubled brow.

People frozen and impassive, like a fisher long at sea!

Yet these hearts are deftly managed and these smiles
    are free.

V. Beyond Modernism: *Hollywooder Liederbuch*

14. "An den kleinen Radioapparat" (To the Little Radio)

Composed by Hanns Eisler
Text by Bertolt Brecht

Du kleiner Kasten den ich flüchtend trug,
Daß meine Lampen mir auch nicht zerbrächen,
Besorgt vom Haus zum Schiff, vom Schiff zum
    Zug,
Daß meine Feinde weiter zu mir sprächen,
An meinem Lager und zu meiner Pein
Der letzten nachts, der ersten in der Früh,
Von ihren Siegen und von meiner Müh.
Versprich mir, nicht auf einmal stumm zu sein.

O little box I carried in my flight
So carefully your lamps and tubes protecting
From house to boat, from boat to train held tight,

So that my enemies could still address me,
Beside my bed and much to my dismay
Last thing each night and first thing every day,
About their victories (defeats for me).
O please do not fall silent suddenly!

* English adapted from Eric Bentley

15. "Hotelzimmer 1942" (Hotel Room 1942)

Composed by Hanns Eisler

Text by Bertolt Brecht

An der weißgetünchten Wand steht der schwarze
    Koffer mit Manuskripten.
Drüben steht das Rauchzeug mit dem kupf'rnen
    Aschenbecher.
Die chinesische Leinwand, zeigend den Zweifler,
    hängt darüber.
Auch die Masken sind da.
Und neben der Bettstelle steht der kleine sechs-
    lampige Lautsprecher.
In der Frühe drehe ich den Schalter um
Und höre die Siegesmeldungen meiner Feinde.

The black suitcase with manuscripts stands against the
    whitewashed wall.
Over there stands the smoking stuff with a copper
    ashtray.
The Chinese canvas showing the doubter hangs over it.

The masks, too, are there.
And next to the bedstead stands the six-lamp loudspea-
    ker.
In the morning, I turn on the knob
And hear the victory reports from my enemies.

16. "Der Kirschdieb" (The Cherry Thief)

Composed by Hanns Eisler

Text by Bertolt Brecht

An einem frühen Morgen, lange vor Morgengraun,
Wurde ich geweckt durch ein Pfeifen und ging
    zum Fenster.
Auf meinem Kirschbaum—Dämmerung füllte den
    Garten—
Saß ein junger Mann mit gflickter Hose
Und pflückte lustig meine Kirschen.
Mich sehend nickte er mir zu,
Mit beiden Händen holt er die Kirschen
Aus den Zweigen in seine Taschen.
Noch eine ganze Zeitlang, als ich wieder in meiner
    Bettstatt lag,
Hört' ich ihn sein lust'ges kleines Lied pfeifen.

Early one morning, long before cockcrow
I was awakened by whistling and went to the window.

In my cherry tree—gray dawn filled the garden—

Sat a young man, with patched-up trousers
Cheerfully picking my cherries.
Seeing me, he nodded,
And with both hands pulled the cherries
From the branches into his pockets.
For quite a while as I lay once more in bed

I heard him whistling his lovely little song.

English translation by Willett and Manheim in Brecht
1976.

17. "Über den Selbstmord" (On Suicide)

Composed by Hanns Eisler

Text by Bertolt Brecht

In diesem Lande und in dieser Zeit	In this land and during these times
Dürfte es trübe Abende nicht geben,	There may not be gloomy evenings,
Auch hohe Brücken über die Flüsse,	Also high bridges over the rivers,
Selbst die Stunden zwischen Nacht und Morgen	Even the hours between night and morning,
Und die ganze Winterzeit dazu,	As well as the entire wintertime,
Das ist gefährlich.	All this is dangerous.
Denn angesichts dieses Elends	For because of this suffering
Werfen die Menschen in einem Augenblick	People throw away their unbearable lives
Ihr unerträgliches Leben fort.	In only a moment.

18. "Vom Sprengen des Gartens" (On Watering the Garden)

Composed by Hanns Eisler

Text by Bertolt Brecht

O Sprengen des Gartens, das Grün zu ermutigen!	Oh, water the garden, the greenness to embolden!
Wässern der durstgen Bäume!	Water the thirsty trees!
Gib mehr als genug, gib mehr, gib mehr, gib mehr als genug.	Give more than enough, give more, give more, give more than enough.
Und vergiß auch nicht das Strauchwerk,	And don't forget the shrubs,
Auch das beerenlose nicht, das ermattete!	Also those without berries, those already weary!
Und übersieh nicht zwischen den Blumen das Unkraut,	And don't overlook the weeds between the flowers,
Das auch Durst hat.	Which are also thirsty.
Noch gieße nur den frischen Rasen	Do not just water the fresh lawn
Oder den versengten nur:	Or only that which is dried out:
Auch den nackten Boden erfrische du,	Also freshen the naked earth,
Erfrische du.	You should freshen that.

19. "Die Heimkehr" (The Homecoming)

Composed by Hanns Eisler

Text by Bertolt Brecht

Die Vaterstadt, wie find ich sie doch?	My hometown, how does it seem to me?
Folgend den Bombenschwärmen	After the massive bombing
Komm ich nach Haus.	I am coming home.
Wo liegt sie mir? Wo liegt sie mir?	Where is it? Where is it?
Dort, wo die ungeheuren Gebirge	There, where the monstrous mountains
von Rauch stehn.	of smoke rise.
Das in den Feuern dort ist sie.	That's it, in the fires.
Die Vaterstadt, wie empfängt sie mich wohl?	My father city, will it welcome me?
Vor mir kommen die Bomber.	The bombers came before me.
Tödliche Schwärme melden euch meine Rückkehr.	Deadly swarms announce to you my return.
Feuersbrünste gehn dem Sohn voraus.	Firestorms precede the son.

All translations by Philip V. Bohlman unless otherwise noted. Several Brecht translations are adapted from the standard translation of the poet's works: Bertolt Brecht, *Poems*, edited by John Willett and Ralph Manheim (London: Methuen, 1976).

Mitchell Ash is Professor für Neuere Geschichte at the University of Vienna. His research interests range widely across the history of science and the history of modern Central Europe, with special interests in the connections among science, politics, society, and culture in the nineteenth and twentieth centuries, as well as German history since 1750. He holds positions at numerous research centers and academic associations, including the Berlin-Brandenburgische Akademie der Wissenschaften, the Austrian Society for the History of Science, and the Austrian Society for Exile Research; he also serves as the president of the Society for the History of Science. Among his many edited or co-edited volumes are *Forced Migration and Scientific Change: Émigré, German-Speaking Scientists after 1933* (1996), *Mythos Humboldt: Vergangenheit und Zukunft der deutschen Universitäten* (1999), and *Psychology's Territories: Historical and Contemporary Perspectives from Different Disciplines* (2006). His *Gestalt Psychology in German Culture, 1890–1967: Holism and the Quest for Objectivity* (1995)

was awarded the Morris D. Forkosch Prize by the *Journal of the History of Ideas* for the best book on intellectual history in 1995.

Philip V. Bohlman is Mary Werkman Distinguished Service Professor of the Humanities and of Music at the University of Chicago, where he also served as chair of the Committee on Jewish Studies from 2003 to 2006. He is a Corresponding Fellow of the British Academy, which awarded him its Derek Allen Prize for musicology in 2007. His publications range widely across the humanities and social sciences, and among his most recent books are *The Folk Songs of Ashkenaz* (2001, with Otto Holzapfel), *World Music: A Very Short Introduction* (2002), *Jüdische Volksmusik: Eine mitteleuropäische Geistesgeschichte* (2005), and *Jewish Music and Modernity* (2008). His current projects include a monograph on music for the operatic and cabaret stage in the Holocaust and a translation of Johann Gottfried Herder's writings on music and nationalism. In 2007 he delivered the

Royal Holloway–British Library Lectures in Musicology on "The Silence of Music." He is artistic director of the Jewish cabaret troupe the New Budapest Orpheum Society and was president of the Society for Ethnomusicology from 2005 to 2007.

Sander L. Gilman is Distinguished Professor of the Liberal Arts and Sciences at Emory University. A cultural and literary historian, he is the author or editor of over seventy books, whose topics range across the social and medical sciences, and the humanities. He taught for twenty-five years on the Cornell University medical and humanities faculties before serving on the faculties of the University of Chicago and the University of Illinois at Chicago. He has served as a visiting professor at universities throughout the world and has been awarded an honorary professorship at the Free University in Berlin and a Doctor of Laws (*honoris causa*) at the University of Toronto. The subjects of his books range across disciplinary boundaries, with many of his publications making critical contributions to fields as diverse as German literature and the history of psychiatry, Jewish studies, and musicology. Among his most recent works are a biography, *Franz Kafka*, and an edited special edition of the journal *History of Psychiatry* titled *Mind and Body in the History of Psychiatry*.

Pamela M. Potter is professor of music and German at the University of Wisconsin–Madison. She has written extensively on music and politics in twentieth-century Germany and is best known for her work on the history of German musicology (*Most German of the Arts: Musicology and Society from the Weimar Republic to the End of Hitler's Reich*, 1998; German ed., 2000) and on the connections between music and national identity (*Music and German National Identity*, co-edited with Celia Applegate, 2002). She has contributed entries on Wagner to *Antisemitism: A Historical Encyclopedia of Prejudice and Persecution* (2005) and *The Cambridge Companion to Wagner*

(forthcoming), as well as articles on the question of Nazi aesthetics in the journals *Central European History*, *The Musical Quarterly*, and *Contemporary European History*. Jewish music, particularly in modern European and American vernacular history, weaves its way into both teaching and research topics. She was the 1997 recipient of the Alfred Einstein Award of the American Musicological Society.

Edwin Seroussi is the Emanuel Alexandre Professor of Musicology and director of the Jewish Music Research Centre at the Hebrew University in Jerusalem. He has written on various aspects of Jewish liturgical music, with emphasis on traditions from North Africa and the Middle East, Judeo-Spanish folk song, and popular music in Israel. Among his works are *Spanish-Portuguese Synagogue Music in Nineteenth-Century Reform Sources from Hamburg* (1996), the *Cancionero sefardí* by Alberto Hemsi (1995), and *Popular Music and National Culture in Israel* (co-authored with Motti Regev, 2004). He has contributed entries on Jewish and Israeli music for major encyclopedias, among them *The Revised New Grove Dictionary of Music and Musicians* (2001), *Garland Encyclopedia of World Music* (2002), and the *Diccionario de la música española e hispanoamericana* (2002). He edits the Yuval Music Series and the CD series Anthology of Music Traditions in Israel at the Jewish Music Research Centre. His most recent book, *Incipitario sefardí: El antiguo cancionero judeoespañol en fuentes hebreas (siglos XV–XX)* was published in Spain in 2007.

Kay Kaufman Shelemay is the G. Gordon Watts Professor of Music and professor of African and African American Studies at Harvard University, where she won the Phi Beta Kappa and the Levenson Memorial Teaching Prizes in 2006. She has carried out fieldwork in Ethiopia, the United States, Mexico, and Israel. Her numerous research areas include African and Jewish music, and American music. Among her current research projects is the comprehensive study, with Carol Oja, of Leonard Bernstein's Boston years, and she is now at the beginning stages of research on the music of the new African immigrants in North America. Her book *Music, Ritual, and Falasha History* won both the ASCAP–Deems Taylor Award (1987) and the prize of the International Musicological Society (1988), while *Let Jasmine Rain Down: Song and Remembrance among Syrian Jews* was a finalist for the 1998 National Jewish Book Award. Her textbook *Soundscapes: Exploring Music in a Changing World* appeared in a revised second edition in 2006. She is a member of the American Academy for Arts and Sciences and the American Academy for Jewish Research.

Michael P. Steinberg is director of the Cogut Center for the Humanities, Barnaby Conrad and Mary Critchfield Keeney Professor of History, and professor of music at Brown University. He also serves as associate editor of *Musical Quarterly* and *Opera Quarterly*. His main research interests include the cultural history of modern Germany and Austria, with particular attention to German Jewish intellectual history and the cultural history of music. He has received fellowships from the American Council of Learned Societies, the National Endowment for the Humanities, and the John Simon Guggenheim Memorial Foundation, as well as the Berlin Prize from the American Academy in Berlin. He is the author of studies of Hermann Broch, Aby Warburg, Walter Benjamin, and Charlotte Salomon, and of *Austria as Theater and Ideology: The Meaning of the Salzburg Festival* (2000), the German edition of which (*Ursprung und Ideologie der Salzburger Festspiele*, 2000) won Austria's Victor Adler Staatspreis in 2001. Most recently he has published *Listening to Reason: Culture, Subjectivity, and 19th-Century Music* (2004) and *Judaism Musical and Unmusical* (2007).